JOSEPHINE

The Empress and her Children

JOSEPHINE

The Empress and her Children

NINA EPTON

WEIDENFELD and NICOLSON
LONDON

George Weidenfeld and Nicolson Limited,
11 St John's Hill, London SW11
Printed in Great Britain by
Willmer Brothers Limited, Birkenhead
ISBN 0 297 77012 8

CONTENTS

ILLUSTRATIONS

PROLOGUE

The Empress Josephine lurks decoratively, graceful as the swan that she adopted for her emblem, in the background of the vast historical landscape of the Napoleonic era. She glides into learned biographies, which usually devote as many pages to her illustrious husband and his numerous military campaigns as to her. She is depicted waiting for his return from the battle front, presiding over court ceremonies, dutifully accompanying her husband on his progresses and finally cast off – a melancholy figure for ever melting in tears. It is true that she wept frequently and could be tiresomely jealous, but there is another side to her. There is Josephine the mother, in the role of umpire in the intimate family circle, which consisted of herself, Napoleon and Eugène and Hortense, her children by her first marriage to the Vicomte Alexandre de Beauharnais. This is the aspect that has intrigued me and upon which I have concentrated: these four interlocked lives from which Josephine emerges less as a vague myth-figure – the 'Creole born to be empress' – and more as a creature of flesh, blood – and heart.

Portraits probably do not do her justice. She was not particularly beautiful, but she had a mysterious 'aura'. Those who knew her intimately believed that her greatest charm lay in the mobility of her expression, her sweet voice and her graceful movements. Kindness, gentleness, femininity were her chief characteristics. Yet she could be firm. She could, and did, fight for her rights and those of her children. In her short lifespan – barely fifty-one years – she went through experiences that would have left most women hardened and arrogant. But Josephine never changed. She looked on life through her heavy-lidded eyes, with her tight-lipped smile, hoping for love, and receiving it from her children, if not from her two husbands, who paid court to other women. Such was her nature, however, that she ended by forgiving and returning good for deep hurt. She bore no malice.

Josephine was born under an extraordinary, but not a lucky star; she enjoyed few moments of real happiness. After Napoleon's exile to Elba when she was alone, helpless and fearful for her children's future, the burden proved too much for her to bear. Yet had she but known it, her grandson, rather than Napoleon's son, was to ascend the throne of France – an ironical, posthumous twist of fate for an empress who had been repudiated because she could not bear her husband a child.

I

THE VICOMTESSE DE BEAUHARNAIS

On a rainy day in October 1779 people gathered round the harbour of Brest to watch the arrival of the storeship *Ile de France*, convoyed by the frigate *La Pomone*, which had just sailed in from Fort-Royal in Martinique. It had been a rough passage, but at least they had not been intercepted by the English. The few passengers who disembarked were green from seasickness, particularly Monsieur Joseph-Gaspard Tascher de la Pagerie, who totteringly escorted his little party down the gangway. It consisted of his spinster sister Rosette, a mulatto servant, Euphémie, and his eldest daughter, Marie-Josèphe-Rose, a sixteen-year-old girl with dark chestnut hair, wide brown eyes, a well-formed mouth (which she kept closed most of the time so as not to reveal her bad teeth) and the sallow complexion peculiar to Creoles, as people of European descent born and bred in the islands were called. Known to her family as 'Yeyette', she signed herself 'Marie-Rose' at this date. Only later, much later, was her second husband to call her by the name that posterity has made famous – Josephine.

As she set foot on French soil and drew her cloak round her shapely shoulders in the chill wind blowing off the sea, Marie-Rose must have looked at the grey buildings encircling the harbour and wondered with a beating heart what would be her future in this land of her dreams; and especially whether her fiancé, Alexandre de Beauharnais, would correspond to her Aunt Edmée's description: 'He has a pleasant face, a charming bearing, wit, intelligence ; all the qualities of heart and soul are united in him. He is loved by all who surround him.' (This circle included his mistress, Marie-Françoise-Laure de Longpré, who was subsequently to cause much mischief.)

The marriage had been fixed after two years of negotiations

3

by forceful Aunt Edmée, whom Marie-Rose could scarcely remember. She had left for France years before to live with the ex-governor of Martinique, the Marquis de Beauharnais, who had been recalled to his native land in 1761 after having failed to organize a relief expedition for Guadeloupe, then besieged by the English. He was pensioned off, thanks to his connections at court, with the title of marquis and 12,000 *livres* a year. He was also given the rank of fleet commander. The liaison between Edmée Renaudin (Alexis Renaudin was the 'cover' husband provided for her to still gossiping tongues, but they were now separated) and the Marquis de Beauharnais had begun soon after she became his wife's companion. She was godmother to his second son, Alexandre, who was considered to be too young to endure the voyage to France and had been placed in the care of Edmée's mother at Fort-Royal for five years. This was the boy – now aged nineteen and enrolled in the army under the patronage of the liberal Duc de La Rochefoucauld – to whom Edmée was determined to marry one of her three nieces, no doubt with the dual objective of assuring her own position and of helping her impoverished family.

Edmée's brother Joseph-Gaspard (Marie-Rose's father) was not a pushing man and malaria had helped to undermine his not very robust constitution. Edmée had arranged his marriage (in 1761) with Rose-Claire des Vergers de Sannois, a girl (a spinster in those days at the advanced age of twenty-five) from one of the oldest families of the colony. The Taschers de la Pagerie belonged to the lesser French nobility from the Orléanais. Through an uncle, canon of Blois and Viscount of Abbeville, who had been appointed almoner to the Dauphine Maria Josepha of Saxony, Joseph Tascher had obtained a post as page to the dauphine at court, where he was in attendance at the time of the birth of the future Louis XVI. Back in Martinique he helped to defend Fort-Royal against the English during their attack in 1762. The little town was under fire for only ten hours but Joseph's part in the defence secured him a royal pension of 450 *livres* a year. His main and rather meagre resources came from his sugar plantation at Trois-Ilets, across the bay from Fort-

Royal. The big house was destroyed by a hurricane when Marie-Rose was three years old and since then the family had lived on the upper floor of the sugar-refinery, among mango and banana groves and a profusion of tropical flowers that Marie-Rose remembered all her life.

There were no flowers in the grim little port of Brest. But Brest was not Paris, the splendid city of which her father, not to mention the dancing and drawing masters who had taught her during the four years she had been a boarder in a convent at Fort-Royal, had so often spoken. 'When I was at court....' How often Marie-Rose's frustrated father must have retold his memories to the members of his family, the only one who was really interested being Marie-Rose. Her mother had no wish to visit France, and neither had her two younger sisters Catherine and Marie-Françoise (known as Manette). The former had originally been destined to marry Alexandre de Beauharnais, but she had died of a malignant fever during the exchange of correspondence with Aunt Edmée. Manette, the youngest, aged eleven, did not wish to be parted from her mother. 'You know what these Creole mothers are like,' Joseph wrote apologetically to his sister. 'Send any one of your daughters' was the gist of Edmée's impatient reply, and so the name of the bride was left blank in the authorization sent from Paris to publish the banns of marriage in Fort-Royal.

Alexandre was anxious to marry, as on that event depended his inheriting an annual income of 40,000 *livres* from his mother's properties. He hoped, however, that his father would not force him to marry 'this young lady [Marie-Rose] if she and I should feel a mutual repugnance, but I do not doubt, after the description that has been given of her, that she will please me. I hope to be so happy as to inspire in her the feelings that I shall experience.... The affection and desire that this young person shows to make her aunt's acquaintance decide me in her favour....'

Joseph had written that Marie-Rose had 'a great desire to know her dear aunt and to deserve her kindness and that of the Marquis de Beauharnais' – which was a little beside the point, one would have thought. He had also sent a fairly objective description of his eldest daughter, who had 'on several occasions asked me to take her to France. . . . She has a very good skin, good eyes, good arms, and a surprising taste for music. I gave her a teacher for the guitar while she was at the convent, and she made full use of this and has a pretty voice. . . . It is a pity that she has not the advantage of an education in France. . . .' This sentiment was echoed by Marie-Rose's bridegroom (now a *sous-lieutenant* in the infantry regiment of the Sarre), who hastened to Brest, accompanied by Aunt Edmée, as soon as they heard that Joseph and Marie-Rose had actually arrived. The irregularity of sea passages had prevented the latter from announcing their departure from Martinique in advance.

In the meantime the Creole party was probably housed privately by one of the port officials, since the Marquis de Beauharnais was nominally a fleet commander and had many acquaintances in the various ports. Marie-Rose slowly recovered from her seasickness. Her father had suffered even more and was feeling wretched.

There is no record of the bride and groom's first encounter but it must have been in the nature of an anticlimax, with Joseph Tascher ill in bed, Marie-Rose probably inclined to be tongue-tied, conscious of her Creole accent and of the difference between her unpolished colonial Aunt Rosette and worldly Aunt Edmée, who was tall, blonde, blue-eyed and commanding. As for her opinion of Alexandre, she must have been bowled over by the handsome young vicomte who, dressed in the latest style, was dashing, gracious and extremely voluble. He was irrepressible both as a talker and as a letter-writer. Marie-Rose must have been subjected to a torrent of words and elegant, slightly pedantic phrases. Alexandre probably asked her a thousand questions about life in Martinique that she was utterly incapable of answering.

An ardent disciple of Jean-Jacques Rousseau, Alexandre was interested in the condition of 'noble savages', and indeed in all social problems, as well as in the education of women. It did not take him long to discover that Marie-Rose presented him with a challenge. From the first day of their meeting he made up his mind to improve her education and 'make up by his zeal for the neglect of her first sixteen years'. A convent education had given his bride little knowledge beyond the three R's and a smattering of the usual 'young lady' accomplishments of sketching, singing romantic airs and strumming the guitar. The latter instrument was not considered fashionable in France. Marie-Rose must learn to play the harp. As for conversation, all that she had heard was that of the young officers invited to the house of her uncle, Baron Robert Tascher, director of ports and harbours ; she had spent most of her weekends from boarding school at Fort-Royal with him and her grandmother.

From Brest, Alexandre wrote guardedly to his father in Paris : 'Mademoiselle de la Pagerie will perhaps appear to you less pretty than you expected but I think I can assure you that the uprightness and sweetness of her character surpass all that you have been told about it.' That word 'sweetness' was indeed the key to Marie-Rose's character, as Alexandre had so correctly discerned. Had he been more mature he might have made a better Pygmalion, but he was too impatient and he wanted more from Marie-Rose than she was capable of. Theories did not interest her, nor did books. She was a child of tropical nature, intuitive, warm and – no doubt – at that time naive.

But that was only one side of Marie-Rose's character. She also had an abundant share of those characteristic feminine weaknesses : jealousy and possessiveness, twin defects that have alienated so many husbands through the ages, and which were to alienate hers. Alexandre, accustomed to doing as he pleased, leading the double life expected of gentlemen, with a charming mistress, Laure de Longpré, who was about to bear him a son, indulged in by his godmother Edmée, to whom he candidly recounted his love affairs, was the last man to put up with a suspicious, acquisitive wife. This, unfortunately, was what Marie-Rose soon proved to be.

It was almost inevitable that she should feel possessive and jealous of this Prince Charming whom destiny had placed in her path. She must have felt inadequate and unsure of herself, for she had never met such a man before. She could not fathom his mind or judge his intelligence, but his good looks and polish fascinated her. Did Aunt Edmée drop a discreet hint about the conduct she should observe in order to preserve his budding affection for Marie-Rose *la douce*? Ah, if only her niece had been educated in France, as she had suggested so many times in her letters to her brother, but he had never been able to summon up the cash or the courage.

At this crucial moment, when the wedding details were being finalized, Aunt Edmée was extremely concerned about Joseph's health. The man was so weak that their journey to Paris had to be interrupted so that he could rest in a hotel at Rennes. Supposing he were to die? Edmée took precautions before they left Brest and hauled Joseph before a notary to sign full powers for her to act for him in all matters relating to the marriage and dowry. She was a calculating woman. The cost of the 3,793 franc journey was evenly divided between her and Joseph, who paid her his share at the end of it. Edmée was helpful, but businesslike. It was not necessary for Marie-Rose to contribute a dowry, the marquis had said, but for the sake of appearances the hypothetical figure of 120,000 *livres*, based on uncertain profits from Joseph's plantations, was inserted into the marriage contract.

Travelling at the rate of thirty miles a day in a large hired cabriolet, the little party at last reached the two-storied Hôtel Beauharnais in the rue Thévenot, where Marie-Rose was to spend the first two years of her married life. It was a tall, narrow house set at the end of a garden between trees, with small rooms for the servants in the attics and large rooms below full of heavy ornaments. The narrow rue Thévenot, north of the leather market, had come down in the world since the marquis had inherited it from his grandmother ; he and Edmée had moved into it so that the young couple could live with them. The house was damp and gloomy. How different from the

8

open verandahs and smiling landscape of Trois-Ilets and the freedom of its tropical gardens!

The banns were published during the first week of December in three parishes: that of Saint-Sulpice, which Edmée had just left, Saint-Sauveur, to which she had just moved, and Noisy-le-Grand, where the wedding was to be celebrated. The contract was signed on 10 December in the rue Thévenot, in the presence of the two fathers, Alexandre's elder brother, François, his uncle and cousin, and the Abbé Tascher, almoner to His Most Serene Highness the Duc of Penthièvre and a distant relation, who acted as proxy at the wedding when Joseph had a relapse. Aunt Edmée presented Marie-Rose with her house at Noisy-le-Grand and furniture.

The marriage finally took place on the chilly morning of 13 December 1779. Laure de Longpré's husband had died a week before; she had been delivered of a son who was christened Alexandre, and the fond father was most eager to see him. His frequent escapades from home, allegedly to visit his patron, the Duc de la Rochefoucauld, at the château of La Roche-Guyon, allowed him to do so, but Marie-Rose, not unjustifiably, soon became suspicious.

How boring that first winter in Paris must have been for the little bride from Martinique! The rooms in the dark house of the rue Thévenot were cold; she had to become accustomed to French food and formal meals; the mulatto servant Euphémie, though devoted, was miserable, and social life was limited. If Marie-Rose had once believed that she would be received at court through the Beauharnais connection, her illusions were rapidly dispelled. The marquis, because of his notorious liaison with Aunt Edmée, was ostracized by polite society. Their entourage was middle-aged to elderly. Among their visitors, however, Marie-Rose found two very different female friends: Alexandre's aunt, Marie-Anne-Françoise Mouchard, Comtesse de Beauharnais, divorced wife of the marquis's brother and known as 'Aunt Fanny' by the family; and the more conventional but very gracious Duchesse de Montesson, morganatic wife of the Duc d'Orléans.

Aunt Fanny presided over a minor *salon* in the rue de Montmartre, and later in the rue du Tournon, near the Luxembourg Palace. There she received a bizarre group of lesser poets and artists (with one of whom she visited Italy) and that nocturnal wanderer and reporter of Parisian low life, Restif de la Bretonne. Aunt Fanny was amusing, extravagant, eccentric, a great contrast to down-to-earth Aunt Edmée.

There was no one of Marie-Rose's age except Alexandre, so it is not surprising that she clung to him and behaved, if one is to believe him, like a dictatorial child. It must be remembered that they were both in their teens, although at nineteen Alexandre's experience of the world had made him far more mature than his sixteen-year-old Creole bride. He tried to interest her in Rousseau, Diderot, Voltaire. Her eyes widened uncomprehendingly. He gave up.

In 1780 he rejoined his regiment, hoping that in the meantime Marie-Rose would improve her mind. She wrote touching little letters assuring him that 'she was trying to educate herself'. They were childish, badly written letters that did not satisfy him at all. Finally he suggested that she should send him the first drafts so that he could correct them. It was enough to crush all spontaneity. Then Aunt Edmée tried to help, but her influence was soon detected and Alexandre complained. Only one of Marie-Rose's letters seems to have met with his approval and he replied benevolently : 'How tender, how pleasing is the letter I have just received from you ; the heart that dictated it must be sensitive indeed and worthy of being loved. So it is. Yes, my heart, I truly love you. I long greatly to see you and this expected moment, however near it may be, seems all too far away.'

Their first child, Eugène-Rose, was born on 3 September 1781. He was destined to become Viceroy of Italy and to have three of his children on royal thrones (those of Sweden, Portugal and Brazil).

A further series of domestic tensions ended by Alexandre

appealing simultaneously for help to Aunt Edmée ('Can't *something* be done about my wife's letters?') and to his ex-tutor with a name like a Molière character: Patricol. This earnest gentleman had been appointed tutor to the nephews of the Duc de la Rochefoucauld and it was through him that Alexandre had been introduced to the duke, with whom he was spending more and more time at La Roche-Guyon. Alexandre explained the situation to Patricol, who became a temporary go-between:

Marie-Rose is indifferent and has little will to learn. She wants me to occupy myself solely with her, she wants to know what I say, what I do and what I write and she never thinks to acquire the true means of gaining my confidence. . . . When I first saw her I thought that I could live happily with her. At that moment I formed the plan of beginning her education again. . . . I continued with my plan until I perceived in her an indifference and an absence of desire to instruct herself that convinced me I was wasting my time. . . . Instead of remaining at home with an object who has nothing to say to me, I am going out much more often than I intended, and resuming in part the life of my old bachelor days. She has become jealous. . . .

Patricol was not much use as a marriage-guidance counsellor. He recommended that the whole family should interest themselves in Marie-Rose's education by reading selected passages from the poets with her and encouraging her to memorize speeches from the classical dramatists. He himself offered to teach her history and geography and he devised a course of studies, which included the four volumes of the Abbé Vertot's *Roman History*. It could not have been much fun.

Aunt Edmée, anxious to keep the marriage going and to please both parties, suggested a change of scene for Alexandre and helped to raise funds to send him to Italy. He left two months after Eugène's christening and returned in July 1782, delighted with all he had seen and apparently enchanted to be reunited with Marie-Rose. They moved to a house in the rue Neuve-Saint-Charles, near the church of Saint-Philippe du Roule, a more fashionable residence and quarter. The new house was rented in Alexandre's name. Joseph Tascher de la Pagerie now returned to Martinique with Aunt Rosette. He must have long outstayed his welcome. Perhaps he had tried to obtain a post in France ; if so, he had been unlucky.

Marie-Rose soon found herself pregnant again and Alexandre wrote to her – from La Roche-Guyon – that he was happy to hear of it. This letter was to be of crucial importance in the later separation proceedings.

Perhaps Joseph Tascher's departure gave Alexandre the idea that he too might visit the islands. Martinique was once again threatened by the English. Alexandre asked for leave from his regiment. Laure de Longpré's father had died in Martinique and she decided to go back to settle his affairs. The lovers arranged to travel together on a ship appropriately named *La Venus*. Alexandre bought forty volumes of Voltaire's works to take to his father-in-law as a present, asked Aunt Edmée for a game of lotto to play with Laure during the voyage and sailed without bidding his wife farewell. Perhaps he feared a scene. He wrote to her before boarding his ship :

Will you forgive me for having left you without farewell, for having gone away without warning, for having fled without having told you again a last time that I am all yours? Alas, what can you not read in my soul : love of my wife and love of glory, each rules supreme in my heart. You disapprove of me today. This afflicts me cruelly, but the day will come, *tendre amie*, when you will be grateful to me for having the courage to make so many sacrifices.

Such blatant hypocrisy met with what it deserved : complete silence on the part of Marie-Rose. She never wrote to Alexandre from the moment he left La Rochelle, though she did write to members of her family in Martinique, informing them that she had been looking after Aunt Edmée, who had been ill, and her ten year-old cousin. (This cousin was Baron Robert Tascher's son Gaspard, sent to France for his education and Marie-Rose's protégé – one of many she was to take throughout her life.) In February 1783 Alexandre wrote to his wife from Fort-Royal with news of the family : Grandmother Sannois was hale and hearty at sixty-five, her father's health was improving, her mother missed her. Sister Manette had been marked by an attack of scurvy and he had suggested an inoculation – a remedy advocated by his idol Jean-Jacques Rousseau. 'Keep busy,' he wrote smugly. 'This will counteract the indolence that has always been the primary cause of your neglect of your duties.'

Marie-Rose was delivered of a daughter on 10 April 1783. She was christened Hortense-Eugénie and was destined to become Queen of Holland and mother of the future Emperor Napoleon III. Her godmother was the eccentric Aunt Fanny. Marie-Rose's financial position was so poor that she was obliged to sell a medallion given to her by Alexandre as a wedding present to pay for the christening expenses. Alexandre's reaction to the birth was shattering. He wrote, on 8 July 1783, that he could not possibly be the father of Hortense, who must therefore be illegitimate!

Sunstroke, or his infatuation for Laure de Longpré, could not account for his subsequent letters and actions, which were those of an unbalanced mind. He made a tour of the plantation, bribed frightened slaves, announced that his wife had had affairs before her marriage and wrote to her:

My stay in this country has made known to me your abominable conduct here, the full details of your intrigue with M. de B. an officer in the Maritime regiment, and that with M. d'H. . . . who sailed on the *César*. . . . What of this last child born eight months and a few days after my return from Italy? I am forced to accept it, but I swear by the heavens that enlighten me it is another's; a stranger's blood flows in its veins. It shall never know my shame. . . . Make your arrangements. Never will I put myself in the position of being abused again. . . . Be good enough to betake yourself to a convent as soon as you receive my letter. This is my last word. . . . I will come to see you on my arrival in Paris, once only. I wish to have talk with you. . . . But, I repeat: no tears, no protestations. . . . You probably are not aware of the way in which I managed to unveil all these horrors, and I shall tell it only to my father and your aunt. . . .

Alexandre's conduct during his stay in Martinique was not above reproach; he was hardly in a position to blame his wife, even if she had been guilty. Marie-Rose's mother wrote to the Marquis de Beauharnais: 'I would never have thought that he would have let himself be led around so by Madame de Longpré....' Joseph Tascher offered to take his daughter back. The marquis wrote angrily to his son: 'So this is the result of your journey and of the fine campaign which you were counting on making against the enemies of the State! You got as far as making war on your wife's good name and the peace of the family.' So both the Taschers and the Beauharnais were on Marie-Rose's side. Fortunately, she had kept the letters in which Alexandre had expressed his joy at the news of her second pregnancy and which he had by then forgotten.

Rather ironically, his tirade – in which he called Marie-Rose 'the vilest of creatures' – was delivered in person by Laure de Longpré on her return from Martinique. She had then forsaken Alexandre for Count Arthur Dillon, an Irishman in the service of France as Governor of the island of St Christopher. (Dillon followed her to Paris where she established herself in a fine house in the rue de la Chaise and married him two years later. The wedding contract was signed by Louis xvi and Marie Antoinette. Dillon was elected to the Estates-General like Alexandre and died on the guillotine. Later Marie-Rose – or Josephine as she was by then – was magnanimous enough to protect Alexandre's bastard child and to secure a pension for the widowed Madame Dillon.)

Not having found a congenial occupation in Martinique, Alexandre decided to return to France and he called upon his mother-in-law to bid her goodbye. She wrote to the marquis afterwards:

I saw that he was troubled and moved. He seemed anxious to get away from me speedily to avoid my presence. His heart was already reproaching him for such mistaken conduct. . . . It is hardly possible for my daughter to remain with him unless he gives proof of a genuine desire to return to her and a perfect forgetting of what has happened.

To Marie-Rose she wrote: 'My poor daughter, all your

sorrows are in my breast ; they leave me without rest both day and night. Come, mingle your tears with those of a tender mother. All your friends do you justice ; they love you always and will console you.' She also gave the marquis details of the bribes Alexandre had offered to slaves to make false reports: 'He gave fifteen *moedes* to Thomas. What slave could not one corrupt with this amount of money, and which of them would not sell his master for the half!' She had the offending slave put into chains by way of punishment.

Aunt Edmée and the marquis made a vain attempt to organize a reconciliation. Alexandre landed at Rochefort on 15 September 1785 and stayed for a month with Laure's relations at Châtellerault. On 20 October he wrote severely to his wife : 'On my arrival in France I learned with astonishment from my father's letters that you were not yet in a convent . . . I have a fever caused by your conduct. . . .'

Marie-Rose hurried from Noisy to the house in the rue Neuve-Saint-Charles to plead with Alexandre, but he refused to go near her. He put up first in a hotel off the boulevard des Italiens, then took up residence at the Duc de La Rochefoucauld's town-house on the left bank. He now sold the furniture of the house in the rue Neuve-Saint-Charles, so the marquis, Edmée and Marie-Rose were obliged to return to Noisy. In these circumstances there was no alternative for Marie-Rose but to take herself off to a convent as her extraordinary husband insisted.

Aunt Edmée and Aunt Fanny both agreed that the place to go to was the convent of Penthémont, which was under the direction of the Abbess Marie-Catherine de Béthisy de Mezières and who attracted the cream of the many ladies afflicted with domestic troubles. In this large, comfortably furnished mansion in the rue de Grenelle, with a view of the gilded dome of the Invalides only a few hundred yards away, ladies could choose lodgings according to their means, costing from 300 *livres* a year for a single room to 1,200 *livres* for an apartment of six rooms. Board cost 800 *livres*. The lady abbess, who had con-nections in high society through a brother at court, was well placed to offer remunerative consolation to ladies in need of a fashionable, well-patronized retreat. It was as cosy as a club, with just the right degree of independence for each individual boarder, and no discipline demanded except for a formal attendance at chapel on Sundays. What more – and indeed, what less – could be asked from well-bred *femmes du monde*?

Incidentally there is no record in any of the numerous memoirs of the time of Marie-Rose's (or in later life Josephine's) attitude towards religion, except the remark that she knelt very gracefully in church. That, and a later habit of distributing rosaries to old ladies during her travels as empress, is all that a biographer has to go by. In all the reports of dramatic scenes and events written by ladies-in-waiting, secretaries, readers and valets, there is not one reference to an impassioned appeal to the Deity, the Virgin Mary or the saints. In moments of crisis, Marie-Rose brought out the pack of cards she invariably carried on her person and proceeded to tell her fortune. No devotional pictures, crucifixes or statuettes appear in the inventories of her possessions or the descriptions of her dwellings. To religion she appears to have been quietly indifferent. If the Abbaye de Penthémont opened new vistas for her, and all her biographers agree that it did, they were not of a religious, but of a social order.

Leaving little Hortense with a wet nurse at Noisy, Marie-Rose moved into the convent with Eugène, accompanied by Aunt Edmée, who obviously felt responsible, as the erstwhile match-maker, for her injured niece. All attempts at reconciliation having proved fruitless, Edmée urged Marie-Rose to fight Alexandre, since she had no cause to feel guilty. As soon as they had settled in she summoned an official of the Châtelet to the guest parlour on the second floor. To be precise, this occurred at 11.30 am on 8 December 1783.

There, Monsieur Louis Joron, counsellor to the King and commissioner at the Châtelet, proceeded to question the twenty-year-old Vicomtesse de Beauharnais and to draw up her formal complaint against her husband. Marie-Rose informed Monsieur Joron about Alexandre's 'dissipations and frequent absences from home', his indifference at the birth of his son, their temporary reconciliation, then his visit to Italy and subsequent departure for Martinique at a time when he knew that she was pregnant. At this point she showed him the letter he had sent to her from Italy and, to conclude, his two tirades of 8 July and 20 October 1783, 'containing the most atrocious imputations'. Alexandre had not visited his wife since his return from Martinique and in the whole of the four years they had been married he had spent no more then ten months in her company. (No doubt Aunt Edmée was responsible for this piece of arithmetic.) The petitioner, Monsieur Joron noted gravely, 'desires legal separation of body and habitation. It is not possible for her to suffer patiently so many affronts. To do this would be lacking in what she owed to herself and to her children and to expose herself to the most terrible fate'.

On 3 February 1784 the Provost of Paris issued an order authorizing Marie-Rose to stay at Penthémont until the court reached a decision. Alexandre was to pay for her support and the education of the children ; he was also made to pay the salary of the mulatto maid.

Since Alexandre could not substantiate the wild allegations he had made in his letters he turned on his father, whom he accused of abusing his trusteeship and refusing to render accounts. He claimed he was overdrawn by 300,000 *livres* and that to meet his debts he had been obliged to sell the furniture from his house in the rue Neuve-Saint-Charles. He was still being pursued by his creditors. He also sued his wife for the return of the jewelry he had given her as wedding presents, including the medallion she had sold to pay for Hortense's christening and which he alleged was part of his inheritance. Yet he found the money for a full social life. Perhaps the Duc de la Rochefoucauld, whose aide-de-camp he hoped to become, settled his protégé's expenses and felt sorry for the excitable young man who was making such a muddle of his life. Alexandre was genuinely fond of his children and he paid a quick visit to see Hortense at Noisy, taking an armful of toys. The local *curé* reported this to Marie-Rose, adding that the young vicomte had told him that he was 'enjoying himself greatly in Paris'.

Marie-Rose spent the following year at Penthémont, acquiring the social graces for which she was later to be famous. The convent was said to be the best finishing-school in France. Whether or not she made intimate friends with ladies of a higher rank is open to question, but the abbess appears to have befriended her and set an example of refinement and *savoir faire* that did more for her than the four tomes of the Abbé Vertot's *Roman History*.She learned by observing and imitating ; she also had a prodigious memory for names and dates, which was to prove very useful in her later exalted career. But the one thing she never learned from the shrewd ladies with whom she was then most in contact – Aunt Edmée and the abbess – was how to administer her budget. Not having any money of her own except the little provided by Alexandre, and that irregularly,, she was entirely dependent on her aunt and her parents, to whom she constantly wrote for assistance. She was in debt all her life but, like many people who follow this pattern of existence, though her financial position occasionally worried her, she always got by.

One day in February 1785 Marie-Rose returned to Penthémont after a shopping expedition with Aunt Edmée and called to Eugène, whom she had left playing in the walled garden. There was no reply. After a frantic search upstairs and downstairs, for the child was mischievous and fond of playing pranks, a servant reported that Eugène had driven away in a carriage with a 'charming gentleman' whom he evidently knew and had been delighted to see. Marie-Rose uttered a shriek and nearly had a fit of hysterics. Then she found a note in her drawing-room, left by Alexandre. 'The boy will be better with me. This place is too full of women. It is not suitable for Eugène.'

While she wrung her hands and wept (Alexandre had once referred to her readiness to shed tears, but she had not yet fully developed her lachrymose powers), Aunt Edmée, practical as ever, firmly declared: 'This is a matter for the authorities. You must write to the provost at once to have the child restored to you. Alexandre has no right to behave like this. It will go against him.'

Edmée was right. Eugène was restored to his mother and his parents were summoned to appear at the Châtelet on 5 March 1785, for a confrontation before Maître Trurat, notary of Paris. The case was settled in his study, out of court, and ended in a complete victory for Marie-Rose. Alexandre threw in his hand, withdrew his charges and confessed, rather lamely, to having been led astray by 'the passions and follies of youth'. He was made to pay for them: Marie-Rose was free to live wherever she pleased, to administer her own affairs, to receive directly the interests on her dowry. He was to make her an annual allowance of 5000 *livres*; Hortense was to remain with her mother until her marriage and he was to pay an additional 1000 *livres* a year for her upkeep. Eugène was to stay with Marie-Rose until the age of five, after which he would be brought up by his father, but would be allowed to spend his summer holidays with his mother. There was no further argument about Hortense's paternity.

And so, at the age of twenty-one, Marie-Rose found herself separated from her husband, with no real home of her own and the prospect of having to give up her son in less than two years' time. She was still half a prisoner, unable to remarry and financially insecure.

The Marquis of Beauharnais no longer had control over his son's inheritance, while his properties in Santo Domingo had suffered from a combination of bad weather and bad stewardship. (Joseph Tascher was much to blame for the latter.) Aunt Edmée was in bad health and the troubles of the past few years had soured her temper. It may have been the wise abbess of Penthémont who suggested that it would be cheaper, and more pleasant for Marie-Rose to live outside Paris. In Fontainebleau, for instance, she could introduce her and her relatives to her nephew, the Vicomte de Béthisy and his wife. There she would find congenial company among people more or less attached to the court. The king went to Fontainebleau every year to enjoy the boar hunting in the dense forests around the château.

A move was made and a house rented, although Marie-Rose kept on her apartments at Penthémont. In November 1785 she wrote to the income-tax collector: 'Now I receive a demand for a poll tax amounting to the sum of sixty-six *livres*, three *deniers*; I have the honour to inform you, Monsieur, that I am still legally bound to my husband, who makes his residence in Paris, and that I have no more than an amicable separation from him. If you insist on my paying a tax I venture to submit that I am being taxed at an exorbitant price in relation to my resources.' There is a note in the margin of this letter, preserved in the Paris archives, to the effect that the tax was reduced to 30 *livres*. Marie-Rose was beginning to stand up for her rights.

The husband from whom she stated she was 'amicably' separated wrote to her almost every week and she replied. The letters were mostly about the children, in whom Alexandre continued to take a keen interest. In September 1786 Eugène was sent to his father, and boarded at the Institution de la Jeune Noblesse in the rue de Berry. Josephine felt the separation keenly although life in Fontainebleau was not unpleasant. The now-widowed Aunt Fanny took up residence there and could be relied upon to provide a note of gaiety. The Béthisys introduced Marie-Rose to the governor of the château, the Comte de Montmorin, and through him she was occasionally able to follow the royal boar hunt at a distance. It was the nearest she ever got to the royal presence.

In the spring of 1787 Marie-Rose's uncle, Baron Robert Tascher, came over from Martinique to visit his son, now at a naval college. With him he brought the sum of 2,789 *livres* from his brother for Marie-Rose. Disappointed, she wrote: 'This makes me hope that you are seriously trying to provide me soon with more considerable sums. . . . You know me well enough, dear papa, to be quite sure that were it not for a pressing need of money I would speak of nothing but my tender sentiments for you.' In a further letter she added:

I am occupied at the moment in looking after my daughter, whom Monsieur Beauharnais has wished to be inoculated; I thought I ought not to oppose this request in this delicate situation; up to the present I have nothing to reproach myself about since the child is as well as could be desired. She is my consolation, she is charming in face and character. She already often speaks of her grandpapa and grandmama la Pagerie. She does not forget her Aunt Manette and asks me: 'Mama, shall I see them soon?' Such is her prattle at the moment. Eugène has been at a school in Paris for four months. He is wonderfully well. He could not be inoculated because of his double teeth, which are coming early, as you see. . . .

During the three years when Marie-Rose resided most of the time at Fontainebleau she made useful and pleasant contacts, mostly through the Montmorins. Gentlemen paid court to her: the Comte de Cresnay (Madame de Montmorin's brother-in-law), the Duc de Lorge, the Chevalier de Coigny. Did they become her lovers? We do not know. All we can affirm is that she had plenty of opportunities to exercise and develop her charm and coquetry.

For reasons that biographers have found obscure, Marie-Rose made up her mind to return to Martinique in July 1788 taking Hortense with her. A year had gone by since her enforced separation from Eugène and it is natural to suppose that she must have been feeling melancholy and in need of a change of scene. Nine years had elapsed since she had left home and she was anxious to show Hortense to her parents. Perhaps Baron Tascher, during his visit to France the year before, had hinted that a return visit would put a stop to any gossip and unfriendly comment provoked by her known separation from Alexandre. Perhaps, too, she thought that she could persuade her father to part with more money if she was there to explain her position in person. And maybe she was finding domineering Aunt Edmée a little trying. There are a number of plausible explanations for her decision.

Hortense was five years old, too young to know anything about her mother's reasons for wanting to return home; in her memoirs she merely states: 'My mother wanted to see her own country again.' By a strange coincidence, in 1814 Hortense revisited the house where she had stayed with her mother at Le Havre while they were waiting for a ship. The owners, Monsieur and Madame Dubuc, were still there and they recalled how bravely Marie-Rose had agreed to sail in a fierce storm and how impressed the captain had been by her courage. Considering what a bad sailor she was, her motive for leaving France must have been strong indeed. (The Dubucs' house, incidentally, had been recommended by a banker friend, Monsieur de Rougemont. All through her life Marie-Rose was to cultivate the useful friendship of bankers and financiers.)

She had borrowed 1000 *livres* from Aunt Edmée, as she was short of cash to pay for the voyage. No doubt Aunt Edmée charged her interest. Business was business even when the family was concerned and sentiments were never allowed to interfere. Marie-Rose, always so generous herself, was beginning to find her a little hard and demanding.

The island had scarcely changed since she had left it. There were the familiar buildings of Fort-Royal and, across the bay, the settlement of Trois-Ilets with its little stone church and fifty old wooden houses belonging to the *grands blancs*, as the local French aristocracy were called. And there was the family plantation, much as she had recollected it, but even more dilapidated, for Joseph Tascher de la Pagerie was as apathetic as ever. Beyond a stream, named La Pagerie after the family surname, was the round sugar-refinery on pillars with its red-tiled roof, the chimney of the furnace just visible above the fruit trees, the acres of sugar-cane, coffee, tobacco plants, the slave huts surrounded by little kitchen gardens. There was the rock-hewn basin by the stream, shaded by tamarinds and mango trees, where Marie-Rose and her sisters had bathed when they were children. She must have pointed it all out to little Hortense, whose eyes glowed at her first sight of the brilliant flowers and birds. It was paradise for a child, and that is how she was always to remember it.

And there, lined up waiting on the wide verandah, were Grandmama Tascher, Grandpapa, Aunt Manette, who looked so frail (she died in the following year), and the slaves – about

twenty of them, the women colourful in their bright headscarves, the men already bursting into songs of greeting
accompanied by drums and tambourines. Hortense, with her
good ear for music, picked up the tunes almost at once. She
only hoped there would not be an earthquake during their stay,
or a hurricane like the one her mother had told her about. This
had taken place in her childhood and had razed the family
home to the ground; forty-eight ships had been sunk at sea,
trees had been uprooted and swept away. It was after this
catastrophe that the family had taken to living in the sugar-
refinery, as they had no money to rebuild. And then there was
the ever-present danger, which had not receded, of an attack
by the English, who had blockaded the island so many times.
She saw her mother fervently embrace her parents and her old
wet nurse, the slave Marion, to whom she was greatly attached
and whom she never forgot. (In 1807 Napoleon bestowed an
annual pension of 1200 francs upon her, 'in gratitude for the
services she rendered to our beloved spouse in her youth'.)

At first life was easy and pleasant; Marie-Rose relaxed in
the warm sunshine, waited on hand and foot by the slaves, to
whom she was always friendly and generous. Hortense had
observed her mother giving them money and on one occasion,
as she relates in her *Memoirs*, seeing piles of coins in her grandmother's room she thought they were destined for the slaves
and proceeded to distribute them herself, to Madame Tascher's
wrath.

Soon after her return home Marie-Rose wrote to Aunt Edmée
asking her to forward her evening dresses. This seems to
indicate that she had not originally intended to stay long on the
island. Otherwise she would surely have taken her entire ward-
robe with her – unless, of course, she had deliberately made a
quick get-away, fearing that her husband might forbid her to
return to Martinique with Hortense. It also indicates that she
was finding life at Trois-Ilets dull. Uncle Robert was the leader
of whatever social life was available at Fort-Royal, the little
capital, and Marie-Rose must have been a great attraction.
There were no doubt a few admirers to flirt with. The Vicom-

tesse de Beauharnais had been welcomed back and there were no whispers about a suspect past. She was probably pitied on account of her husband's outrageous behaviour, which everybody who mattered well remembered since it had occurred only four years before ; the legal separation had been in her favour. She had come from France, the fount of civilized life, the convent schoolgirl who had left nine years earlier transformed into a sophisticated woman. She must have brought the new fashionable clothes à l'Anglaise (a few years later all things British, or of British provenance, including Indian muslins, became taboo by order of Bonaparte). Tight jackets over loose flowing skirts, round tall hats, free, unpowdered hair – Marie-Rose wore everything with airy elegance. She must have been bombarded with questions about life in Paris and at court. The young Marie-Rose who had been interrogated by her politically minded husband on conditions in Martinique had been caught unprepared and had been unable to give satisfactory answers. Now, to the ladies and gentlemen of Fort-Royal, she could elaborate on her friendship with the Comte and Comtesse de Montmorin, the Duchesse de Montesson, the Vicomte and Vicomtesse Béthisy. With a little imagination and pardonable embellishments she could even give a description of court life at Fontainebleau and of the royal boar hunts she had followed – at a distance. Uncle Robert was proud of his niece. Marie-Rose never forgot his hospitality, for, as countless instances will show later, she possessed that rarest of virtues – gratitude.

This easy-going colonial life continued until the following year, 1789. Disturbing news from France had reached Martinique and Marie-Rose sought advice from her relatives as to what she should do. The country was in turmoil ; great political changes were imminent and both Alexandre and his brother François (who held rigidly royalist views) were taking an active part in bringing them about. Both brothers were elected in the summer of 1789 when the Estates-General met at Versailles, Alexandre was elected to represent Blois and François for Paris. Alexandre was in his element – at last he had found an outlet for his progressive ideas and his love of rhetoric. He joined the Breton, (later known as the Jacobin) Club and was one of 47 nobles out of 235 who voted that the three estates (nobility, clergy and commons) should sit together.

No letters have survived from that period but Alexandre must have written to his wife to give her news of Eugène, and Aunt Edmée, too, must have kept her *au fait* with developments. Should she return to France? Was Eugène being neglected by his busy father? Events settled the issue for her early in 1790.

In France the Society of the Friends of Negroes had worked for the emancipation of slaves in the colonies and the Duc de la Rochefoucauld's family (who had property in the islands) were ardent supporters of the movement. When the news that a member of the Constituent Assembly in Paris had demanded the abolition of slavery reached Martinique, there were Negro revolts and street brawls in Fort-Royal; the soldiers, out of sympathy, were reluctant to fire on the rioters. Marie-Rose decided to go back to France, since she was worried about Eugène's safety; Alexandre was too involved in politics to look after him properly. Her parents and Manette, who was dangerously ill, had always been just to their slaves ; they would doubtless be respected and had nothing to fear. Events proved her right.

But would there be a ship available to take her and Hortense back to France? Those in the harbour had been driven out by the rebels, who were virtually in charge of Fort-Royal ; she had taken Hortense there on a hurried visit to confer with her Uncle Robert, the port commander. During her visit he had attempted to parley with the Negro rioters, but had been seized and held hostage. The insurgents captured one of the forts and threatened to bombard the town. A friend of Marie-Rose's uncle, Captain Durand de Braye, commander of the frigate *Sensible* (described in some accounts as a warship) got an urgent message through to Marie-Rose, who had meanwhile taken refuge in her uncle's abandoned house. He intended, he wrote, to make a bid to leave the port that night, before the mob seized control and disarmed his ship. It was her last chance to leave for France. If she hurried she might be able to make it. It was risky. The decision was up to her.

Marie-Rose did not hesitate. It was the only time in her life that she abandoned all thought of clothes. Grabbing Hortense by the hand she made her way from the house and ran across the open fields to the edge of the sea, with bullets whizzing over her head. Eventually she reached a boat and was rowed out to the *Sensible*, which was just on the point of sailing. They left the harbour under heavy fire from the batteries of Fort Bourbon, where Baron Tascher was still held hostage. Civil war was about to sweep the island.

Marie-Rose was seasick during most of the voyage from Fort-Royal to Toulon, but little Hortense, less delicate then than she was to be later, made friends with the sailors and entertained them by her rendering of Negro songs and dances – proof that she had mixed freely with the Negro slaves on her grandparents' plantation. One day Marie-Rose noticed that the child's feet were bleeding ; Hortense confessed that there were holes in her shoes and that she had danced barefoot. She possessed only one pair of shoes. An old sailor overheard the conversation and made Hortense a pair of sandals from scraps of leather so that she could continue to dance without hurting her feet. Years afterwards Marie-Rose – then Josephine – recounted the story to her ladies-in-waiting, adding characteristically that she was sorry she had never asked the sailor's name. He was called Jacques, that was all she knew. The sandals were one of the most precious gifts she had ever received, she said, and she would dearly have liked to reward the kind donor now that she was in a position to do so.

From Toulon Marie-Rose made her way to Fontainebleau to rejoin Aunt Edmée and the marquis and to find out what had happened to Eugène and his father. Eugène, she was informed, was still at boarding school, and was a great admirer of his father's oratory. Alexandre, one of the three secretaries of the Constituent Assembly, became its president and, as a professional soldier, also had a seat on the military committee. He had advocated free public education for all children and was proving himself to be a faithful follower of his hero, Jean-Jacques Rousseau. He was in the chair of the Constituent Assembly on 21 June 1791 when the news came that the king and his family had fled from the Tuileries, and it was he who made the announcement reproduced in so many textbooks: '*Messieurs*, the king has fled during the night ; let us proceed to the order of the day.' All the books he had read, all the liberal theories he had imbibed poured forth in torrents of prose ; he made speeches about pensions, hospitals, the general staff, the navy, religion, Jews, the press. . . .

Marie-Rose now went to Paris to be nearer Eugène and was first housed in the rue d'Anjou. Later she shared a house in the rue Saint-Dominique with a Creole woman of her own age, Madame Hosten-Lamotte. It seems that people of Creole origin kept together in a little separate society of their own.

Marie-Rose and Hortense were often joined by Eugène on his free days and his father appears to have been on at least civil terms with his mother. A surviving letter to the Marquis de Beauharnais from Alexandre contains the sentence: 'I embrace my children. Tomorrow I shall try to write to Madame de Beauharnais.' The vicomte must have met his wife in society, for they both frequented the salons of liberal aristocrats such as Prince Frédéric de Salm-Krybourg and his sister Princess Amélie of Hohenzollern-Sigmaringen, members of the Jacobin Club, as well as the minority of ultra-revolutionaries known as 'The Mountain'. Marie-Rose, perhaps partly on the advice of Aunt Edmée, partly on the basis of her own strong instinct for survival, made – or tried to make – friends in every camp, so as to be sure of some support from whoever turned out to be on the winning side. Most of her friends were wealthier than she was and she incurred debts so as to be able to dress and keep up with ladies like the Marquise d'Espinchal, Madame de Genlis, the Marquise des Moulins and the members of their literary salons.

Alexandre's moment of glory was shortlived. At one time he was virtually the ruler of France and Eugène was greeted in the streets of Fontainebleau by cries of '*Voilà le Dauphin!*'. But the Constituent Assembly was brought to an end in September 1791. The Convention gave Alexandre the rank of chief of staff of the Army of the Rhine and he went to Strasbourg where he placed Eugène in school.

Marie-Rose's friend Madame Hosten-Lamotte had rented a house in the village of Croissy near Paris and there, after the execution of the king and queen in 1792, Marie-Rose joined her with Hortense, so as to be further away from the Terror. (The house in Croissy, incidentally, had belonged to the late queen's first lady-in-waiting, Madame Campan, whom Marie-Rose and her family were to know so well later.)

At Croissy Madame Hosten-Lamotte introduced Marie-Rose to the mayor, Jean Chanorier, a popular *ancien seigneur* interested in market gardening. In his house she met Tallien, the revolutionary who was to save her life ; Pierre-François Réal, attorney at the Châtelet and later councillor of state and deputy minister of police under the Consulate ; and Madame de Vergennes, one of whose daughters, the future Madame de Rémusat, would become one of the empress's ladies. Marie-Rose used her 'red' friends to protect the Vergennes but the day came when these aristocratic connections landed her in trouble. She was actually arrested on the same day as Monsieur de Vergennes.

In September 1793 a Law of Suspects was promulgated ; this referred to 'those who by their conduct, their connections, their remarks or their writings, show themselves to be the partisans of tyranny ; also the relatives of any who have emigrated and those who have been refused certificates of citizenship'. Marie-Rose quickly dropped her title of vicomtesse, and became plain Citoyenne Beauharnais, and applied for a certificate at Croissy.

In July 1793 Alexandre, as commander-in-chief of the Army of the Rhine, had failed to relieve the besieged city of Mainz, which was surrounded by Prussians and Austrians, and his enemies took the opportunity to bring him down. He resigned and retired to his estate at La Ferté-Beauharnais. Aristocrats, however liberal, were now a proscribed caste. On 2 March 1794 the Committee of General Security ordered his arrest and the seizure of his papers. Little Eugène, aged only twelve, left his school at Strasbourg and made his own way to Croissy to join his mother. Thoroughly alarmed, Marie-Rose, whose first thought was for the safety of her children, sent them both with Princess Amélie to Saint-Martin in the province of Artois, where Prince de Salm had a country house. Brother and sister were planning to emigrate to England but Alexandre, hearing of the plan, sent word to Marie-Rose to have the children recalled at once. Princess Amélie brought them to Croissy herself; her brother was arrested and later guillotined. Without knowing it, he had sacrificed his life for the future Queen of Holland, the mother of Napoleon III.

The liberal Duc de La Rochefoucauld had been hacked to pieces at Gisors by an inflamed mob who had heard of the invasion of France by the Prussians; his nephew was murdered, and his town house was confiscated and converted into a warehouse. Alexandre's brother François, who had tried to organize a plot to release Louis XVI and his family from the Temple, had emigrated across the Rhine after their execution and became a major-general in the army of the Duc de Condé.

In the village of Croissy people were less fanatical than in Paris, but children everywhere were now expected to learn trades – hands were considered to be as important as brains, as in twentieth-century Maoist China. Since the children's schools had been closed, Marie-Rose apprenticed Eugène to the local carpenter at Croissy, while Hortense learned the rudiments of dressmaking from her governess, Madame Lannoy. They seem to have enjoyed the experience and Hortense never forgot it. In later years she impressed upon her sons that they should learn a trade, for nobody knew what vicissitudes life might bring. Eugène, always cheerful and adaptable, endeared himself to everybody, whatever their station, and began to take upon himself the responsibilities of an adult. He even signed the wedding register on the occasion of the marriage of the gardener, Pierre Foy, as his mother was absent in Paris. She had gone to Paris to seek advice – and money – from her friends.

At this early age Eugène had already begun to assume the protective guardian role towards his mother that he continued to exercise discreetly and affectionately throughout his life.

Marie-Rose kept up her little establishment at Croissy and wielded her pen in favour of the persecuted. Her self-appointed task was to pull strings and draft petitions; this she did courageously and at considerable risk to her own safety. For instance, as soon as she heard that Françoise de Beauharnais, the divorced wife of Alexandre's *émigré* brother, had been arrested and sent to the prison of Saint-Pélagie, she wrote to Vadier, the head of the Committee of General Security, to plead for her release. Her letter was as much a plea for her own husband as it was for Françoise:

> ... I would very much regret, Citizen Representative, if you were to confuse Alexandre in your mind with the elder Beauharnais. . . . Alexandre has never deviated from these principles [liberty and equality]. He has constantly kept to the line. If he were not a Republican, he would have neither my respect nor my affection. I am an American and know him. . . . My household is a republican household. Before the Revolution my children were not distinguishable from *sansculottes* and I hope they will be worthy of the Republic.
>
> I write to you frankly, as a *sansculotte*. . . . I appeal to your sympathy and humanity on behalf of an unfortunate citizeness. . . .

One cannot refrain from smiling at the thought of Marie-Rose as a *sansculotte*. But the means justified the end and she had to practise the art of dissimulation in order to survive. People were to say later that she was an inveterate liar. One can counter that accusation by saying that she nearly always lied in a good cause and not solely in self-interest.

Vadier never replied to Marie-Rose's letter, but as he did not tear it up it has survived the troubled years and can still be read in the archives of the City of Paris. Did he think it could be used as a weapon against her? He was the first to sign the arrest warrant for Alexandre and to pretend to believe in the alleged prison conspiracy for which Alexandre was imprisoned and subsequently guillotined. Among the signatures on the letter from the Committee of General Security ordering

Alexandre's arrest was that of Jacques-Louis David, artist and patriot, who – ten years later – was commissioned to paint the official picture of Napoleon and Josephine's coronation in Notre Dame. Josephine, the widow of the man he had helped to send to his execution! People changed, circumstances changed. Where was truth to be found? What *was* truth? People lied – life itself was a lie, and Marie-Rose adapted herself like a chameleon. From *sansculotte* to empress – an astonishing metamorphosis.

It was a lie, too, that sent her to prison in her turn, the basest form of lie: an anonymous letter denouncing her as a traitor to the republic. She was arrested on 20 April 1794 with a warrant to search her home in the rue de l'Université, where she was spending the winter. Nothing was found there except a bunch of patriotic letters written by Alexandre. On 21 April she was taken to the prison of Les Carmes, a former convent in the rue de Vaugirard, where Alexandre was also incarcerated. Husband and wife managed to meet briefly, although the sexes were confined to separate quarters, and they exchanged letters. There was never any question of a last-minute reconciliation ; love had died long ago, but they showed a common concern for their children. It is greatly to Marie-Rose's credit that she never uttered a word against Alexandre to Eugène and Hortense. She must have impressed upon them that their parents' disagreements were of a private nature. Alexandre, she insisted and they believed, was a true patriot and had been a brave soldier. Eugène admired his father deeply and – by one of fate's curious twists – it was because of this fervent, childish admiration that his mother was to meet her second husband : General Napoleon Bonaparte.

During the 108 days of Marie-Rose's imprisonment (from 21 April to 6 August 1794) Eugène and Hortense were looked after by the faithful Madame Lannoy and they spent Sundays with Princesse Amélie, herself a suspect with a republican guard in her house. The children's protectors must have contacted their mother's business advisers and bankers, perhaps even Aunt Edmée, of whom nothing is heard during this period except that she and the marquis had taken out certificates of citizenship at Fontainebleau. The petitions sent by Eugène and Hortense in May and June to the Convention and the Committee of General Security were clearly not composed by them, however precocious they may have been:

> Two innocent children appeal to you, Citizen Representative, for the liberty of their beloved mother, who can be blamed for nothing but the misfortune of having entered a class to which she has shown that she considered herself to be a stranger, since she has never associated with any but the best patriots, the most excellent members of the Mountain. . . . Citizen Representative, you will not permit the oppression of innocence, patriotism and virtue. Give back life to these unfortunate children whose age is not fit for sadness: Eugène Beauharnais (aged 12) Hortense (aged 11).

The children walked disconsolately to the grim ex-convent every day to try and catch a glimpse of their parents. It has been stated over and over again that they succeeded in getting messages through to their mother by concealing them under the collar of Marie-Rose's pet pug, Fortuné; yet it is difficult to believe that the little creature was allowed to trot in and out of the prison unnoticed by the gaolers, even if the gardener and his wife, who lived in the lodge beside the entrance, had been bribed. Nevertheless, the fondness that Marie-Rose displayed toward Fortuné, the special treatment meted out to him after her release, point to his having made a useful canine contribution towards easing her anguish. (He has been described by those who knew him only too well as an ugly, black little animal of an aggressive disposition, and he has passed to posterity as the only creature who ever dared to bite Napoleon's leg.)

This was the worst period – physically – that Marie-Rose ever had to endure. Separated from her children, in fear of losing her life and of seeing Alexandre lose his, she was driven frantic by the thought of Eugène and Hortense being left orphans and at the mercy of the revolutionaries. There are conflicting accounts of her behaviour during these trying times. She herself, in later years at Malmaison, assured her listeners that in prison she was sustained by the prophecy of her old Creole nurse, Marion, that 'she was destined to become queen of France, but not for long' and that this gave her courage. But her cell-mates, including the Duchesse d'Aiguillon, insisted that she was in the depths of despair and wept copiously. As an aristocrat with the proverbial stiff upper lip, the duchess was dismayed and slightly contemptuous. Those of her class and rank went to the guillotine with their heads held high. One historian has suggested that if they had let themselves go, wept and wrung their hands, they might have aroused pity in the hearts of their executioners and the spectators ; but it could be argued that the reverse attitude could have been aroused – their tears might have given their executioners sadistic pleasure. Judging from Marie-Rose's inclination to shed tears at the drop of a hat, one may safely assume that she shed many in her captivity ; it is almost certain that she never gave a thought to Marion's prediction, which would have appeared absurd in the circumstances, but tell her own cards she did, over and over again. The results might have been contradictory, since she derived no comfort from her own fortune-telling.

Les Carmes was a sinister place ; Marie-Rose shared a damp, dirty cell, which measured seven and a half feet by thirty, with eighteen other detainees. It had a vaulted roof and an iron-barred window overlooking an overgrown garden. The outline of two swords drawn in blood had been traced on the wall by the Septemberists of 1792, who had been imprisoned there after they had massacred the Archbishop of Arles and many priests.

Every day a list of people executed appeared in the papers and these were smuggled into the prison and eagerly scanned by the inmates for news of their relatives. On 25 July Marie-Rose read the name Alexandre de Beauharnais on the fatal list. He had been executed the day before and buried in a communal grave. She fainted, partly no doubt from genuine grief and partly for fear that her turn was imminent.

Before his execution Alexandre had written her a long letter

33

from the Conciergerie, the pre-guillotine prison to which he had been transferred on 21 July. It was evidently intended for publication and it appeared on the streets of Paris later in the form of a pamphlet. The style is characteristic of this strange, impassioned eccentric:

> I regret . . . having to leave a country that I love, for which I would willingly have given my life a thousand times, which I will be unable to serve and which will see me depart believing me to be a bad citizen. This intolerable thought requires me to entrust my reputation to you. Work to redeem it, by showing that a life wholly dedicated to the service of one's country and to the triumph of Liberty and Equality must, in the eyes of the people, repudiate those odious calumniators who themselves belong to the class of suspects. . . .

And there was much more in this flamboyant vein.

Marie-Rose, it must be repeated, faithfully carried out Alexandre's last request. In Eugène's eyes his father was a hero and she never said or did anything to make him believe otherwise.

Three days after Alexandre's execution Robespierre fell. The Terror was over. Marie-Rose endured a few last moments of personal terror when her gaoler entered her cell to remove her straw mattress. She asked whether he had come to change it and he replied with an ugly leer that 'she would have no further use for it'.

It is generally believed that she owed her release to the intercession of Jean Tallien, a member of the Committee of General Security, whom she met at Croissy and to whom Eugène had appealed. Thérésa de Cabarrus, Tallien's mistress, had been released from the prison of La Force a week before her, but nobody knows for sure whether the two women, who were to become inseparable friends, already knew one another. In any case the official order for Marie-Rose's release was signed by Tallien, and Eugène confirmed this fact in his memoirs.

Another story relates that Marie-Rose may also have owed her life to that resourceful employee of the Committee of

General Security, the former actor Delperch de la Bussière, who removed the dossiers of 'favoured prisoners so that their trials, through lack of documents, were indefinitely postponed. It was alleged that the formidable total of 1,153 dossiers was made to disappear, and by the most extraordinary method imaginable – La Bussière actually chewed and swallowed the incriminating documents! (This feat does not appear to have impaired his digestion ; the last we hear of him is in 1803, when a group of benefactors who owed their lives to him organized a charity performance at the Théâtre de la Porte Saint-Martin for the benefit of the impoverished actor. Josephine attended with Bonaparte and sent him a purse containing the sum of 1000 francs, with the revealing note: 'In grateful remembrance'.)

But at the time of her release from prison she was the one who was impoverished. She found herself alone in the chaotic post-revolutionary world, a widow with two growing children to support. She was thirty-one, an almost unmarriageable age in those days. She had her own life to live ; she could no longer burden Aunt Edmée and the ageing marquis with her troubles, and most probably she did not wish to do so. They had enough troubles of their own. Hardly any money was coming from colonial plantations and Martinique had again been seized by the British.

Marie-Rose now appealed to her banker friends, no doubt exercising her considerable charm to obtain loans from them. On 1 January 1795 she wrote plaintively to her mother :

You have doubtless heard of the misfortunes that have befallen me, leaving me and my children with no means of subsistence except your charity alone. I am a widow, deprived of my husband's fortune, as are his children. You see, my dear mama, what need I have to come to you. Without the care of my good friend Emmery [a Dunkirk banker often resorted to by the Tascher family] I do not know what I should have done. I am too certain of your affection to have the least doubt about the anxiety that you will show to procure me the means of living and of showing my gratitude by paying back what I owe to M. Emmery.

(Seven years later she was in a position to lend Monsieur

Emmery and his partner 200,000 francs, and she refused to accept any interest.) She begged her mother to send money to Hamburg or London bankers, who could then transmit it to Dunkirk. Madame Tascher does appear to have sent her daughter some money, but it was not enough. It never could be enough for Marie-Rose, who was determined to hob-nob with fashionable society. She was not beautiful but (to quote Oscar Wilde's phrase) she behaved as if she was ; she was not rich, but she lived as if she was.

She rented an apartment from Madame Krény at 371 rue de l'Université. Tallien supported her petition to be allowed to recover the furniture and clothes that had been looked after during her imprisonment by the devoted Madame Lannoy. Aunt Edmée advanced her 50,000 *livres* in the currently inflated currency, which enabled her to pay a visit to Hamburg to see the banker Matthiessen and to draw bills on her mother for 25,000 *livres*. After a short period of service under General Lazare Hoche, who had known Alexandre, and who had been entrusted with an expedition against the Chouan and Vendean rebels of western France, Eugène was sent to the newly established Collège Irlandais run by Patrick McDermott at Saint-Germain-en-Laye. Marie-Rose thought Eugène needed further education before entering the army permanently.

Hortense was placed as a boarder next door to Eugène at a newly opened school for girls under the direction of Madame Campan. This school became so fashionable that pupils were sent there to be 'finished' from all over Europe. They later formed a kind of 'old girls' club' that proved useful to many of them. Resourceful Madame Campan had successfully weathered the revolutionary storm and had adapted herself to changing circumstances without relinquishing one iota of her strict moral code and conduct.

Marie-Rose was – had to be – more flexible. Having no education or background that counted, she could only fall back on her feminine charms in the realization that time was against her. With the help of her friend Thérésa Tallien (Marie-Rose became godmother to her daughter, who was born very soon after her marriage) she threw herself with the zest of the re-prieved into the frenzied life by which people sought to efface from their minds the horrors of the Revolution. The *bals à la victime* were a particularly macabre form of entertainment to which relatives of guillotined victims were invited. They wore their hair short, as if in preparation for the block, and tied a thin red ribbon round their throats. *Muscadins* and *Incroyables* were the titles bestowed upon young men who affected grotesque frock coats, flattened their hair in the 'dog's ear' style and always carried a knotted cane ; they wore stiff collars and high cravats and could hardly turn their heads. The women, in contrast, adopted the flimsy dress of the goddesses of antiquity, wore sandals instead of shoes and rings set with cameos and jewels on their toes. They were appropriately known as the *Merveilleuses* and would not have looked out of place in London's Kings Road in the 1970s. The outrageous was in vogue, but there were limits to what the public would take. Marie-Rose's Creole friend Madame Hamelin was mobbed when she walked from the Champs-Elysées to the Luxembourg Palace in a topless dress. There is no record of Marie-Rose ever having exposed herself in this way, but she, Madame Tallien and Madame Récamier were the undisputed trend-setters of Parisian society in that fateful year of 1795, during which Marie-Rose fought for survival. As she was gifted with a lithe, graceful figure that required no support, the Greek fashion was admirably suited to her ; yet she was not statuesque – indeed it appears that she was little over five foot tall, though well-proportioned.

At first political power was in the hands of Tallien, Barras and Fouché. Then, after the new constitution had been pro-claimed in September 1795, the executive power was shared by five directors, of whom Barras, the ex-aristocrat, ex-officer and corrupt careerist, played the dominant role. Madame Tallien had introduced Marie-Rose to him ; true to form, she almost immediately petitioned him for the release of her sister-in-law Françoise, and for that of Madame de Montmorin, her friend from Fontainebleau, whose husband had escaped to England.

Marie-Rose now began to preside over the dinner parties Barras gave in La Chaumière, his house off the Champs-Elysées. She also reopened her house at Croissy and lively parties were held there. Sometimes there were not enough forks and knives for so many guests and some had to be borrowed from neighbours. Chancellor Pasquier, who was living at Croissy at the time, recorded in his memoirs: 'As one often finds among Creoles, there was a certain ostentation about Madame de Beauharnais's house. There was superfluous luxury and at the same time a shortage of essentials. The kitchen was crammed with poultry, game and rare fruits (though there was an extreme shortage of food at that time) but lacked saucepans, glasses and plates, which had to be begged from our paltry stock.' Rather fun, one would have thought, compared to the stiff ceremonial meals of later imperial days, although even then it is curious to read the memoirs of guests who noticed the absence of adequate cutlery amid an abundance of silver and gold plate.

From the back garden of the house at Croissy Marie-Rose sometimes looked across the Seine to the rooftops of an abandoned but handsome residence situated in acres of meadow and park land near Rueil. She was told that it was called Malmaison and belonged to a family of bankers, the Lecoulteux. It caught her fancy.

Marie-Rose had now become Barras's mistress. Sure of his backing, she began to restore her financial position and was emboldened to make a formal appeal to the Committee of General Security to give her two horses and a carriage in compensation for those that Alexandre had had to leave when he relinquished his command of the Army of the Rhine; she asked for her husband's silver, furniture and books from his property at La Ferté; she also wished to be compensated for the loss of the Beauharnais family plantation at Santo Domingo, which had been looted by insurgents – they could indemnify her in sugar and coffee, she added shrewdly in her petition, since these commodities were expensive to buy and could therefore be sold at handsome profits on the black market.

This last request, however, does not appear to have been granted to Citoyenne Beauharnais.

In October 1795 she moved into a house in the rue Chantereine for the large sum of 4000 francs a year in metallic currency ; it had been used as a love nest by the actor Talma's estranged wife Julie Carreau.

This house was demolished in the nineteenth century when the *grands boulevards* were constructed. It was situated near the Gare Saint-Lazare and was delightfully secluded, like one of the aristocratic mansions in the Faubourg Saint-Germain on a miniature scale. From the porter's lodge, adjoining which were stables and a coachhouse, a tree-lined drive led through a small shrub-filled garden to the diminutive two-storied house with its semicircular verandah and mansard roof. There were five reception-rooms, one of them oval, and a narrow circular staircase led up to the principal bedroom, which had an adjoining bathroom and dressing-room lined with mirrors. There was a dark sitting-room and smaller bedrooms for the children when they came on holiday. The servants slept in the attics. Soon new bedroom curtains were made in pale yellow silk tufted with red and blue ; a harp was bought, plus a walnut writing table with a marble top and a bust of Socrates. Four mahogany chairs, upholstered in the new fashionable horsehair with bronze inlays, were ordered. There was not much money left over for new clothes: one muslin dress and one of silk taffeta, three pairs of grey silk stockings, a shawl – that was all Marie-Rose could afford that autumn when she moved into her new abode. But for the first time in her life she could arrange her home the way she liked, invite friends and play the role of hostess, an art she soon developed to perfection.

Of course she had to have a livery and servants, but she had to make do with the bare minimum : a coachman, a manservant, a cook, a chambermaid and a personal maid. The latter was Marie Lannoy, whose salary of 600 francs a year was rarely paid ; in fact she often had to lend money to her improvident mistress.

Through her friend Thérésa Tallien, Marie-Rose now met the

latter's new lover, the financier Ouvrard. This was a useful connection and one that opened the door to profitable transactions. Everybody who could do so was making money out of necessities – and, later, out of army supplies. Marie-Rose swam with the tide, encouraged no doubt by Thérésa, who was herself the daughter of a clever Spanish financier. Thérésa's mother was also Spanish and she made the most of the vivacious good looks she had inherited. Was it she who suggested that Marie-Rose should make the most of her exotic Creole charm ? At parties Marie-Rose often wore brightly coloured headscarves in Creole fashion ; her swaying, sensuous way of walking was Creole too, and so was her soft drawl. These traits distinguished her from the more beautiful women who surrounded her, and they were soon to captivate the raw young general whom Barras had known and admired during the siege of Toulon against the English.

Marie-Rose's 'Creole pose' may have been partly innate, but it has misled many people, including her biographers, into assuming that she was of an indolent, lazy disposition. It is true that Alexandre had found this, but that was some time ago. She was very different now. From the moment she became mistress of her destiny, after her release from prison, she bestirred herself tirelessly and resourcefully. She called upon influential people, she wrote endless petitions on behalf of herself and her friends, she travelled to Hamburg and Dunkirk to interview bankers and merchants, she moved into the rue Chantereine, she was a splendid hostess, she visited her children regularly at Saint-Germain-en-Laye and brought Hortense over to attend suppers given by Barras. It cannot therefore be said that she was indolent or that, in her busy social rounds, she neglected her children. By showing Hortense in public she made no pretence of concealing her age (until the time came to state it on her marriage certificate). And if Hortense was invited to these supper parties one assumes that the conversation and behaviour were in keeping with the presence of a *jeune fille* from Madame de Campan's proper establishment. Barras had manners, even if he was deficient in morals.

Napoleon Bonaparte had come to Paris from Toulon in May 1795. The state of the capital and the life led by France's rulers shocked his still provincial, puritanical Corsican outlook. 'Women are everywhere in the ascendent!' he wrote to his elder brother Joseph, half-contemptuously and, perhaps, half-afraid of being enmeshed himself. He had nearly married Désirée Clary, Joseph's young sister-in-law, who later married Jean Bernadotte, a marshal of France and later King of Sweden – and who always disliked Josephine. He had then turned to a Corsican friend, Madame Permon, the widow of a government contractor. (Her daughter later married General Junot and became the Duchesse d'Abrantès. The Duchesse relates in her memoirs that Bonaparte proposed to her mother, although she was fourteen years his senior.)

When the new constitution of 1795 was submitted for popular ratification, some of its provisions were objected to and there were threats to attack the government. Barras entrusted Bonaparte with the command to quell public demonstrations ; his ruthless but effective cannonade charge from outside the church of Saint-Roch on the rue Saint-Honoré dispersed the hostile mob at a cost of only two to three hundred casualties and the government was saved. From being a general of a division Bonaparte was appointed second in command of the Army of the Interior. This was announced in *Le Moniteur* (the official gazette) of 14 October, together with a report of Barras's statement to the Convention that all unauthorized weapons in the districts of Lepelletier and the Théâtre-Français were to be handed in to the authorities. Commissioners were sent out on house-to-house searches to enforce the law and one of them called on Madame Beauharnais in the rue Chantereine while Eugène was spending a few days' holiday with her.

The only weapon in the house was the late Alexandre de Beauharnais's sword and this the loyal, spirited Eugène refused to surrender. He argued persuasively with the commissioner and told him that he would never consent to part with this souvenir of his brave father who had been so unjustly executed despite his patriotism. Perplexed and astonished by the boy's outburst, the commissioner passed the buck – to the commanding general of Paris at his headquarters in the rue des Capucines, Napoleon Bonaparte. He alone could grant Eugène permission to keep the sword.

Marie-Rose must have been aware of Barras's opinion of Bonaparte. She may even have seen him at the Luxembourg Palace. It is not quite clear when they first met, but if she had not already hooked him at a dinner party (at which Bonaparte would probably have been timid and unsociable without a formal introduction to the charmer) she succeeded most effectively when, the day after he had given Eugène permission to keep his father's sword, she presented herself at his headquarters to thank him for his generosity. In all probability she had no intention of seducing the twenty-six-year-old general for herself but, intuitively realizing that he was on his way up, she must have calculated that he could further Eugène's military career ; she had used General Lazare Hoche for a similar purpose.

Bonaparte was impressed by this gracious woman, who belonged, or so he thought, to the remote aristocratic class he secretly admired, though he affected to despise it. He believed that she was part of the fashionable, well-connected Faubourg Saint-Germain set ; in fact the ex-vicomtesse had never been received in aristocratic circles. Bonaparte came from a family of Corsican/Italian minor nobility ; he had a military man's respect for hierarchy and, as time would soon prove, he was no submissive egalitarian republican. Even then there was little left of the concepts of Liberty, Fraternity and Equality in France's top echelons of the day.

Some biographers believe that Bonaparte hoped to better himself financially by marrying Marie-Rose or, as I shall refer to her from now on, Josephine. This is what Bonaparte decided to call her, from her middle name – Josèphe. He told General Bertrand in after years that he had been led to infer that she possessed a fortune ; he was, however, canny enough to make inquiries from her banker Emmery and to discover the truth – – and it did not deter him. Josephine's mother had a plantation worth about 50,000 francs a year, from which Emmery was authorized to draw from 20,000 to 25,000 francs yearly at Josephine's request.

But what about the money she received from Barras? Surely Bonaparte could not have been naive enough to be unaware of their relationship? Had it been broken off by the time he met her? That is a distinct possibility. The lively Thérésa Tallien appealed more to Barras's sexual taste.

He was not the sort of man to appreciate *la douceur*, whereas Bonaparte was in a phase of his life when he was still fundamentally insecure and an outsider. A later allusion, in one of his letters to Josephine from Italy, to the 'afflicting scene that took place a fortnight before our marriage' may well have been provoked by a full confession by Josephine of her liaison with Barras. Even if it was not, there were plenty of people in Bonaparte's entourage who could have acquainted him with the fact, as they were to when she was unfaithful to him during his Egyptian campaign. Yet for the time being, and until Bonaparte seized power as first consul, both he and Josephine remained on the friendliest terms with Barras, and Josephine continued to send him most affectionate letters.

Although one must read Barras's memoirs with the utmost caution, there may be a grain of truth in the callous description of what went on behind the scenes before the marriage:

Shall I admit it? Yes, I shall, since I am writing my memoirs without giving them the pompously modest description of confessions. Going as far as a Frenchman brought up in the principles of chivalry can, I have said that I was on terms of familiarity, long established, but none the less genuine, with Madame de Beauharnais. There is no boasting – some might say I am being very modest – in this revelation. None the less a situation resulted that could hardly escape the notice of people who were aware of my private life. So Madame de Beauharnais was generally regarded as one of my first liaisons and Bonaparte, who was often at my house, was one of those who could hardly have any doubts about the real position. But it seems that, unlike ordinary men, it was a matter of complete indifference to him and that he was quite above such things. So when he was contemplating marriage with Madame de Beauharnais and could not believe our association was over, he himself brought his future wife to the Directory; she was already a tool in his designs, as she had been of his original advancement. As there was always something he wanted from me he thought it was less insidious if he passed his requests through her. Having frequently wanted me to see her alone, she simply used to ask me to see her in my private room without anyone else present. Bonaparte would wait for her in the salon, talking to anyone who happened to be there.

One day Madame de Beauharnais had something particularly private to talk about and our meeting lasted longer than I wanted. She let herself go about the affection she had always had for me; her projected marriage would not mean the end of it. Hugging me close, she reproached me for ceasing to love her and repeated that she had never loved anyone more than me and could not break with me at the moment when she was to become the wife of 'the little general'.

I was almost in the situation of Joseph *vis-à-vis* Madame Potiphar. But I would be lying if I said that I had been as cruel as Pharaoh's young minister.

I emerged from the room with Madame de Beauharnais, not without considerable embarrassment.

Lucien Bonaparte, admittedly one of Josephine's enemies, wrote in his memoirs: 'Barras undertook to provide Josephine's dowry, which was the supreme command of the Army of Italy' – implying that this was the price the general paid for it.

Napoleon himself told General Gourgaud on St Helena: 'Barras did me a good turn when he advised me to marry Josephine, assuring me that she was of the *ancien régime* as well as the new. Her house was the best in Paris, and that would make people forget my Corsican name. Best of all, the marriage would make me wholly French.' This is not a very convincing statement in view of the fact that Josephine was a Creole. His later statement to General Bertrand ('I married Josephine only because I thought that she had a big fortune. She herself said she had. But there was nothing') flatly contradicts the known facts that he had had an interview with Emmery and later sent a letter to Josephine from Italy asking whether she needed money, adding that 'you never spoke about business matters to me'. Her almost immediate extravagances and borrowings did not elicit expressions of surprise or resentment at any deception on her part.

In such a web of diverging statements it is difficult to ascertain who was the biggest liar. Both parties seemed to want to convince people that they had entered matrimony unwillingly. Even Josephine confided later to Comte Ségur that she 'had had to overcome a feeling of repugnance before I could bring myself to marry 'the little general'. That, of course, was when she was playing at being a member of the *ancien régime* and wished to convince people that she was not a *parvenue*.

Bonaparte held back at first, in an attempt to control his emotions, for, as he confided to Gourgaud: 'I was passionately in love with her and our friends were aware of this long before I even ever dared to say anything about it.'

A few days after the visit to the rue des Capucines Bonaparte was put in charge of the Army of the Interior and was obviously too busy to indulge in social life. Josephine sent him a letter dated 28 October in which she gently chided him: 'You no longer come to see a friend who loves you. You have completely abandoned her. You are very wrong, for she is tenderly attached to you. Come tomorrow to lunch with me. I want to see you and talk to you about your affairs. Good night, my friend. *Je vous embrasse.*' It was a clever little note. Josephine had made much progress as a letter-writer since those far-away days when Alexandre had asked to see her drafts. In a few sparse lines she managed to assure Bonaparte discreetly of her affection, and entice him to a meal in her house, where he would be captive, the very next day, so that he had no time to think it over, and all in his own self-interest to discuss *his* affairs! Her friendship with Barras no doubt enabled her to play the role of go-between, or to pretend to play it, since she did not in fact have much influence over Barras at that time.

The following letter from Bonaparte may or may not have

been in reply to the above: 'I cannot understand what made you write as you have. No one desires your friendship as much as I do, or is as ready as I am to prove it. If my affairs had permitted, I should have brought this letter to you myself. . . .' Guarded in tone, this is the letter of a friend but not, yet, of a lover. Josephine was playing her cards carefully, obviously not wishing to give the impression that she was a *cocotte*. Bonaparte paid several visits to the rue Chantereine; friends of both parties were already suggesting marriage.

Josephine no doubt consulted Aunts Edmée and Fanny, as well as her bosom friend Thérésa Tallien. Bonaparte was six years her junior; he had no money. Her business adviser, Monsieur Raguideau, exclaimed scornfully: 'What will he bring you? A cloak and a sword?' (Actually Bonaparte was present when he said this, standing beside the window unnoticed, and he laughed heartily, agreeing that Raguideau was quite right. But he did not take offence. On the contrary, he thought Raguideau should continue to advise Josephine.) Bonaparte had personality and a compelling magnetism that attracted Josephine, although she was not yet 'in love' with him. The tone of her letters to Bonaparte during the Italian campaign, her conduct in his absence were certainly not those of an infatuated woman.

Hortense was present at a dinner party given by Barras in January 1796 at the Luxembourg Palace. She was awkwardly placed between her mother and Bonaparte and she observed in her memoirs that he 'annoyed me by pressing forward to talk to my mother with so much vivacity and perseverance that I was obliged to sit back in my chair'. She remarked that he was 'pale, but had a beautiful expression'. But she did not like him, and confided her fears to Eugène. Both children tried to dissuade their mother from remarrying, but that was chiefly because they were afraid of taking second place in her affections. They were never to do that – except on the unfortunate occasion of Hortense's marriage to Bonaparte's brother Louis.

On the further occasions when Hortense saw Bonaparte he

resorted to his habitual heavy-handed teasing of the women-folk present. He never gave up this habit, even after he had become emperor and had assumed airs of grandeur. Hortense concluded that he did not like women, since he tormented them so. The only point she found in his favour was that he was a good story-teller, particularly of ghost stories.

Bonaparte's first love letter to Josephine, the one that appears at the beginning of the various collections of his letters, is undated but was evidently written before their marriage ; no doubt Josephine had given her consent and the couple were already engaged. Now it was no longer a matter of friendship but of a mad infatuation on his part. It was written at seven in the morning : 'I awake full of you. Your portrait and the memory of the intoxicating evening of yesterday leave my senses no rest. Sweet and incomparable Josephine, what a strange power you have over my heart ! ... a thousand kisses, but give me none in return for they make my blood burn. ...'

The banns were published in February 1796 and the brief civil wedding service was held on 9 March, almost secretly, in the office of the mayor of the second *arrondissement* at 3 rue d'Antin, a building that had once been the private Hôtel Mondragon, and had been taken over by the municipal authorities after the Revolution. One can still see the gilded salon where the two legendary figures were married, now the office of the head of the Banque de Paris et des Pays-Bas. Josephine arrived in the company of Barras, Tallien and Jérôme Calmelet, one of her business advisers who had also been tutor to her children. They waited and waited but Bonaparte did not turn up and the weary mayor left, investing a minor official, Collin-Lacombe, with the authority to deliver the marriage certificate if and when the groom arrived. He did – after making his bride wait for over two hours. The time had flown by, he explained, no doubt to Barras's satisfaction, while he was studying maps of Italy ; he had been appointed commander of the Army of Italy and already had one foot in the stirrup. The one candle in the room had dwindled and it was to the spluttering sounds it made before finally going out that the wedding register was hastily signed. Josephine's birth certificate was conveniently in far-off Martinique so she took four years off her age while the gallant bridegroom added one to his, to make them equal.

II

MADAME BONAPARTE

Bride and groom departed for the rue Chantereine and their first night of lawful connubial bliss, slightly marred by the presence of the dog Fortuné. Bonaparte told visitors subsequently, as the poet Antoine Vincent Arnault recalled in his *Souvenirs*: 'See that fellow – he took possession of Madame's bed on the night I married her. I was told frankly that I must either sleep elsewhere or share the bed with him. Not a very pleasing alternative. Take it or leave it, I was told. The darling creature was less accommodating than I was. . . .' He then displayed the scar made by Fortuné's sharp teeth on his left leg.

Hortense and Eugène were told about the marriage by tactful Madame Campan, who had been taken into Josephine's confidence and who had most probably advised her to marry the promising young general, if only for the sake of the children. 'She won't love us so much,' Hortense exclaimed sadly. Later, after Bonaparte's first Italian victories at Montenotte, Millesimo, Dego and San Michele, Madame Campan tried to arouse Hortense's enthusiasm for her stepfather: 'Your mother has united her destiny to that of an extraordinary man. What talents he has, what a worthy man, at every instant making new conquests!' 'Madame,' Hortense replied stiffly, 'let him make all the conquests he likes, but I shall never forgive him for having conquered my mother.' The usually dignified Madame Campan burst out laughing and Hortense's *mot* was related and repeated by the exclusive members of Faubourg-Saint-Germain society. What an amusing child she was, this pretty Hortense with the long, pale golden hair and forget-me-not-blue eyes! She herself laughed at her own sally in later years. She had become as fond of Bonaparte as if he had been her own father and the sentiment was reciprocated. It even gave rise to scandalous gossip.

In the meantime, however, she wrote acidly to her step-father: 'I have just learnt about your marriage to my mother. What has astonished me most is that you, whom I have heard saying so many things against women, should have decided to take one for your wife.' Bonaparte replied amiably to his stepdaughter, whom he visited, as well as Eugène, the day after the wedding, when he accompanied Josephine to Saint-Germain-en-Laye. It is significant that Josephine's first thought, after the wedding night, was to introduce her children formally to their stepfather, who was leaving for Italy the following day.

The general was received with every mark of respect and graciousness and Madame Campan listened attentively to his views on women's education. Unfortunately they have not been recorded, but judging from his low opinion of blue-stockings like Madame de Staël, they could not have been very advanced ; yet they were pronounced by Madame Campan to be '*très justes*'. Bonaparte in turn was so impressed by the tone of Madame Campan's establishment and the rank of her young lady boarders that he promised to send her his sister Caroline to be educated there. 'She knows absolutely nothing,' he warned her candidly. Before leaving he exclaimed warmly : 'If I made a Republic of Women, you should be the head of it!' Royalist Madame Campan must have smiled a little grimly at such an unlikely prospect. She was a serious, plain little woman who always dressed in black, stressed the necessity of 'manners, morals and modesty' and reproved Hortense for giggling im-moderately. She herself wrote a book about her views on education for girls, in which she deprecated the development of useless talents: 'For myself I have a powerful objection to the amount of time demanded to acquire them. Moreover, the enthusiasm they inspire exalts the young imagination and in females this is not the last harmful result. . . .' And yet, Hortense, her favourite pupil, became extremely talented at music, singing, composing and drawing. The latter talent was taught at Madame Campan's by the painter Jean-Baptiste Isabey, whom she had befriended after meeting him at Versailles, where he had helped to design the costumes for masquerades. Through Hortense, Isabey met Josephine and Bonaparte and they entrusted him with taking Eugène and Hortense to and from boarding school and their mother's house in the rue Chantereine on holidays.

Before leaving for Italy Bonaparte wrote briefly to the president of the Directory, Letourneur: 'I have asked Citoyen Barras to inform the Executive Directors of my marriage to Citoyenne Tascher Beauharnais. The confidence that the Directory has on all occasions shown in me makes it my duty to keep it informed of all my actions. This is a new tie binding me to my country; it is a token of my firm resolution to entrust all my fortunes to the Republic.' This note was signed: 'The General in Chief of the Army of Italy, Bonaparte'.

It is difficult to see in what way Bonaparte believed, if he really did so, that his marriage was 'a new tie binding him to his country'. In any even the directors took the view that it might momentarily bind him less to it and they withheld the passport asked for in the name of Josephine, so as to keep her in Paris and prevent her from distracting the general during his forthcoming campaign against the Austrians and Sardinians.

He found time, during the brilliant campaign that has fascinated military historians ever since, to send Josephine a flood of ardent love letters. Although she did not reply to half of them she preserved them to the end of her life, when reading them must have been a bitter experience; eventually they joined the immense collection of Bonaparte's published correspondence. Nothing he ever wrote equalled the ardour and spontaneity of those first love letters to Josephine.

He began to write *en route* for Italy. From the posthouse at Chenonceaux, on 14 March, he sent the following message:

Every moment separates me further from you and every moment I have less energy to exist so far from you. You are the constant object of my thoughts. . . .
I cannot pass a day without loving you. I cannot even drink a

cup of tea without cursing the glory and ambition that keep me apart from the soul of my existence. . . .

Before reaching Nice he stopped at Marseilles to see his family and break the news of his marriage to his austere mother, Madame Letizia Bonaparte, and to his sisters. They belonged to another world and Bonaparte was well aware of it. He had not even informed his eldest brother Joseph, let alone asked his advice. The Bonaparte clan were horrified to learn that their son and brother had married a Creole widow with two children. No doubt Bonaparte himself drafted the formal letter he forced his mother to write and dispatch to her daughter-in-law in answer to the gracious letter he had handed to her:

I have received your letter, Madame, which could only strengthen the good opinion that I had formed of you. My son has informed me of his happy union and from that moment you possess my esteem and my approval. Nothing is wanting to my happiness save the satisfaction of seeing you. Be assured that I feel for you all of a mother's tenderness and that I love you as much as my own children. My son gives me the hope, and your lettter confirms me in it, that you will pass through Marseilles in going to join him. I rejoice, Madame, in the pleasure that your sojourn here will afford me. My daughters join with me in hoping that you will hasten the happy moment of your journey. In the meantime be assured that my children, following my example, have vowed for you the same friendship and tenderness that they feel for their brother. Believe, Madame, in the attachment and affection of Letizia Bonaparte *mère*.

Since Madame Mère, as she was later to be called officially, could not spell and did not know French well, it has been assumed that the above letter was submitted to a family council before being forwarded and that it was delayed so that it could be shown to Joseph, who was now in Genoa.

A little later Joseph went to Paris on Bonaparte's behalf to explain to the directors the motives that had made him accept the Italian armistice, and at the same time he was the bearer of a letter to Josephine begging her to join her husband in Italy. Unlike modern warfare, the enemies were not engaged in battles every day and when battles took place they did so only in fairly limited, well-defined areas. In the cities, far from the battlefields, civilians were more or less safe. Josephine could not make up her mind.

In one of her rare letters she reverted to addressing her husband by the formal 'vous' instead of 'tu'.

How can you have written such a letter [he raged]? How cold it is! You have been four days without writing to me. What have you been doing? I do not demand eternal love from you, nor fidelity, but only: truth and unlimited frankness. Remember what I have sometimes told you: nature has given me a strong and decided character. She has made you all gauze and lace. Have you ceased loving me? The day you tell me you love me less will be the last one of my love and the last of my life.

Occasionally, however, he came down to earth: 'I do not know if you need money. If you do, ask my brother Joseph who has two hundred *louis* of mine. If there is anybody you wish placed, send him to me and I will place him.' Josephine, true to form, immediately found somebody who needed placing – the husband of her friend Madame Hamelin (who had worn topless dresses in the hectic post-revolutionary period). Bonaparte obliged.

On 26 April he again complained of Josephine's negligence, which he attributed (probably correctly) to the busy social life she was leading in Paris. He added severely, no doubt recalling his native Corsican *mores*: 'In countries where morality is adhered to everybody stays at home ; in those countries they write to their husbands, think of them and live for them. . . .' In a letter from Milan he analysed their respective situations bitterly: 'When you write to me the style, the paucity of words never reveal deep sentiments. You fell in love with me through a passing whim ; you already realize how ridiculous it would be to engage your heart. I believe you have already made your choice and that you know to whom to address yourself to replace me.'

How right he was! In the spring of 1796 General Leclerc returned to Paris from Marseilles with a handsome young officer of the Hussars in his suite. The officer's name was Hippolyte

Charles; he was nine years younger than Josephine, slim, dashing, high-spirited and a clever mime, with black hair, an olive skin and merry blue eyes. He was worldly, unlike Bonaparte, a good conversationalist, also unlike Bonaparte, who was more of a 'man's man' than a drawing-room prattler.

Bonaparte, who must have heard, perhaps from Josephine herself, that the directors were opposed to her going to Italy, appealed to them directly. He wrote to General Carnot: 'I wish to thank you particularly for the attentions you have shown to my wife. I recommend her to you; she is a sincere patriot and I love her madly.' The rather incoherent juxtaposition must have provoked an indulgent smile. On the same day he wrote to Barras: 'I wish my wife to come and join me via Piedmont. She won't be near the scene of war because I have securely defended fortresses behind the lines and in addition there are fine plains in which important towns are situated.' When Murat informed Bonaparte that Josephine was ill – there was even a false rumour that she was pregnant – he was beside himself with tender anxiety. 'Rather than know you are melancholy,' he wrote extravagantly, 'I think I would give you a lover myself. Be cheerful and happy and know that my happiness is entwined with yours.' To Barras he wrote: 'Murat tells me that my wife is ill. This grieves me to an extent that you cannot begin to imagine.' He then went on in a more prosaic vein: 'I should like you to do me a great favour: persuade Frèron not to marry my sister Pauline. This marriage would not suit any member of my family.' (Pauline, the youngest of Napoleon's three sisters and the one who was to dislike Josephine most intensely, had fallen for this older, married man.)

His outpourings to Josephine continued unabated:

My life is a perpetual nightmare. A fatal foreboding prevents me from breathing. I cannot see. I have lost more than life, than happiness, more than peace. I am almost without hope. I send you a messenger. He will stop only four hours in Paris and will then bring me your answer. Write me ten pages. That alone will console me a little. You are ill, you love me, I have grieved you, you are pregnant, and I cannot see you. I accuse you of lingering in Paris and you are ill there. Forgive me, my dear one, the love you have inspired in me robbed me of reason, and I shall never recover it.

It is amazing to think that the man who could write that he had been robbed of reason was at that very moment using his very considerable reasoning powers for the methodical conquest of Italy.

Two interesting points emerge from the many letters the couriers bore tirelessly back and forth. One is Bonaparte's admission that if Josephine 'had been more naive, younger, I would not have loved her so much'. (That was the letter in which he referred to the 'afflicting scene that took place a fortnight before our marriage'.) 'Everything about you pleased me,' he wrote, 'even the memory of your mistakes.' The second point is a reference to her 'lovable jealousy', which in later years he was to find so irritating. Alexandre, too, had had occasion to complain about his wife's jealousy. In the first case she had been justified; in the present one she was anticipating future events, and tempting fate.

The general shed tears in the privacy of his tent: 'My tears cover your portrait, which never leaves me. Scarcely have we been married, scarcely have we been united, and already we are separated. ...' That, of course, was one of the main reasons for the passionate love letters that took the place of embraces. He preserved all his illusions about his *princess lointaine*; he was in the position of a troubadour *vis-à-vis* his unattainable lady love. There was no thought of his being unfaithful to his wife: 'You know that I have never loved anybody but Josephine – you are the first woman whom I have adored. ...'

Josephine communicated some of these letters to the poet Arnault, a frequent visitor to her house:

I can still hear her reading a passage in which, apparently trying to smother the anxieties that obviously tormented him, Bonaparte wrote: 'But if it was true [that she had been unfaithful] fear Othello's dagger!' and I can still hear her saying in her Creole accent, and with a broad smile: 'What a funny fellow he is, this Bonaparte!' The love she inspired in so extraordinary a man flattered her less than the man himself. She was proud to know that he loved her

57

nearly as much as his glory. She adored that glory, a glory growing greater every day, but it was in Paris that she loved it, to the accompaniment of the frantic cheers that greeted her wherever she went, whenever news of the Army of Italy arrived. Her annoyance was very great when she saw that there was no hope of further postponement of her journey to Italy.

'As if a pretty woman could abandon her habits,' Bonaparte reproached her. 'Her friendship with Madame Tallien, a dinner with Barras, a performance of a new play, the dog Fortuné – yes, Fortuné! You love everything more than you love your husband; for him you have only a little respect, merely a part of the general kindliness in which your heart abounds. Millions of kisses, even to Fortuné, in spite of his bad temper. . . .' To his brother Joseph he wrote: 'I must see her and press her to my heart. I love her to the point of madness, and I cannot continue to be separated from her. If she no longer loved me, I would have nothing left to do on earth.' There were letters that he did not send: 'In a month I have received from my *bonne amie* only two letters of three lines each. Is she having affairs? . . . A day will no doubt come when I shall see you, for I cannot believe that you are still in Paris. Then I shall show you pockets full of letters that I have not sent to you because they were too foolish.' He appealed to Barras again: 'I am desperate. My wife does not come. Some lover keeps her in Paris. I curse all women but I heartily embrace all my good friends. . . .' To Josephine he recalled intimate bedroom memories: 'I don't forget the "little visits" – you know what I mean – the "little black forest". I kiss it a thousand times. . . .'

Only one of Josephine's letters appears to have been really loving; she must have made an effort. Bonaparte, delighted, replied (on 3 April 1796): 'I have received all your letters but none has made such an impression on me as your last. What eloquence, what feelings you portray! They are of fire, they inflamed my poor heart . . . Away from you there is no joy; to live for Josephine – that is the history of my life.'

It may seem surprising that such a society-loving woman as Josephine should have expressed a desire to live in the country ; yet this topic had been discussed by the couple before Bonaparte left for Italy. In one of his letters to Joseph he wrote:

If Josephine wants to buy a country residence as we had agreed between us, each of us would contribute half of the price. I would advance 30,000 francs and she would put up an equal sum. I would take this money from the 40,000 francs that remain from the reserves we have withdrawn from Corsica. When you have come to an agreement with my wife you can take out a bill of change on your brother-in-law Clary.

(Clary was an industrialist and businessman.) Josephine had been brought up close to an exuberant nature and she spent large sums of money on flowers with which to decorate her rooms in Paris. A country residence, not too far from the capital, a view, drives in nearby woods – the idea appealed to her. It would not mean leading a country life (going for long walks or hunting), but a country residence would provide an oasis from which to look out at the world of nature in the company of intimate friends, relatives and loved objects. It would be nice, too, for the children. (On 17 July 1796 Bonaparte told Josephine that he had heard from Eugène and bid her 'write for me to those charming children of yours and send them some trinkets. Be sure to tell them that I love them as if they were my own.')

Josephine now remembered Malmaison, the charming house she had spied from the garden at Croissy when life had been so insecure. She had spoken to Bonaparte about it before he left and now she opened negotiations for buying it. How marvellous to be able to buy the house of one's dreams, even if it meant borrowing and haggling and using up a whole year of one's income in advance. Fairyland was expensive, but it could be bought – with perseverance. Josephine played with money as she played with cards. Something would turn up at the last minute, something, from somewhere, from someone – it always did. She asked the artist Isabey to contact the owners of Malmaison, the Lecoulteux, and to have a look at the house. Would it cost much to repair and decorate? A great deal, he told her. 'The children saw it and were enchanted.' That settled it. Malmaison would be hers.

During an inspection visit in the Piedmont Bonaparte accidentally dropped the minature of Josephine which, as he had assured her, he always carried on his person, and the glass broke. General Marmont later recounted in his memoirs that Bonaparte turned pale as he stooped to pick up the fragments, exclaiming: 'This is a bad omen; either my wife is ill or she is being unfaithful to me.'

Bonaparte's belief in destiny was very strong; allied to this was his conviction that Josephine contributed to his luck in some intangible way. References to his interest in the supernatural appear in several of his letters to his wife, notably one written in Abenga on 4 April 1796, when he was mourning the death in battle of his friend and brother-in-arms Chauvet:

What is the future? What is the past? What becomes of us? What magnetic fluid surrounds us and hides from us the most important things that we should know? We pass, we live, we die in the midst of the marvellous. Is it surpising, therefore, that priests, astrologers and charlatans should have taken advantage of this penchant, this singular circumstance, to lead our thoughts to their own ends? Chauvet is dead. His last words were that he was leaving to rejoin me. And so it is. I see his shadow, he wanders in the middle of battles, he whistles through the air, his soul is in the clouds, he will be propitious to my destiny

Was Josephine really ill, or was she being unfaithful, as the broken glass had prophesied, according to Bonaparte? Perhaps a little of both. As far as her health was concerned, in letters to her family one frequently comes across allusions – then and afterwards – to migraines and a general feeling of being below par, though the doctors who examined her could find nothing wrong. She may have been a bit of a hypochondriac. A year or less before her death (at the age of almost fifty-one) Hortense's reader Mademoiselle Cochelet found her looking more radiant and youthful than her own daughter. The migraines seem to have occurred when she was travelling in the highly uncomfortable conditions of the time. Jolting carriage journeys on badly made roads fatigued her.

Biographers cannot account for her delay in joining Bonaparte in Italy. True enough, she was first prevented from going by the members of the Directory and it was only on 21 May 1796 that General Carnot, a member of the Executive Directory, wrote to her impatient husband:

It is with great reluctance that we yield to the desire of Citizeness Bonaparte to join you. We were afraid that the attention you would give to her would turn you from the attention due to the glory and safety of your country. Hence we had long resisted her wishes and we had agreed with her that she could set out only when Milan was yours. You are there, and we have no more objections. We hope that the myrtle with which she will crown you will not detract from the laurels with which you have already been crowned by victory.

Yet Josephine did not leave until a month later and she wrote very little to her husband during that period. He was still under the impression that she was pregnant. 'How goes your pregnancy?' he wrote. 'I imagine constantly that I see you with a protuberant little belly – it must be charming.' Nothing was farther from the truth. 'Where will this letter be delivered?' he wrote in June. 'If in Paris, my misfortune is certain. You no longer love me. I would have nothing to do but die. . . . Could it be possible? . . . My condition is terrible. . . . And your conduct? . . . But must I accuse you? No. Your conduct is that of your destiny. . . .'

Could General Carnot have been lying when he informed Bonaparte on 22 June: 'Your dear wife is at last about to rejoin you, though she has not yet fully recovered. She takes with her the particular regards of my entire family. . . .'

Passports were at last issued on 24 June. Captain Hippolyte Charles was one of the party, which included Joseph Bonaparte, Nicholas Clary, his brother-in-law, General Junot, Louise Compoint (Josephine's companion), four servants and last but not least the Duke of Serbelloni, in whose splendid palace outside Milan Bonaparte had made his headquarters (and Josephine was also to be housed there). Other members were Antoine Hamelin, for whom a post had been promised, and of course Fortuné. So it cannot have been frustrated love for Hippolyte that caused Josephine to burst into tears when she left Paris. Arnault remarked that she 'sobbed as though she were about to be led to the torture chamber ...' – which is hardly flattering to Bonaparte.

One is forced to the conclusion that her marriage had as yet made little impact, that she was not sexually excited by her husband and, also, that she bitterly regretted having to leave behind her children, her friends, her new home, perhaps even Aunt Edmée, who had married the gouty old Marquis de Beauharnais. Josephine had begun to take an active interest in black-market speculations, no doubt advised by Barras and his current mistress Thérésa Tallien. At the moment of her departure for Italy, however, she had certainly not become rich on the proceeds, since she was obliged to borrow 4000 francs from Madame Hamelin before she finally set off, dabbing a lace handkerchief to her eyes.

It is possible that after only three days' marriage to a man she knew so slightly she felt – at a remove of three months – as if she had not been married at all. One wonders, too, from subsequent allusions – Antoine Hamelin describes in his memoirs that Bonaparte 'played with Josephine in public' and adds that the Corsican's rough caresses embarrassed him as well as others present – whether he was too brusque and awkward a lover for a woman who, by all accounts, was dainty, fastidious and perhaps slow to be aroused sexually? This side of their life together can only be guessed at, but the raw young general who teased women so rudely and behaved so boisterously in public can surely not have been as refined or versatile in bed as, say, Captain Hippolyte Charles.

It may be, incidentally, that Josephine's frequent migraines, between which she obviously enjoyed good health and led an active life, were caused by painful menstrual periods and that this very real 'curse' was the reason for the delay of her departure for Italy. None of her biographers has put forward this likely explanation, but Napoleon himself provided an interesting clue when, on St Helena, where he talked so much, he said that Dr Corvisart had told him some years after his marriage that Josephine had long since ceased to have periods, that Creoles often matured early and also reached the menopause early. So she may already have begun to suffer from menopausal symptoms in 1796, though she would naturally take pains to conceal these from her husband.

It is difficult to judge the degree of a person's sensuality from portraits, particularly official ones, yet if one examines closely those of Josephine painted by artists such as Isabey, David, Gros or Prud'hon a certain consistency of expression, of features, of attitude emerges, none of which inclines one to the view that one is looking at the face of a sensual woman. 'All gauze and lace' was how Bonaparte described her – a revealing expression that encompasses more than clothes or external appearance. The sweetness of her expression, the shape and firmness of her rather thin lips, her swaying walk, which so many observers commented on, suggest tender passivity. Did Captain Charles inspires more, much more than that? It is probable. Josephine may have been one of those women who can be roused by words and pre-love play, in both of which talents – so characteristically French – Corsican Bonaparte was surely lacking. All this belongs to the realm of conjecture, but the signs are there, and they cannot be lightly dismissed.

Josephine and her party took two weeks to reach Milan and during that time, as inevitably occurs when men and women are thrown together in the course of a journey, with the many occasions it offers for intimacies, there were flirtations. Junot, in particular, was later alleged to have made advances to Louise Compoint, Murat to Josephine, although this, in the presence of Charles, seems doubtful.

When they finally drove up to the Serbelloni Palace on 10

July it was to find that Bonaparte was away, dealing with civil affairs in another part of Italy. But he had left instructions for a courier to be dispatched to him as soon as his wife arrived. He returned three days later, overjoyed to be reunited with her and – as Hamelin related – unable to contain himself in public. Their host, the urbane Duke of Serbelloni, president of the directorate of the newly created Cisalpine Republic, must have been amused by his victor's boyish behaviour in the presence of his wife.

Very soon, however, Bonaparte was back on the battlefield ; at the end of July he asked Josephine to join him at Brescia, in northern Italy, where General Wurmser nearly took him by surprise. The governor of Brescia, a secret ally of the Austrians, had invited Bonaparte and Josephine to a reception on the day they had intended to depart. Josephine, who had had one of the premonitions in which Bonaparte placed so much faith, refused so firmly that she finally persuaded her husband to leave at once. They were only a few miles from Brescia when the Austrians advanced; they could both have been killed or taken prisoner. From Verona Bonaparte sent Josephine to safety by way of the shore of Lake Garda, where her carriage was fired upon by an Austrian boat and two of her horses were killed. She made her escape in a local cart and reached Castiglione, where Bonaparte rejoined her. As she threw herself into his arms in a fit of near-hysteria, he assured her : 'Wurmser will pay dearly for those tears.' They reached Milan by skirting Mantua, which was being besieged by a French force. Under the walls of this town Josephine was again fired upon. She was greatly relieved to return to Milan while Bonaparte drove his armies across Venetian territory on to Austrian soil. In July he wrote to his wife. 'I love you more than ever. Your tears take away my powers of reasoning, burn my blood.' Josephine never forgot the effect of her tears upon her husband, but with the passage of time their impact steadily decreased.

In between battles Bonaparte told her that he had visited Virgil's village by the lakeside and had not for a moment forgotten his beloved Josephine. Casual paragraphs referred to his military activities. He had had two hundred men killed or wounded by the enemy who had lost five hundred in his precipitate retreat. . . . He had lost his tobacco pouch and asked her to send him a replacement, together with some of her hair.

Josephine must have heard that the voluptuous Italian ladies of the conquered cities were only too willing to surrender themselves to the conqueror of their country ; as yet she had no cause to be jealous but she must have complained because on 22 July Bonaparte wrote to her reproachfully from Castiglione : 'I am in despair, *ma bonne amie*, that you should believe my heart could open to any other but you. It belongs to you by right of conquest and this conquest will be enduring and eternal. I don't know why you mention Madame T. who concerns me not at all, and the ladies of Brescia. . . .'

Back in Milan domestic bliss was resumed. The painter Gros was now commissioned to paint a portrait of Bonaparte ; the subject was too restless to remain stationary for long periods at a time and the only way to retain him was for Josephine to take him on her knees. The sessions usually took place after breakfast. There were endless fêtes and receptions but Josephine does not seem to have enjoyed them very much. She wrote to Aunt Edmée : 'Ah well, I would prefer to be an ordinary individual in France. I don't like the honours of this country and I am often bored. It is true that the state of my health does much to make me sad, for I have much discomfort.' (She gives no further details, but the word 'discomfort' might well be a euphemism for menstruation pains.) She went on : 'If happiness could ensure health, then I should be doing well. I have the best husband in the world. All day long he adores me as if I were a goddess. . . . He couldn't possibly be a better husband. He often writes to my children, for he loves them very much.' He had recently sent Hortense a fine repeating watch surrounded by pearls and Eugène a handsome gold watch. 'I shall try to send some money,' Josephine went on in a familiar vein, 'for the purpose you describe, as soon as possible.' She may have borrowed, as indeed she had done not so long before from the

65

same Aunt Edmée ; it was a habit and she was always willing to reciprocate. By the same courier – in this instance the Duke of Serbelloni, who was on a visit to Paris – Josephine sent letters to her children and to Barras, and various presents : a Leghorn straw hat for Madame Tallien, sausages for Tallien, a necklace for their daughter (Josephine's goddaughter) and liqueurs for Barras.

Josephine recalled the capital with regret. Bonaparte wrote to her from Rimini : 'You are melancholy and ill ; you want to go to Paris. Write to me, think of me and love me.' His constant absences and preoccupations with military affairs irked her. She was growing very weary of Italy. 'I cannot accustom myself to being separated so long from my children,' she replied. This was remedied in part when Eugène came to join Bonaparte as his aide-de-camp. A little court began to form in Milan. Excursions were arranged to Lakes Como and Maggiore, and then, before the hot season began, a move was made to the Villa Cerutti at Mombello, outside Milan on the road to Como. It was charming but too small for receptions so a large tent was erected for that purpose in the gardens.

It was in Mombello, in June 1797, that Josephine at last made the acquaintance of her husband's mother and sisters. Both she and Bonaparte must have anticipated the confrontation with misgivings ; he knew that Madame Mère was displeased at his marriage but he also knew that she was not in a position to be too disdainful because she wished to obtain his approval of his sister Elisa's marriage to Prince Baciocchi, a member of a poor but noble Genoese family. He had been against the marriage but his family pretended that his letter had reached them too late and the civil wedding had taken place in May. Elisa, at twenty, was a serious, ambitious young woman ; tall, thin, with prominent brown eyes, she later became Grand Duchess of Tuscany. Bonaparte had meanwhile arranged a marriage for his seventeen-year-old sister Pauline – the one about whom he had written to Barras, deploring her infatuation for womanizer Fréron, who had several illegitimate children. Pauline believed that Josephine had persuaded Bonaparte to effect the break with Frèron, and she therefore hated her sister-in-law. (At Mombello she was often caught putting her tongue out at her behind her back.) The intended husband was Bonaparte's friend and member of his staff Victor-Emmanuel Leclerc (later to become a general) had been in love with pretty Pauline for over three years, ever since he had met her when he was stationed at Marsailles. He was twenty-four, handsome, well-educated and in every way a worthwhile suitor. Caroline Bonaparte, at fifteen, was about to be sent to join Hortense at Madame Campan's, as her brother had decreed.

Josephine behaved graciously as always and the Bonaparte ladies must have felt awkward and unpolished in her presence. Madame Mère, being strong and matriarchal, an austere biblical figure, held her own and was icily polite to her daughter-in-law. Preparations for the double wedding kept them all busy, for Bonaparte had decided that Elisa too should have the benefit of a church wedding. (He did not, incidentally, consider it necessary to put himself right with the Church as far as his own marriage to Josephine was concerned, but it seems strange that nobody should have raised the question at this point. It was rectified only seven years later, at Josephine's request.)

After the double wedding the family dispersed. Madame Mère left for Ajaccio, with Elisa and her husband ; Caroline and the youngest brother, Jérôme (then thirteen years old) were sent to school in Paris ; Joseph was appointed minister in Rome ; Louis was made a captain of cavalry ; Lucien became a commissary of the first class. Only Pauline remained behind with her husband. Since Hippolyte Charles had been on Leclerc's staff it must be presumed that he told her about Josephine's infatuation for him. Charles was now dismissed from the army on the pretext of having improper dealings with army contractors and narrowly escaped being shot. He was sent to Rome and Paris but stayed behind in Italy for several months. Pauline confided later to the Duchesse d'Abrantès : 'My sister-in-law nearly died of grief. I consoled my brother, who was very unhappy.'

During that summer the primadonna of the Scala opera

house, Madame Grassini, was invited to stay at Mombello and virtually threw herself at Bonaparte, though she did not become his mistress at this date. Meanwhile Josephine behaved like an affectionate wife and an eyewitness, the playwright and poet Carrion de Nisas wrote that she 'frequently caresses her husband, who seems very devoted to her'. Josephine herself wrote to Barras: 'Bonaparte sends you his warmest regards. He still loves me to the point of adoration.'

The couple moved to the castle of Passeriano while Bonaparte discussed the terms of the treaty of Campo Formio with the Austrian ambassador. Fêtes were given and gifts began to pour in from officials and private individuals. But a tragic event had occurred before the move: Josephine's pug Fortuné had been killed when, with his customary arrogance, he had taken on the cook's dog at Mombello, despite the disparity in their size. His excessive aggressiveness had been punished at last. 'It was a most tragic death,' wrote Arnault, who was present. 'I leave you to imagine what was his mistress's grief. The conqueror of Italy could not but show his sympathy. He mourned sincerely for an accident that left him sole possessor of his wife's bed. She did as many a woman does to comfort herself for the loss of a lover: she took another.' Fortuné was succeeded by a rough, black-haired dog, one of a long line of pets that accompanied Josephine wherever she went; as the years went by a special kennelmaid (though no imperial dog ever slept in a kennel, but on a cashmere shawl on a chair) was allocated to each pet and food costs rose from 350 to 600 francs a month. Incidentally, Fortuné was the origin of the fortune made by Milanese doctor Mercati, who had looked after him during an illness before his fatal fight. Mercati was brought to Bonaparte's notice and elevated to the rank of count, subsequently occupying several important positions.

Bonaparte asked Josephine to represent him at fêtes that he was unable to attend when he was called elsewhere on duty. When he was invited to Venice, for instance, he sent her in his place and it was she who made the symbolic gesture of planting a 'tree of liberty' in front of the cathedral of St Mark.

The visit lasted four days and included such diversions as a regatta, a picnic on the Lido and a ball in the Doge's Palace. Josephine appeared on all these occasions smiling, graceful and loaded with diamonds. These were added to when the Venetian delegation, headed by the patriot Dandolo, returned with her to French headquarters at Passeriano, hoping to persuade Bonaparte to preserve the independence of Venice. Josephine was offered a 100,000 ducats for her assistance, and a further sum was to be handed over to her in the event of a favourable outcome of the discussions. She spoke enthusiastically on behalf of Venice at a dinner and after the meal a member of the delegation invited her for a walk in the garden, in the course of which he slipped a valuable diamond ring on her finger. Venetian independence, however, was not respected and no more was heard about the ducats – though Josephine appears to have kept the ring.

So many valuable presents were showered on the couple, by the Pope, by the heads of the various Italian principalities and nobles anxious to please, that from then on a collector's lust seized Josephine. It must have been difficult to resist. In retrospect the little house in the rue Chantereine seemed altogether too modest, too small. She wrote to the architect Vautier with detailed instructions as to how she wished the interior to be redesigned, decorated and furnished in the latest style. David designed a frieze for one of the salons and the famous Jacob brothers, cabinetmakers, were ordered to make furniture for which they claimed the exorbitant sum of 130,000 francs. Bonaparte was shattered when the bill was sent to him. Josephine's bedroom was redecorated to look like a military tent and the chairs were covered with chamois leather to imitate drums.

At Rastadt Bonaparte found a letter from the Directory requesting his return to Paris ; everybody was eager to welcome the hero of Italy. Josephine was still in Venice and she made her way back to the capital with Eugène in a slow triumphal progress through the towns of southern France. Detained by fêtes, she arrived in Paris later than had been expected, to the annoyance of the organizers of the grand fête at the Luxembourg Palace. The great hall was hung with trophies, speeches were made, toasts drunk, but Bonaparte, who had little taste for such displays (unless he had arranged them), looked surly and his reply to the directors' compliments when he was formally presented to them by Talleyrand, the minister for foreign affairs, was brusque to the point of uncivility.

On 3 January 1798 Talleyrand gave a reception, which outshone the Directory's efforts, in his magnificent Hôtel Galliffet. Even Bonaparte was impressed. Talleyrand spent lavishly when it suited his purpose, which was to acquire more and more money and indirect power. He spent 12,000 *livres* on the decorations alone, invited 4000 guests and led his guests of honour up the grand staircase to the sound of martial airs played by a band, into a shrine surrounded by a cupola in which he had placed a bust of Brutus presented to him by Bonaparte (one of many objects from the Italian loot). Josephine, attired in simple but elegant Greek style, must have smiled at Brutus, remembering the days when her first husband had made her read ancient Roman history. Little had she realized then that her second husband would bring about so many changes in the territories over which those same Roman emperors had ruled.

The gardens of the Hôtel Galliffet were brightly illuminated, while guards from every regiment displayed their bright uniforms – only Bonaparte was perversely dressed in civilian clothes. He was observed to keep close to his wife and he stood behind her when supper was served at midnight and the ladies were invited to sit down. It was during this reception that bluestocking Madame de Staël, the Swiss financier Necker's daughter, who persecuted Bonaparte with her admiration, approached him to ask personal questions with a directness – not to say tactlessness – comparable to that of contemporary television interviewers. What did he think of women? she wanted to know. What kind of woman did he admire most? He grumpily replied that he most admired those women who produced the most children. Looking at Josephine, the ladies present must have smiled archly behind their fans, but

Josephine herself, anxious for her husband to show himself in the best social light, accused him afterwards of making people think he was narrow-minded. He was unrepentant. He could not stand women with intellectual pretensions.

The house in the rue Chantereine, renamed the rue de la Victoire in Bonaparte's honour, was soon filled with the leading people of the day. It was now bought outright by Bonaparte and spoils from the Italian campaign were crammed into every corner. Yet he disliked Paris more and more every day. Corruption was rife, army supplies were obtained at exaggerated rates through contracts with large-scale, unscrupulous suppliers; Barras, Talleyrand and Ouvrard (Thérésa Tallien's new lover) were making fortunes through loans and currency deals. Hippolyte Charles was still involved with them, and so was Josephine.

Joseph Bonaparte had heard rumours, probably through his sister Pauline, about his sister-in-law's interests in the suspect army supply company of Bodin, and he insisted upon a confrontation with Bonaparte about it. The few but very revealing letters that Josephine sent to Hippolyte Charles (discovered by Monsieur Hastier and published in his book *Le Grand Amour de Joséphine*) provide incontrovertible evidence of her involvement. She describes to Charles the 'savage interrogation' she had been put through by Joseph and Bonaparte and said that they had asked together whether she knew that Bodin had been responsible for obtaining for Hippolyte supply contracts with the Army of Italy. Did Captain Hippolyte Charles lodge with Bodin at 100 Faubourg Saint Honoré and was it true that Josephine went there every day?

I replied that I knew nothing of what he was saying to me; if he wanted a divorce he had only to speak. He had no need to use such means, and I was the most unfortunate of women, and the most unhappy. Yes, my Hippolyte, they have my complete hatred; you alone have my tenderness and love; they must see now, as a result of the terrible state I have been in for several days, how much I abhor them; they can see my disappointment and despair at not being able to see you as often as I wish. Hippolyte, I shall kill myself – yes, I wish to end a life that henceforth would be only a burden if it could not be devoted to you. Alas, what have I done to these monsters? But they are acting in vain. I shall never be a victim of their atrocious conduct.

Tell Bodin, I beg you, to say that he doesn't know me ; that it was not through me that he got contracts for the Army of Italy ; let him also tell the doorkeeper at No. 100 that when people ask if Bodin lives there he is to say that he doesn't know him. Tell Bodin not to use the letters I gave him for Italy until some time after his arrival there, when he needs them. Ah, they torment me in vain! They will never separate me from my Hippolyte ; my last look will be for him.

I will do everything to see you today. If I cannot, I will spend the evening at Bodin's and tomorrow I will send Blondin [a servant] to let you know the time when I could see you in the garden of Mousseaux [afterwards the Parc Monceau]. Adieu, my Hippolyte, a thousand kisses, as burning as is my heart, and as amorous. . . .

Barras was in it too, of course. She told Hippolyte that she had written to Barras asking him to 'return the letters he had promised'. Then she went on to say that she was going to the country :

I shall be back between half past five and six, looking for you at Bodin's. Yes, my Hippolyte, life is a continual torture. You alone can make me happy. Tell me that you love me and only me. I shall then be the happiest of women.

Send me by means of Blondin fifty thousand *livres* from the notes in your possession. Callot is demanding them. Farewell. I send you a thousand kisses. *Tout à toi.*

If Josephine had written to Bonaparte in a similar vein he would never have written to her, as he did in October 1796 from Modena : 'Your letters are as cold as if you were fifty ; we might have been married fifteen years. One finds in them the friendship and feelings of that winter of life . . . It is very bad, very unkind, very undutiful of you. . . .' At least she did not dissimulate to him in writing.

Although the shady business dealings were under scrutiny, Josephine still succeeded in concealing her affair with Hippolyte from her husband ; his eyes were not opened until later.

Outwardly Josephine was enjoying herself immensely. She reigned as a popular hostess in the rue de la Victoire, went to see Hortense act in *Esther* at Madame Campan's, dined with Barras in Bonaparte's company, went with them both afterwards to see the great actor Talma. She arranged a marriage for her niece Emilie, the daughter of François, Marquis de Beauharnais, with aide-de-camp Antoine Lavalette. She also came, discreetly, to the assistance of Françoise, Aunt Fanny's daughter, who had married a mulatto, Charles Castaing, from Santo Domingo, to the embarrassment of the family. Josephine had already appealed to Barras from Italy to see what he could do to smoothe over this family difficulty (as we have seen, he had already been importuned by Bonaparte to intervene in the Pauline/Fréron affair). He was still Josephine's closest friend and confidant. He must have felt at times, as others were to later, that she was a bit of a pest but, as she herself admitted in later years, people pestered her in their turn and she always tried to help them.

One of the most original of Josephine's petitions concerned the infant prodigy Caroline Wuiet, who had played the piano at concert halls at the age of five and before Marie-Antoinette. She returned to France after several years abroad and was received by the Talliens and Josephine. As she was poor and found clothing a major expense she decided to wear men's clothes. This caused difficulties with the police, so Josephine wrote to the chief of police: 'You will see from the attached note, estimable Citizen, that Citizeness Caroline Wuiet, a distinguished artist whom I take the greatest pleasure in helping, wishes to obtain permission to wear men's clothes occasionally. I ask for her your accustomed courtesy since the Citizen Minister has kindly promised to act favourably in her case. Greetings and friendship, Lapagerie-Bonaparte.'

Meanwhile Bonaparte, frustrated, with nothing for him to do in France, went on a tour of the northern coastal towns to study the possibility of an invasion of England. Seeing that the project was impracticable he decided to attack from the east, via England's colonial empire, and to cut her communications with

India by occupying Egypt. Taking Eugène with him as his aide-de-camp (he had already sent his stepson on various missions for him, to Otranto and Corfu where he had acquitted himself well), he sailed from Toulon on 19 May 1798, having travelled to the port in great secrecy and with Josephine, who was unaware of their destination until they had actually arrived. He advised her to take the waters at the spa of Plombières in the Vosges, since they were supposed to promote fertility in women ; she would then join him in Egypt within two months, sailing in the frigate *La Pomone*. (By a strange coincidence this was the ship that had convoyed her from Martinique on her first voyage to France to marry Alexandre. But *La Pomone* did not escort her to Egypt after all ; in the interval the French fleet was destroyed by Nelson during the Battle of the Nile and Bonaparte was cut off from France. In 1799 he crossed the Syrian desert, captured Gaza and Jaffa and re-entered Cairo on 14 June ; on 25 July he annihilated the Turkish army at Aboukir.)

Josephine now returned to Paris via Lyons, from were she wrote to Barras. It is possible that Hippolyte had joined her. She was still much involved in the affairs of the Bodin company : 'I hear, my dear Barras, that General Brune is doing his best to break the Bodin company's contract. Do please write to General Brune in their favour. We each owe them all our interests and I hope, my dear Barras, that you will oppose any action taken against Bodin. You would do them a service by writing for them to General Brune and I beg you not to lose any time. You know how much interest I take in these people.' She then sent a further letter, with another enclosed for Bonaparte, which she asked Barras to forward without delay, 'because you know what he is like ; he would be annoyed not to have news from me. The last letter he sent me was very tender and sensitive. He asks me to join him quickly, saying that he cannot live without me. So I shall hurry to take the cure that has been recommended to me [Plombières] in order to go to him as soon as possible. I am very fond of him [*je l'aime bien*], in spite of his little faults.' For Barras himself she expressed the warmest feelings, asked him to write to her often and assured him of her friendship 'which will last until I cease to live'. (In fact it was to be over within a year.)

Writing later from Plombières, she complained bitterly that her brother-in-law Joseph was doing his utmost to separate her from Bonaparte: 'I am so unhappy to be separated from my husband that I have a sadness I cannot overcome. On the other hand his brother Joseph, with whom he corresponds so closely, acts so abominably towards me that I am always uneasy when I am far from Bonaparte.'

It was with Joseph that she had to deal when she came to buy Malmaison.; after her return to Paris it was he who advanced the money for the purchase from the 40,000 *livres* a year allowance made over to her by Bonaparte. She also sold some jewels, and some of the funds from her interests in the firm of Bodin may have come in useful. Joseph evidently thought that she was being recklessly extravagant, in addition to obtaining funds from a doubtful source.

Hortense wrote to Eugène from her boarding school:

Maman has bought La Malmaison, which is near Saint-Germain. I go there nearly every week. She is living there very quietly and seeing nobody but Madame Campan and her nieces who often go with me. She has given only two big dinners. She asked the Directors and the whole Bonaparte family but the latter always refuse. Of them all only Madame Bonaparte the mother is amiable to us and we of course show her every attention but I believe she is soon going back to Corsica. *Maman* is, I assure you, very upset that the family won't live on friendly terms with her, which must vex her husband whom she loves greatly. I am sure that if she could have gone out to him she would have, but now you know it is impossible.

One detects *Maman*'s hand in this tactful composition which was clearly intended for Bonaparte's eye even more than for Eugène's. *Maman* herself added a postcript:

I love you with all my heart, my dear Eugène. I think of you without ceasing. I await the moment that will reunite me with all I love. I should have nothing more to wish for if only I could have

Bonaparte back as he was when he left me and as he should have continued to be for me. Think, my dear Eugène, of all I have suffered by the absence of you both. Take care of yourself for the sake of your mother and your sister, both of whom adore you.

Far from 'seeing nobody but Madame Campan and her nieces', with an odd dinner or two thrown in, Josephine was in fact seen openly walking in the gardens of Malmaison with Hippolyte on moonlit nights. It was very careless of her. The young hussar had completely turned her head. 'Since I have become a country-dweller,' she wrote to Barras, 'I have become so uncivilized that the fashionable world scares me.' She was living an idyll. Bonaparte was far away – perhaps he would never return. The Army of Egypt was neglected by the Directory. Letters were intercepted by English warships – some of them most revealing – and published in the British press.

It was during the Egyptian campaign that Bonaparte was informed that his wife had been unfaithful to him with Hippolyte. He believed the rumour. Bourrienne overheard an anguished conversation on the subject between Bonaparte, General Berthier, Junot and the aide-de-camp Julien on 19 July 1799. Bonaparte walked up to Bourrienne and exclaimed:

These women! Josephine! If you had cared for me you would have told me all that I have just heard from Junot. He is a true friend. Josephine! And I am six hundred leagues away! You ought to have told me. To think that she should have deceived me. . . . I shall wipe out this race of fops and coxcombs [an obvious allusion to Hippolyte]. As for her, divorce – yes, divorce – a public and sensational divorce! I must write that I know everything.

Bourienne tried to calm him and suggested that in his position he should avoid a scandal and think of his future and glory. 'My glory!' Bonaparte cried. 'Oh, I don't know what I would give not to have to believe that what Junot told me is true. I love this woman so!

If Josephine is guilty I must have a divorce to separate us for ever. I don't want to be the laughing-stock of all the idlers of Paris. I shall write to Joseph. He will get a divorce for me. . . .'

Why should Junot have chosen such an inopportune moment to open Bonaparte's eyes? It was an insensitive thing to do when the cuckolded husband was so far removed from the domestic scene, clicking his heels in an alien land, waiting for arms and aid that failed to arrive.

Bonaparte wrote to Joseph on 26 July; he may also have written before this date, but the letters have not survived. This letter was intercepted by the British and found its way into the archives of the Foreign Office. 'I may be in France within two months,' he wrote. 'I have great domestic trouble; the veil has been entirely torn from my eyes. ... See that I have a country house on my arrival either near Paris or in Burgundy. I expect to spend the winter there and to shut myself up. I am tired of human nature. I need solitude and isolation. Greatness wearies me, feeling is dried up, glory is meaningless. . . .'

Eugène, as his step-father's aide-de-camp, must also have been lurking in the vicinity when the dramatic exchange with Junot and Berthier took place, for he sent a warning letter to his mother, couched in affectionate but guarded terms. This letter, too, was seized by the British, who this time took pleasure in translating, publishing and circulating it widely in both the British and foreign press. 'Bonaparte has been very melancholy these past few days after a talk with Junot and Berthier,' Eugène told his mother. ' . . . What it amounts to is that it appears that Charles went in your carriage to within three post stations of Paris, that you have seen him in Paris, that you have been to the fourth tier of the Théâtre des Italiens with him, that he gave you your little dog, and that he is even at this moment with you. All this I overheard in fragments. . . .' He concluded tactfully by saying that he did not believe these statements.

When the reports of Josephine's infidelity began to circulate in Egypt and became known to the soldiers, Bonaparte took his revenge. Bourrienne records that he asked General Berthier to bring him 'the best-looking women in the country'. When they were presented to him, however, he found them too plump for his taste and ultimately settled for handsome Madame Pauline Fourès, who had disguised herself as a man to be able to follow her husband to Egypt as a soldier in the army. When he began to go for daily rides with Madame Fourès Eugène's position was so embarrassing that he approached Berthier to ask for permission to relinquish his post and join an infantry regiment. A sharp scene with Bonaparte ensued, after which the rides with Madame Fourès ceased, although this was by no means the end of the affair. Bonaparte sent the husband off on a mission, allegedly to deliver important dispatches to the Directory in Paris, but he too was captured by the ubiquitous British ; the British secret service must have been very efficient, for they knew all about the amorous goings-on of the French general. With a wry sense of humour, the British captain put Lieutenant Fourès back on Egyptian soil and he soon reappeared in Cairo, to the consternation of all concerned.

Josephine was dining with the president of the Directory, Monsieur Gohier, and his wife in their luxurious apartments in the Luxembourg Palace when the astounding news arrived that Bonaparte had sailed secretly from Egypt and had disembarked at Fréjus the day before. He would now be on his way to Paris. Josephine turned pale and, fully aware that his brothers Joseph and Lucien would be only too anxious to give him damaging reports about her conduct during her husband's absence, she turned defiantly to her hosts, pushed back her chair and rose, declaring emphatically: 'I am going to meet Bonaparte. It is important for me not to be anticipated by his brothers, who have always detested me.' Gohier, who had advised her to be prudent, as he recounts in his memoirs and had suggested that if she wanted to continue seeing Charles she had better marry him and divorce Bonaparte, must have looked astonished when Josephine went on calmly: 'I have nothing to fear from calumny. When Bonaparte hears that my favourite society has been with you, he will be as flattered as he will be grateful for the welcome I have had in your house during his absence.'

She set out in haste with Hortense from the rue de la Victoire, travelling to Lyons via the Burgundy road. She thus missed Bonaparte who, after enthusiastic receptions in Avignon, Valence and Aix, took the Bourbonnais route to the capital. His brothers Joseph, Lucien, Louis and General Leclerc were more fortunate; they met Bonaparte and Eugène and escorted them back to Paris, pouring gossip into Bonaparte's ears. His mother was waiting in tears, ready to launch into invectives against *la putana* ('the whore'), as she called Josephine. In the evening his sisters Elisa and Pauline came to join in the attack. When Bonaparte's friend, the financier Collot called he declared:

'There's to be no future for Josephine and me.'

'What, are you going to leave her?'

'Has she not deserved it?'

'I do not know, but is this the time to think about it? Think of France. She has her eyes fixed upon you. She expects to see all your energies devoted to her salvation. If she perceives that your thoughts are taken up with domestic quarrels, she will look upon you as a Molière husband. Forget your wife's faults.'

'Josephine must never set foot in this house. When she gets back she must go to Malmaison.'

'She will come and make her excuses, you will forgive her and all will be forgotten.'

'I, forgive her? Never! How little you know me! If I were not sure of myself I should tear my heart out and throw it on the fire.'

Collot shrugged and left him. He knew Bonaparte better than he did himself.

Bonaparte locked himself in his room when Josephine's carriage rolled up to the front entrance. She ran up the stairs in tears, banged on his door and entreated him to open to her. When he refused to reply she summoned Eugène and Hortense (according to some accounts on the suggestion of her maid) to plead on her behalf. Eugène as we know, was well aware of the rumours that had been circulating about his mother and Hippolyte, but what about Hortense? It seems unlikely that she would have heard. According to the Duchesse d'Abrantès, the two children fell on their knees and made an impassioned appeal in a style that Bonaparte, with his highly developed sense of melodrama, found irresistible: 'Do not abandon our mother! She would die. And we poor orphans, already deprived of our natural guardian by the scaffold, are we to suffer the injustice of being robbed of the protector Heaven has sent us?'

At last Bonaparte relented and opened the door to Josephine, who fell into his arms in a dead faint, though she quickly recovered. When Lucien called to see his brother next morning he was admitted into their bedroom, where he found them sitting up together in the bed that had resolved their differences.

Josephine must have assured her husband that her infatuation with Hippolyte was over, as indeed it was. She had sent her lover a letter in February 1799 putting an end to the affair: 'After this interview, which will be the last, you will no longer be tormented by my letters or by my presence. The respectable woman who has been deceived retires and says nothing.' The use of the word 'respectable' sounds a little inappropriate in the circumstances; evidently he had been unfaithful to her. A further brief letter, written in October 1799, deals with the affairs of the Bodin Company and assures him of her tender and lasting friendship. After that the curtain falls. Hastier writes that when Charles was on his deathbed in 1837 he ordered that Josephine's letters to him should be burned – a gallant gesture, but a disappointing one for historians.

Collot had been invited to breakfast the day after Josephine's return and he was received by Bonaparte with a smile of resignation when he arched his eyebrows on hearing movements upstairs that indicated the presence of the mistress of the house.

Well, yes, she is here [Bonaparte admitted shamefacedly]. As she went downstairs weeping after having knocked repeatedly at my door, I saw Eugène and Hortense following her with tears in their eyes. I have not the kind of heart that can bear to see tears flowing. Eugène was with me in Egypt and I have been accustomed to look on him as my adopted son. He is a brave and good boy. Hortense is just about to come out into the world. All who know her speak well of her to me. I confess, Collot, that I was deeply moved. . . .

Bonaparte was just as much of an actor as Josephine when it suited his purpose. His account to Collot of what had happened the night before is palpably false. How could he have seen 'Eugène and Hortense following their mother with tears in their eyes' if he had not opened his door? It is very probable, too, that Josephine had counter-attacked by reminding him that he too had been unfaithful in Egypt, with Madame Fourès. The affair had been notorious. In any event he was still capable of being swept off his feet by Josephine's charms and cajoleries. Furthermore he was to make use of her connections in high places within the next few days to help bring about the 'Coup du 18 Brumaire' (9 November 1799) that propelled him to the Consulate, one step nearer the seat of power. Without Josephine's aid he would never have succeeded.

Josephine was indeed still on good terms with Barras and those in power. From all that Bonaparte had gathered since his journey through France, the people were dissatisfied and were looking for a capable leader. They wanted neither a new Terror nor the restoration of the Bourbons. Fouché, later Chief of Police, the Abbé Sieyès (recently elected to the Directory) and Talleyrand all believed that a *coup d'état* was necessary, but thought that it should be conducted with a semblance of legality. Three of the five directors (Gohier, Moulin and Barras) dissented. Cambacérès, the eminent jurist, had to be won over. On the evening of 9 November Bonaparte and Josephine invited him to dinner with a number of guests who were in the plot. Bonaparte asked his wife to sit at his writing desk and pen a note to Gohier: 'Bring your wife, dear Gohier, and come to breakfast with me tomorrow at 8 am.' It was an open secret that Gohier was in love with Josephine and this was a trap to keep him virtually prisoner while the coup took place. 'Don't fail me,' Bonaparte continued to dictate. 'I have some very interesting things to say to you. Adieu, my dear Gohier. You can always count on my sincere friendship.' Eugène was dispatched to the Luxembourg Palace with the note, but the stratagem failed. The following morning Gohier sent his wife to the rue de la Victoire alone. Bonaparte asked her to write a note to her husband to insist on his coming over, but he did not look over her shoulder and in fact she wrote: 'You were right not to come ; everything here points to the invitation being a trap. I shall lose no time in getting back.' Gohier was not so much in love with Josephine as to make a fool of himself. The extraordinary hour at which he had been bidden had made him suspicious.

Josephine told Madame Gohier later : 'I cannot tell you how grieved I am that Gohier has not accepted my invitation. I planned it with Bonaparte, who wants the President of the Directory to be one of the members of the new government he proposes to set up. When I sent the letter by my son's hands it ought to have shown him the importance I attached to it.' As Madame Gohier insisted upon returning to her husband Josephine begged her to use her influence. 'I must warn you,' she said, 'that at this moment Talleyrand and Bonaparte are with Barras asking him to resign, which he will doubtless not refuse to do. Besides, they are authorized to tell him that Bonaparte is quite determined to use all means, even force, if he ventures to make the slightest resistance.' She assured her friend that Gohier would be given a position in the new Ministry of Justice. Gohier refused, but two years later he was appointed consul general in Holland. Josephine, as usual, had done her utmost to protect her friends. Barras, however, who had been discredited for some time, signed the letter of resignation tendered him by Talleyrand and retired to his château of Grosbois to write vituperative memoirs that presented Josephine as a whore. They were so obviously biased that they were soon as discredited as their author and nobody took them seriously. Bonaparte and Josephine had been ruthless, it is true ; now Barras had served his purpose. He had certainly been extremely useful to them both.

The coup nearly misfired when Bonaparte lost his nerve in addressing the legislative body of the Council of Five Hundred.

The Jacobin members shouted 'Outlaw!' and began to jostle and insult him. His brother Lucien, president of the Council of Five Hundred, exercised his right to call in the troops and, to a roll of drums, the grenadiers swooped in, led by Murat, and emptied the hall. Lucien buttonholed enough deputies in the lobbies to vote that the resignation of the directors should be accepted and that they should be succeeded by three consuls: Bonaparte, Sieyès and Ducos. The masses approved and Paris confectioners sold sugar figures of Bonaparte inscribed: 'France owes him victory; she will owe him peace.' They all knew that Bonaparte was the man who would henceforth lead their destiny, although it was Sieyès who, keeping to the background, worked out the new constitution.

As soon as the coup was known to have succeeded, Bonaparte sent Eugène to the rue de la Victoire to announce the news to Josephine, who was waiting uneasily for the result. It was the first and only time that Bonaparte had let her into his political secrets. In Italy he had used her charm to sugar his military victories; she had been the velvet glove over his iron hand. 'I win victories, Josephine wins me hearts,' he had said graciously. Now she was to be used in yet another role: to help create a new society in which even returning émigrés would feel at ease and would accept the inevitability of Bonaparte's leadership.

On the morning of 15 November 1799 Bonaparte and Josephine moved into the Luxembourg Palace, where they had so often been invited to supper parties by Barras. Now the roles were reversed. They were the hosts.

On 12 December the new constitution was passed and Bonaparte was given executive power and the title of first consul. The other two consuls, Cambacérès and Lebrun, were shadowy figures.

At the Luxembourg Palace the first consul and his wife occupied the right wing overlooking the rue de Vaugirard, less than half a mile away from the former convent of Les Carmes, where Josephine and Alexandre had been imprisoned six years before. During their three months' stay a new life began. The titles of 'Monsieur' and 'Madame' were revived ; 'Citoyen' and 'Citoyenne' fell into disrepute. Bonaparte was even addressed as 'Your Highness'. Women in silks and satins were received by Josephine at what the Princess Dolgorouki described as 'not exactly a court, but no longer a camp'.

Soon the Luxembourg Palace was not considered to be grand enough and on 19 February 1800 a further move was made, this time to the Tuileries Palace :

Well, Bourrienne [Bonaparte exclaimed delightedly] this is the day when we are going to sleep at the Tuileries. You're very lucky because you haven't got to make a show of yourself ; you will go your own way. As for me, I have to go in a procession. It's a great bore, but we must make a show and impress people. The Directory was too simple and so not respected. Simplicity is all very well in the army, but in a large city, in a palace, the head of the government must attract all eyes in every possible way.

He was well aware of the influence of names on the masses. The Tuileries Palace of Catherine de Médicis, Louis XIV, Louis XV, Louis XVI and the Convention was a symbol of power, glory and achievement.

Josephine arrived there first with Hortense and her sister-in-law Caroline and they stationed themselves at the window of Consul Lebrun's apartments in the Pavillon de Flore. The procession began at 1 pm with regiments commanded by Lannes, Murat and Bessières. The first consul rode in a carriage drawn by six white horses presented to him by the Austrian Emperor after the treaty of Campo Formio. Bonaparte sat in the back seat with Cambacérès on his left and Lebrun opposite. The councillors of state and senators followed in hackney carriages with their numbers hidden by pieces of paper, for there were not enough private carriages available.

The route was lined with three thousand picked soldiers and the Place du Carrousel near the Louvre was packed with a cheering crowd. 'Long live the first consul ! Long live Bonaparte !' they roared. Women were heard to exclaim : 'How young he is ! What a fine head and face he has !' Others,

glancing up at the windows of the Pavillon de Flore, added:
'Do you see Josephine? She has brought him luck.' Bonaparte
believed that too. He was delighted with his reception. What
he had said to Bourrienne was quite untrue. He loved show.
The inscription on the guardhouse to the right of the palace
– 'August 10, 1792. Royalty was abolished in France, never to
reappear' – was beginning to be out of date.

The consular guards (which Eugène had joined) lined both
sides of the road from the Carrousel to the door of the Tuileries
Palace. As Bonaparte drove up the troops saluted. The consuls'
carriage passed through the gateway, then stopped. Bonaparte
got out quickly and vaulted onto the horse brought up for him,
while Cambacérès and Lebrun made their way up to the
reception rooms. They were very much in the background. The
march past began with Murat on Bonaparte's right and Lannes
on his left. Madame Mère, who was standing beside Josephine,
wept for joy at the sight.

When the review was over Bonaparte entered the Pavillon
de l'Horloge and briskly ascended the staircase. The newly-
elected minister of the interior, his brother Lucien, formally
presented the consuls to the governing boards of the City of
Paris. Then he inspected his room which had once belonged to
Louis xvi – looking around him with satisfaction. That evening
after dinner he picked up Josephine and carried her to the royal
bed, exclaiming: 'Come along, little Creole, get into the bed of
your masters.' Josephine may have laughed to please him, but
she felt uneasy as she took over the apartments that had been
occupied by Marie Antoinette. She confided to Hortense: 'I
shall not be happy here. I have dark misgivings ... I feel as if
the shadow of the queen is asking me what I am doing in her
bed.'

There were other shadows besides that of the late queen in
those rooms. Josephine's bedroom had also been the seat of the
sinister Committee of General Security during the Terror, that
Committee to which she had sent an appeal for her sister-in-
law and to which the children had written on behalf of their
imprisoned mother. In the entrance hall Robespierre had lain

groaning with a broken jaw in July 1794 while the Committee deliberated on his fate before he was dragged to the guillotine.

'There is an air of monarchy about this place,' Josephine wrote to Hortense after her first few days at the Tuileries, 'that one cannot breathe with impunity, and I am still disturbed by it.' Her misgivings were to be justified nine years later when she left the palace in a carriage bound for Malmaison after her divorce, never to return.

Meanwhile Bonaparte strolled happily through the Gallery of Diana and looked at the busts of his heroes, which had been placed there by his order: Desmosthenes, Alexander, Hannibal, Scipio, Brutus, Cicero, Cato, Caesar, Turenne, Condé, Marlborough, Washington, Frederick the Great and four French generals killed in Republican battles. But he had not lost his sense of reality. 'Getting into the Tuileries isn't everything,' he told Bourrienne. 'The main thing is to stay here.' He ordered the 'trees of liberty' planted in the courtyard of the Tuileries to be cut down. The Revolution was over and it was time to reorganize society – from the Tuileries.

The Tuileries Palace occupied the now empty space between the Pavillon de Flore, overlooking the Seine, and the Pavillon de Marsan, overlooking the rue de Rivoli. There was little privacy; the ground-floor windows gave on to the gardens, which were open to the public. A little room next to Josephine's was reserved for Hortense. 'Do not show yourself at the windows,' Madame Campan advised her. 'The most impudent *Muscadins* will walk below your window after having seen you at some ball or other. Have muslin curtains put up for the summer and canvas for the winter.' The faded tapestries in the reception rooms were dark and oppressive. 'It is very gloomy in here,' Bourrienne observed. 'Yes, like grandeur,' Bonaparte replied tersely.

Josephine realized that a new life had begun for her too; she had to play another, more dignified role than hitherto. She had written to her financial agent Lagrance on 13 December: 'Please wind up my affairs, using all the discretion and delicacy of which you are capable.' The term 'affairs' referred to the companies supplying equipment to the armies. Then she turned her attention to livening up her rooms and furnishing them in the style that was to be known as 'Empire', with its bronze appliqués, sphinx heads and claws. The furniture in the first salon was upholstered in violet and blue taffeta with a design of honeysuckle ; a picture of St Cecilia hung on the wall ; the second salon, was decorated in yellow and brown with draped mirrors ; Sèvres vases adorned console tables of porphyry and marble, crystal chandeliers were suspended from the ceilings and lit by hundreds of candles. A blue-and-white striped cover fringed with gold was placed over the solid mahogany bed in an alcove ; from the adjoining bathroom a small staircase led to Bonaparte's study and dressing-room. (In those early days he slept with his wife every night.) A door from the bathroom led to Hortense's room. Her principal, Madame Campan, was in great demand. Her services were required to settle points of etiquette first for the consular court and later for the imperial court.

Josephine was now thirty-six, elegant and urbane. Her role was to exude social charm and make guests overlook her husband's gaucherie. She had made the most of every opportunity that arose to acquire the polish that rounded off her innate charm : her enforced stay at the Abbaye de Penthémont, her sojourn among aristocrats at Fontainebleau, her social life in Paris before and after the Revolution in milieux of every shade.

Upstairs in Bonaparte's rooms Talleyrand conducted receptions at which the first consul appeared a little stiffly in a newly devised scarlet velvet tunic with gold embroidery.

A few days after the move they gave a reception to the diplomatic corps – 'a splendid display of dresses, feathers and diamonds', according to Bonaparte's valet, Constant. Josephine was dressed with elegant simplicity in a white muslin gown with puffed sleeves ; she wore a tortoiseshell comb in her upswept plaited hair and a pearl necklace that had belonged to Marie Antoinette. She had not been able to resist buying it, at an exorbitant price. Jewellers had begun to pay their assiduous court to her and as usual she had spent too much.

Fearful that Bonaparte would chide her, she appealed to Bourrienne to support her if he were to question its provenance. He did. 'I haven't seen that necklace before, have I?' 'Oh yes you have, Bonaparte. You forget. It was given to me by the president of the Cisalpine Republic, don't you remember?' He turned to Bourrienne. 'Is that so?' Bourrienne shuffled uneasily and nodded.

Josephine's ladies-in-waiting never ceased to be surprised at the interest Bonaparte took in his wife's *toilettes*. He would descend upon her when she was being dressed to give his opinion of her clothes, accessories and jewels – and to ask awkward questions: 'What's this? Where did it come from? How much did it cost?' Whatever the reply to the last question he would invariably exclaim: 'Much too dear!' He had taken after his parsimonious mother Madame Letizia.

First consular 'society' consisted of officials, civil and military, and their wives. Josephine set these timorous ladies, who were unused to drawing-room conversation, completely at their ease by inviting them to breakfasts that were barely disguised lessons in manners.

In my opinion [wrote Madame Junot, later the Duchesse d'Abrantès] it was a delightful custom, that of inviting to such entertainments women who were still too timid to be agreeable in a drawing-room in the presence of men so much their superiors as to alarm them. By talking at these informal breakfasts about the fashions, the new plays, the little commonplaces of society, the young women acquired courage and ceased to be mere wall-flowers in the drawing-room of the First Consul when he sought distraction there. Madame Bonaparte did the honours of the break-fasts with charming grace. Generally there were about half a dozen of us, and all, with the exception of our hostess, were about the same age.

The ladies-in-waiting of the years 1800 and 1801 were succinctly described by the duchess: 'Madame de La Rochefoucauld, a little hunchback, a very kind woman, witty, related to the Beauharnais family ; Madame de Lamèthe, round as a ball and bearded, but good and witty ; Madame de Rémusat, a superior woman and very charming to those who understood her ; Madame de Talhouet, who remembered too well that she had been pretty and forgot that she was no longer ; and Madame d'Harville, systematically impolite and only polite by accident.' All these ladies were to be seen in Josephine's drawing-room on the ground floor, while official visitors went up to the grand reception rooms on the first floor. All shades of opinion, all kinds of people, were to be found at Josephine's side: an *émigré* returned to France only a few days ago could be seen next to a former member of the Convention who, a few years earlier, had condemned his relatives to death ; a republican general talked with a member of the Vendean army. By her tact Josephine was able to enforce if not peace at least a truce. From the beginning of the consulate, wrote the Comte de Saint-Imbert, 'she worked more energetically than anyone to bring about the reconciliation and fusion that her husband desired'.

The receptions on the first floor were called 'mobs' by the ladies on the ground floor. They ascended in their turn every ten days to attend a dinner for two hundred guests. Senators and generals were received on the second day of the *décadi* (or ten-day week, soon to be abolished) ; members of the legislature came on the fourth day ; members of the Court of Appeal on the sixth.

More public and enjoyed by the masses were the reviews of regiments before Bonaparte. He dazzled the men by singling them out and addressing them by name. Josephine told Madame de Rémusat that every night before going to sleep he studied the army lists and learned the names by heart. He also called the soldiers by the familiar '*tu*', which delighted them. The ladies assisted at these reviews from the windows. 'A little before noon,' wrote the Duchesse d'Abrantès, 'Josephine, Hortense, Bonaparte's sisters Caroline and Pauline, pretty women, officials, distinguished strangers appeared at the palace windows. After the parade trumpets sounded, drums beat, Bonaparte appeared on a white horse, his favourite horse Désiré, spoke to the men, who smiled broadly.'

D

Paris in 1800 was eager for pleasure and liberty now meant freedom to enjoy oneself. It was because she had belonged to the old regime, which had upheld pleasure and grace, that Josephine pleased Parisian society, who asked nothing better than to return to the customs of the past. People flocked to Garat's concerts, to the Tivoli, Frascati and other halls. Dancing became a craze. 'Next to money, dancing has become the idol of the Parisians,' wrote a contemporary observer. 'There is dancing at the Carmes, where the crowds are enormous, at the Jesuits' College, at the Seminary of Saint-Sulpice, at the Filles de Marie, at three or four churches, at Ruggieri's, Lucquet's, Wentzel's, at the Thelusson mansion [soon to be acquired by Caroline and her husband Murat]. . . .'

Two articles in *Le Moniteur* of 26 and 28 February 1800 described the reopened opera balls:

People arrive in dense crowds. Five or six thousand persons are massed in a space too small to hold them. Thousands of different disguises, thousands of elegant, odd or amusing costumes call forth jests. Satire has free rein, and nothing is heard but laughter. All faces are radiant with joy. A leader of the riding school, without a mask, elbows a returned exile . . . it shows that the revolutionary leaven has ceased to ferment, that Frenchmen, tired of hatred and fear, now want only to give hands and forgive one another.

Dominoes were hired for 25, 36 and even 48 francs a time. Reproving notes crept into later articles as the fun became a little too boisterous or people showed that they did not know how to behave: 'Last night we saw a good many undignified Spaniards, ungraceful dancing girls, commonplace Orientals ; we saw indiscreet nuns, silent lawyers, solemn clowns and statue-like Harlequins. This is a misfortune but, trusting in the native intelligence of the happy Parisians, we feel sure that they will soon find the talents required by these new pastimes ; there is no occasion for uneasiness.'

The Champs-Elysées, too, were full of dance halls ; returning *émigrés* were astonished to see hackney carriages that had once belonged to them or their friends carrying passengers back and forth from one hall to another. But the church belfries were still dumb. No bells were rung until 1802 and when the Concordat treaty with the Vatican was celebrated.

Bonaparte's mind was on more serious matters, however. On 6 May 1800 he left Paris for his second Italian campaign and did not return to the Tuileries until 2 July. He had had the audacity to take his army across the Alps and the Great St Bernard pass and beat the enemy on the Italian plains. On 22 June came the news of the brilliant victory at Marengo on the fourteenth.

Josephine was proud to learn that Eugène, who had taken part in the battle, had distinguished himself. 'Your son is advancing by giant strides towards immortality,' Bonaparte wrote to her. 'He has covered himself with glory in every action. I look upon him as likely to become one of the first Commanders of Europe.' (This was an exaggeration ; Eugène became a competent commander and no more.) Josephine felt she had done well to marry 'the little general' for the sake of her children. But what about herself ? She had been told that in Milan the singer Grassini had had more success with her husband than at their previous meeting. He was fond of Italian music and performers, so was there anything extraordinary about this invitation to Madame Grassini ? Josephine began to organize a private spy system. When Grassini returned to Paris in 1803 Josephine wrote to her friend and former landlady in the rue de l'Université, Madame de Krény : 'You would be doing me a favour if you send Julie [her maid] ... to find out where this women is staying and to see whether Bonaparte is visiting her.' Bonaparte subsequently made Madame Grassini a monthly allowance of 20,000 francs which continued until she married the violinist Rode, whom she had met in Paris. Bonaparte had in fact tired of her long before then.

During the Italian campaign he had written affectionate letters to his wife, although they no longer resembled his early effusions : 'I love you very much ; I wish you to write to me often and to remain convinced that my Josephine is very dear to me.' And again : 'Within ten days I hope to be in the arms of my Josephine, who is always very good when she doesn't weep or act the coquette . . . I am sending cherries to Hortense ; they are very good here.' This was his first allusion to the fact that he was growing tired of tears and scenes. But Josephine could not help herself. Jealousy devoured her. She constantly looked at herself in the mirror and made extravagant use of powder and rouge. The first consul became so accustomed to red cheeks that he would approach women less heavily made up and rap out: 'What is the matter with you, Madame? You are pale. Go and put on some rouge.'

He was still very fond of his wife. When he returned from Italy to thunderous ovations in the Tuileries, he turned to Bourrienne and said: 'Do you hear the hurrahs of the population, which have not yet ceased? It is as sweet to me as the sound of Josephine's voice.' That voice was one of Josephine's greatest charms. It was low, husky and what we would today call 'sexy'. It charmed people of both sexes. Madame de Rémusat recorded that even the servants would sometimes pause in their duties to listen to the sound of their mistress's voice. Knowing how good she was to them, it may be assumed that she rarely chided them or had occasion to raise her voice in anger.

Twelve days after Bonaparte's return the festival of 14 July, the anniversary of the taking of the Bastille, was celebrated with astute showmanship. Bonaparte had ordered the members of the consular guard (including Eugène) to bring the Austrian flags captured in battle to the courtyard of the Tuileries at 10 am on the morning of the fourteenth, to take part in the celebrations. It was made to look like a happy coincidence. Eugène also accompanied Bonaparte to the Invalides and the Champ de Mars to take part in the reviews and parades. Lucien Bonaparte made a patriotic speech in the Temple of Mars, as the chapel of the Invalides had been renamed. Three bands played the 'Song of 25 Messidor' (14 July) with words by Fontanes and music by Méhul. The soloists and choruses were declared to be perfect. It was the first time – in France – that a concert had been given by three bands, each placed at some distance from the others.

Bonaparte paid a visit to the disabled soldiers in the courtyard behind the dome of the Invalides and distributed five gold medals; then he went to the Champ de Mars, where the minister of war presented to the three consuls the officers who had brought the captured flags. The crowds surged forward from all sides shouting 'Long live the Republic! Long live Bonaparte!' There were public festivities in the evening: foot and horse races, a balloon ascent, fireworks, dancing.... Disabled soldiers were invited to a dinner at which Bonaparte was present.

To celebrate the founding of the republic Bonaparte and Josephine went to the Théâtre Français to attend gala performances of *Le Cid* and *Tartuffe*: Corneille and Molière, the tragedian and the comedian – fitting tribute to the first consul. Lucien made another of his rhetorical speeches.

On two occasions, however, festivities were interrupted by attempts on the first consul's life. On 10 October 1800, while Josephine was dressing to go to the opera in the presence of Bonaparte, General Bessières came in with Eugène and Bonaparte went up to them, saying: 'You don't know, do you, that they want to assassinate me this evening at the opera?' As the two men and Josephine registered horror and surprise, he went on: 'Calm yourselves; the police have taken all the necessary precautions,' and he assured Josephine that he would come to no harm. Bessières was in command of the cavalry of the guard and he ordered Eugène to start off with a picket guard to protect Bonaparte. At the opera house Eugène made half his men dismount, gave them orders and entered the building fifty paces in front of Bonaparte. Preceded by his men, he walked ahead to make people in the passageway think he was the first consul. He then halted his men, formed them into two lines, stepped quickly aside and let Bonaparte pass through the double line into his box. A few minutes later the two would-be assassins, radical malcontents, were arrested in the opera house. Josephine had joined her husband in their box, a little pale but smiling bravely; when the news circulated that the conspirators had been seized the audience stood and applauded vociferously.

The second conspiracy was engineered by the Chouan rebel Georges Cadoudal from his exile in England. He entrusted it to three men: Saint-Régent, who had been a naval officer and was familiar with artillery, Ceracchi, a Roman citizen, and Arena, a Corsican whose brother had been a member of the dismissed Council of Five Hundred. Whenever Bonaparte drove from the Tuileries towards the rue de Richelieu and the boulevards he took the long, narrow (since disappeared) rue Saint-Niçaise ; this was observed by the conspirators, who hired a stable in the street to house a cart containing an infernal machine, a barrel filled with gunpowder. They calculated the time taken by Bonaparte's carriage to reach this spot and arranged for the machine to explode at that instant on 24 December, when he was due to attend the first performance of Haydn's *Creation* at the Opéra. The cart was taken out and placed in front of a house, thus obstructing the street ; at a signal from Saint-Régent, his accomplice was to set fire to the machine when the carriage arrived and then run for safety.

It was to be a great occasion at the Opéra with the famed singer Garat; the orchestra was larger than usual, the choruses had been doubled by engaging that of the Théâtre Feydeau. It was of course a full-dress affair and Josephine prepared to do full justice to it. A trivial detail of *toilette* saved her life – one of those strange twists of fate that can either cause or avert disasters.

Bonaparte was tired and not at all eager to go to the opera, but Josephine and Hortense urged him to rouse himself ; he finally did so, and got into his carriage followed by an escort of mounted grenadiers. Josephine was to ride in a second carriage with Hortense, her sister-in-law Caroline and General Rapp. She tossed a shawl round her shoulders ; it was a recent gift from Constantinople and the first eastern shawl she had ever worn. Rapp, who had been with Bonaparte in Egypt and the Middle East, was bold enough to suggest that she was not wearing it with her customary elegance. 'Very well, General,'

she smilingly replied. 'You have no doubt seen many eastern
ladies in this attire. Pray tell me how it should be draped.'
Rapp gallantly obliged, while Caroline said sharply. 'Do hurry
– I can hear Bonparte's carriage driving off.'

The three of them ran down the staircase and into their
carriage, Josephine and Hortense occupying the back seat, Rapp
and Caroline the front one. They were going through the Place
de Carrousel when Bonaparte was in the rue Saint-Niçaise. A
loud explosion was heard. Rapp stopped the carriage and went
to investigate what had happened. Bonaparte's carriage had
driven safely past the danger spot. A member of his escort had
seen the cart blocking the street, had hit the 'driver' on the
head and pushed it back, averting a catastrophe. 'To the Opéra,'
shouted Bonaparte. His coachman, who was drunk and
believed the noise to have been a demonstration of loyalty,
made full speed and Bonaparte entered his box uninjured.
Several houses had been damaged by the explosion and passers-
by had been killed. Had Josephine's carriage followed
Bonaparte's, as it should have, she would have been killed too.
As it was Hortense's arm was grazed by a splinter of glass, that
was all. Rapp, having ascertained that the first consul had gone
on to the Opéra, went back to Josephine's carriage and they
made a detour. A little late, she and Hortense entered the
consular box, all of a tremor. Bonaparte greeted them with a
smile and asked for a programme. He remained imperturbable.
Word spread during the interval: 'An infernal machine
exploded on the first consul's route – people have been killed
– forty houses have been damaged – Bonaparte and Josephine
have been saved by a miracle.' All turned towards their box
and applauded. The three plotters were seized and executed.
But the frustrated attempt made people begin to ask who was
to succeed Bonaparte if and when something happened to him
or, simply, after his death. The question was raised inside the
Tuileries too. Josephine decided to try the waters of Plombières
once again.

A peep behind the curtains at the Tuileries would reveal

pleasant domestic scenes of 'the family' quietly enjoying one another's company. 'The family' consisted of Josephine, Bonaparte, Eugène and Hortense, whom Bonaparte loved and treated as if they had been his own children. 'Bonaparte,' wrote Madame de Rémusat, 'who generally had a low opinion of women, always expressed his respect for Hortense. In her presence his language was always more reserved and more decorous. He often appealed to her to decide between her mother and himself, and listened to advice from her that he would not have taken from anyone else. "Hortense", he used to say, "makes one believe in virtue." '

The schoolgirl who had objected to her mother marrying Bonaparte had now become deeply attached to him. 'My step-father is a comet and we are the tail ; we must follow him wherever he goes, whether it be to good or to evil fortune,' she once observed fatalistically.

She was Madame Campan's star pupil. She had a gift for music and even composed a famous marching song, 'Partant pour la Syrie', which was to be sung by generations of French soldiers ; her son, Napoleon III, had it played during a state visit to Windsor, though perhaps a little too often, or so it appears from Queen Victoria's diary. She also drew very well. On one occasion, when she was late for dinner, the first consul sat down without waiting for her. Josephine ran up to her room to fetch her and found her daughter engrossed in putting the finishing touches to a sketch. Josephine asked her rather sharply whether she expected to support herself by her skill, since nothing could turn her away from her work. 'Mama, who can say what may not happen in times like these?' that serious young lady replied. Later, as we have seen, she was to warn her sons that they too might have to be able to earn their living. She had never forgotten those days when she had been apprenticed to a seamstress, when life had been full of danger and her father had been guillotined. They had affected her more than her brother.

Everybody liked Eugène who was more light-hearted. According to Madame de Rémusat, and many others agreed with her, 'his figure was graceful, he was skilled in all bodily exercises and he inherited from his father those fine manners of the gentleman of the *vieille cour* in which perhaps the Vicomte de Beauharnais had himself given him his earliest lessons. To these advantages he added simplicity and kind-heartedness; he was neither vain nor presumptuous; he was sincere without being indiscreet and could be silent when silence was necessary.' Madame de Rémusat was a royalist and there-fore attributed Eugène's manners to his father, but Alexandre had had a prickly character and was unstable. Eugène was in fact much more like his mother, though without her suspicious nature. His popularity also came from the fact that he was an excellent dancer and 'music mad'.

Laure Junot, the future Duchesse d'Abrantès, who was about to become attached to Josephine's household, described her first visit to the Tuileries at the age of sixteen. She arrived, trembling, to be presented to Bonaparte and Josephine after their return from the opera. She had been summoned for ten o'clock and she was dead on time but General Duroc, now governor of the palace, exclaimed: 'How late you are!' She thought there must have been some mistake and was terror struck. There was a click of folding doors upstairs and a young man in dark-green uniform ran down and greeted her affably. It was Eugène. He immediately put her at ease by telling her that his mother had heard a carriage arrive and feared that Madame Junot might have been denied admittance, for she had not heard anyone coming up the stairs. He led her upstairs and whispered: 'You have nothing to fear: my mother and sister are so kind.' He gave her his arm and they entered the salon together. It was dimly lit by two branched candlesticks, which had been covered with gauze to decrease the glare – Bonaparte liked soft lighting. Madame Bonaparte, wrote the future memorialist, was sitting with a tapestry frame before her; Hortense had been reading; her fine golden hair was spread round her shoulders like a halo. The first consul was standing in front of the fire with his hands behind his back.

The solicitude displayed by Josephine and Eugène was typical of them – these were the considerate ways by which they endeared themselves to so many people.

It was at Malmaison, however, that Bonaparte and Josephine enjoyed their greatest domestic bliss. 'Nowhere did I see Bonaparte more happy than in the gardens of Malmaison,' Bourrienne wrote. In September 1800 the architect Fontaine reported: 'The decorators have finished the ceilings of the library and the frieze in the room of the First Consul, on the first floor, above the drawing-room. Madame Bonaparte takes a lively interest in everything we do. She is ordering some new decorations and wants us to give our attention to the gardens, the waters, the hothouses, in short: to everything that can make this place more agreeable, for she regards it as her own private property.' A bathroom was put in near Bonaparte's bedroom with, on the side, a dressing-room and another small bedroom. Two small staircases were built, one from Bonaparte's room to the gallery on the ground floor, the other from the first floor to the library and council chamber.

Visitors drove along an avenue of palm trees to the main courtyard, where the three-storied mansion, what the French called a *gentilhommière*, or manor house, confronted them. Under a tent-shaped verandah surmounted by gilded crescents stretched a great hall paved in black and white marble, with a view of the park beyond. The vaulted roof was upheld by four stucco columns. To the left of the hall were the dining-room, council chamber and the library ; to the right, the billiard-room, Josephine's boudoir and drawing-room, and the picture gallery that she was to fill with a valuable collection of paintings, most of them spoils of war. (In years to come, when the engraver and antiquarian Denon told Napoleon how much they were worth, the great man, in one of his not infrequent moments of pettiness, exclaimed: 'If I had known they were so valuable I should not have given them to her. They should be in the Louvre.') The dining-room was decorated with statues of six nymphs, and a large plate window separated it from the hall. On the mosaic floor a rose marked the spot where

Josephine sat at table. The library door was painted with motifs of helmets, war trophies and inscriptions from the days of chivalry. Medallions of Plutarch's heroes were scattered profusely in the arches between the windows. A passage led from the library into the garden and to a tiny bridge across the moat. In 1800 it was covered by a canvas tent, which gave Bonaparte an extra room in which to work. He had his table carried there and often walked in and out to think, as he found fresh air conducive to 'the expansion of ideas'.

Josephine began to be a little possessive, as he recorded on St Helena. 'She was ever present. . . . Not one of my thoughts, not one of my actions, escaped her ; she followed, grasped, guessed everything – a fact that sometimes inconvenienced me in my occupations.'

When he was not working Bonaparte played prisoners' base on the lawn. On fine days meals were eaten out. Among the younger set of women were Hortense, who always came first in games, Bonaparte's sisters Caroline and Pauline ; Madame Campan's nieces, Eglé and Adèle Auguier (one became the wife of Marshal Ney, the other Madame de Broc) ; Mademoiselle Cochelet (later Hortense's reader) ; a Miss Clarke, who may have taught Hortense English until Bonaparte forbade her to learn the language of his greatest enemy ; Mademoiselle de Lolly Tollendal ; Stéphanie de Beauharnais, Josephine's niece, later Grand-Duchess of Baden, who was educated at Josephine's expense at Madame Campan's ; another niece, Emilie, who had married General Lavalette ; Mademoiselle Hervas, who married General Duroc ; and Elisa Monroe, daughter of the future president of the United States, who was then ambassador. Among the men were Bonaparte's brothers Lucien, Louis and Jérome ; Eugène ; General Lauriston (married later to a lady-in-waiting) ; the painter Isabey, General Rapp, General Savary and Bourrienne, who left a record of the fun and games and of how Bonaparte used to chase Hortense round the gardens. All this gaiety subsided in 1802, with the 'disappearance of republican simplicity'.

In the evenings the company played whist, trick-track, chess and billiards (at which Hortense excelled) and Bonaparte talked endlessly, holding his audience enthralled with stories about the Revolution, comments on philosophy, the East – which had captured his imagination – and ghost stories, which also fascinated him. Josephine does not appear to have taken a very active part in these diversions. She preferred card games and the contemplation of flowers, birds and animals.

In 1802 a little theatre was built for amateur performances. Fontaine wrote:

It is now some time since a love of theatrical performances has begun to appear in the household of the First Consul. . . . We made a sort of portable theatre, which was set up for this purpose in the gallery near the drawing-room. Then we contrived to construct a little hall by taking a corner of one of the largest rooms in the north pavilion on the second floor, but this last plan, although it gave more space, was less convenient for it required that the spectators should leave the drawing-room, and go up two flights of stairs, to sit in a narrow room that was neither large nor handsome.

At last the First Consul yielded to long-continued supplications and he has commissioned us to build, as cheaply as possible, a little theatre, entirely isolated, in the courtyard on the side of the farm. He has given us a month to do it in, and we shall set to as soon as he has approved the cost. Yesterday we made a plan and an estimate and gave them to Bourriene who, with Mamemoiselle Hortense, is one of the most enthusiastic actors.

The estimate of 30,000 francs was approved and the theatre was built in thirty days, as Fontaine had promised. It was a wooden structure, polygonal in shape, covered with slates, and had ample room to seat two hundred people. The ceiling was decorated with printed calico. It contained a pit, a row of boxes, a gallery, an orchestra pit and two small greenrooms. A floor was built above ground level to avoid damp and was on occasion made to serve as a dance floor. A canvas gallery led to the theatre from the ground floor. It was formally inaugurated on 12 May 1802 by a troupe of Italian actors, who performed the *Serva Padrona*, said by the spectators to be 'not a very amusing play.'

Hortense, who had been a success in *Esther* and other classical plays at school, delighted in appearing at the Malmaison theatre. The Duchesse d'Abrantès wrote: 'Eugène de Beauharnais acted remarkably well. I am not prejudiced when I say that Junot had really great talent. Monsieur Didelot made a capital Crispin. I got through my parts tolerably well and General Lauriston made a noble Almaviva or any other lover in court dress. But the best of the company was Monsieur Bourrienne ; he acted serious parts to perfection.' Bourrienne himself commented on the actors: 'Hortense acted admirably ; Caroline only tolerably. Eugène, very well ; Lauriston was a trifle heavy, Didelot passable and, I may say without vanity, that I was not the worst in the company. If we were not very good it was not for lack of good advice and instruction. Talma and Michot used to come to make us rehearse together and separately. How many lessons I have received from Michot when walking in the beautiful grounds!' The company owned a fine collection of props. The first consul gave each of the actors a collection of plays, richly bound, and, as the company's patron, had elegant and expensive costumes made for them.

Bonaparte took great pleasure in these performances [Bourrienne wrote]. He liked to see comedies acted by his friends ; sometimes he even complimented us. Although I liked it as much as the others I was obliged to tell him more than once that my occupations left me very little time to learn my parts ; then he would assume his caressing way and say: 'Oh, nonsense! You have such a good memory. You know what pleasure I get from it ; you see how these plays light up Malmaison. Josephine is very fond of them. Get up earlier.' 'And I sleep so much as it is, don't I?' 'Come, Bourrienne, do it to please me. You do make me laugh. Don't deprive me of this pleasure ; I haven't too many, as you know....'

And so Bourrienne would set about learning his roles to please Bonaparte and Josephine.

Sometimes the plays were followed by concerts or a ball, three or four quadrilles going on at a time. The first consul danced with untiring energy and on such occasions would ask the muscians to play old tunes that reminded him of his boyhood.

There was nothing more delightful than a ball at Malmaison [recalled the Duchesse d'Abrantès], in which the women who composed what was really, though without the name, Madame Bonaparte's court took part. All were young, many were pretty, and when they were dressed in their white crêpe gowns, carrying flowers and wearing garlands as fresh as their young, laughing faces, radiant with gaiety and happiness, it was lovely to see them dancing in the hall in which were the first consul and the men with whom he was weighing the fate of Europe.

Bourrienne added:

Away from the cares of government, which, so far as possible, we left behind us at the Tuileries, we were often very happy in our colony at Malmaison; but then we were young, and what does not youth beautify? In the salons the conversation was most animated and varied and I may say truthfully that gaiety and freedom were the essence of the conversation and made its whole charm. There were refreshments of every sort and Josephine did the honours with such grace that everyone felt that she had been more occupied with him than with anyone else. After these delightful entertainments, which generally finished at midnight, the guests would return to Paris.

Hortense made a hit in *The Barber of Seville*. It is strange to think that that same play had been performed at the Petit Trianon in 1785 with Marie Antoinette in the role of Rosine. The memory of the court of Versailles was indeed still very fresh and Madame Campan kept it alive by instructing her young ladies in the traditions of the *ancien régime*, with its old-world courtesies. The country balls at the Trianon, the taste for pastorals and idylls, the sheepfolds, the Swiss chalets, the fashion for wearing white dresses, the English gardens, rustic life – all these reappeared at Malmaison.

Like Marie Antoinette, Josephine delighted in parks with retreating paths and winding walks, where the grass was covered with violets and daisies. She had always loved flowers and Malmaison gave her full scope for this interest. She wanted her gardens to be world-famous. In this she imitated the former owners of Versailles, for the cult of gardens and exotic plants was a traditional royal leisure-time occupation. Yet Josephine made others benefit by it, generously distributing bulbs and seeds throughout France. These were to have many descendants and in some obscure, subconscious way they perhaps made up for the children she was unable to give her husband and France. It was a way of ensuring continuity. In March 1804 she wrote to her gardener: 'I want Malmaison to become a source of wealth for all the Departments of France. That is why I have sent them so many trees and shrubs . . . I want each one of them to possess – in ten years' time – a collection of precious plants issued from my nurseries.' 'These are *my* conquests,' she had smilingly told Lord and Lady Holland during their visit in 1802, pointing to her roses from Damietta and lilies from the Nile. Plucking a branch of jasmine from her native Martinique, she added: 'The seeds were sown and tended by my own hands – they remind me of my country, my childhood and the ornaments of my adolescence.'

As early as 1798 she had met the famous flower-painter Redouté, who was lodged at the Louvre. This botanist and artist from the Ardennes, broad-shouldered, heavily built, with thick, almost deformed hands and a lively sense of humour, had worked in London, had met Sir Joseph Banks, president of the Royal Society, and had visited Kew. Josephine's greenhouses were inspired in part by what Redouté had seen at Kew. The great botanist Ventenat knew Redouté well, and when Josephine commissioned him to write a book about the Malmaison gardens, Redouté was asked to illustrate it. The two volumes, now extremely rare, were published in 1803 and 1804. The second Malmaison book, *Les Liliacées*, contains five hundred colour plates by Redouté, who was also editor and publisher. It was a great success. Chaptal, the minister of the interior, considered it to be a 'status symbol' for cultural France. Bonaparte willingly subscribed to eighty copies, which he had sent to heads of states, ambassadors and statesmen.

Its present value is estimated at 100,000 francs. Redouté's more widely known book, *Les Roses*, was published after Josephine's death (between 1817 and 1824) but it is believed that the first paintings for it were made during his association with her ; several of his flower paintings adorned the walls of her bedroom.

Josephine particularly loved roses and camellias. Mademoiselle Ducrest recounts in her memoirs that the other ladies of the household sulked when Josephine presented her one day with a particularly beautiful specimen of a camellia as a mark of friendship. Josephine collected all the varieties of roses then known and assembled 197 of them in the first rose garden to be created in France. She also encouraged the work of the best-known growers of the time, Laffay and Dupont, though the variety known as 'Souvenir de Malmaison' was not developed until after her death. The two celebrated Spanish botanists Ruis and Pavon created and dedicated to Josephine the *Lapageria rosea*, a pink liana with falling bells that still figures in some horticultural collections. A plant of South African origin discovered in a Dutch garden was also dedicated to her and named *Amaryllis Josephinae* (now renamed *Brunswigia Josephinae*).

Through Redouté and Eugène's friend (and later steward) Soulange-Bodin, a nephew of Josephine's financial adviser, Jérôme Calmelet, who became one of the first horticultural advisers at Malmaison, Josephine developed her knowledge of botany. Plants had begun to arrive as early as 1800 from Raffeneau Delile in Egypt. From England Sir James Smith sent her seeds and Sir Joseph Banks obtained from her the tobacco plant *Nicotiana undulata*. Political considerations were waived in the pursuit of flora and Bonaparte did not object to his wife receiving plants from the land of his enemy. 'Some plants have arrived for you from England,' he wrote to her when she was taking the waters at Plombières in 1801. Kennedy & Lee of Hammersmith sent her a collection of Cape heathers that became one of the glories of Malmaison and new varieties were obtained from them. Then in 1802 the German naturalist Alexander von Humboldt sent her the seed of *Cactus speciosus ambiguus* and of *Cactus phyllantuides*, which did not flower until 1811. He also sent her, among other things, several dahlias. From Mogador came *Picridium ligulatum*, from Tenerife, *Cheiranthus longifolius*, from South Africa, gladioli and pelargoniums ; Michaud of Charleston sent her an andromeda, others sent purple magnolias, rhododendrons, asters, phlox, from South America came *Araucaria imbricata*, from Australia eucalyptus and *Hibiscus diversifolius*. Rare plants poured in regularly and were carefully tended and propagated by a succession of gardeners, beginning with the Englishman Howatson. Bonaparte objected to him after he made a muddle of transporting some shrubs from Belleville to Malmaison and, more important, because he considered the bill excessive. Howatson was dismissed in 1805.

Josephine did not, after all, have *carte blanche* at Malmaison, for her despotic husband interfered here, as in other details of her life. He dismissed a subsequent chief gardener and supervisor, Charles Mirbel, for having a shrub removed without imperial authorization and – the usual complaint – for spending too much. (Josephine would spend as much as 3000 francs on occasion for a rare bulb – almost as much as the price of a rare jewel.) She was very attached to Mirbel and had him reinstated ; when he left Malmaison he became a professor at the Sorbonne and wrote books on horticulture.

The landscape gardener Jean-Marie Morel designed the grounds, which were traversed by a stream called 'the English stream' ; the stream was bordered by weeping willows and crossed by a wooden bridge. Here too were 'Napoleon's lake', a 'temple of love', also on the edge of the pool, surrounded by banks of rhododendrons, and a magnificent hothouse beside a pond, with a salon in the middle furnished with settees and tables set between coloured marble columns entwined with creepers. From this vantage point Josephine contemplated the lovely blue lotus of the Nile (*Nymphaea caerulea*), the sacred fig tree of India (*Ficus religiosa*) and its Bengal relative (*Ficus benghalensis* ; between 1803 and 1814 two hundred species bloomed for the first time, among them the tree peony *Paeonia*

moutan, Canna flaccida and the Japanese lily *Magnolia yulan.*
Stretched on a sofa she would listen to the tinkle of a miniature
cascade constructed in an artificial rock, exulting in her self-
created paradise. She always brought guests here and her ladies,
less enthusiastic botanists, grew weary of hearing the lengthy
Latin names rattled off over and over again for the benefit of
newcomers.

It would no doubt be an exaggeration to say that Josephine
was a botanist, but with her facility for memorizing names
she must have been able to impress her friends and visitors
with information supplied to her by experts. For flowers as for
antiques she developed more of a collector's lust than a deep
knowledge of the subject. Rare fruits were also cultivated in
the hothouse, so that when Madame Junot was pregnant and
developed a craving for pineapples this was gratified with a
splendid specimen from the hothouse at Malmaison.

As late as 1809, the year of their divorce, Bonaparte sent his
wife plants from Schönbrunn. She was then in a position to
buy some adjacent land and a house she had coveted for some
time. They had belonged to a spinster, Mademoiselle Julien,
who had refused to sell at any price. When she died Josephine
informed Bonaparte that she intended to buy. He promptly
replied: 'They aren't worth more than a hundred and twenty
thousand francs. But if you want to, go ahead and purchase
them – so long as you don't pull down the house and replace
it by some shapeless boulders.' He scoffed at 'artificial land-
scapes'. Josephine did not pull down the house but had it
redecorated, and her personal physician, Dr Horeau, moved
into it, together with various members of her staff. The domain,
Boispréau, was attached to Malmaison and very much beautified.
Little of it now remains as it was in her time.

In 1801 Fontaine wrote: 'The château of Malmaison, in spite
of all we have spent, and all the additions, is too small for the
First Consul, who requires a country house. He has thought of
taking Saint-Cloud and having it put in condition. Madame
is averse to giving up Malmaison, which she is having decorated

and which she prefers to any spot on earth.' Saint-Cloud was a
royal palace, whereas Malmaison was much more intimate
and in keeping with her personal tastes. But Bonaparte insisted
on adopting Saint-Cloud for his summer residence from 1802.
He also took over Rambouillet as a hunting lodge and spent
half a million francs on repairing it. But Fontainebleau became
his favourite palace. 'The real abode of kings and the house of
the ages,' he called it romantically ; he spent over 1 million
francs in restoring it and 3 millions on the furniture. Hunts
were organized from Fontainebleau, as in the time of the
former kings of France, but Bonaparte was not really fond of
hunting. He sometimes forgot what he was supposed to be
hunting and galloped off through the woods, leaving the hunt
behind. Josephine frankly disliked the sport ; she followed
the chase in a carriage and wept whenever, as sometimes
occurred, a frightened deer sought refuge underneath it,
pleading for it to be spared.

Bonaparte was interested in animals and before leaving for
his second Italian campaign, he had paid a visit to the Jardin
des Plantes to look at a lioness acquired from Constantinople ;
she gave birth to three cubs, one of which was named Marengo,
as it was born on the day of that great victory. Josephine had
gone to see the cubs and hold them in her hands. They inspired
her with the wish to add animals to Malmaison and in the
course of the next few years exotic creatures accompanied
dispatches of seeds and plants from foreign parts : antelopes,
zebras, kangaroos, flying squirrels, monkeys, a parrot that
spoke Spanish, danced and uttered the name 'Bonaparte' with
astonishing clarity, and an orang-utan that ate with a knife and
fork and slept in a real bed in a chemise. More useful were the
flock of Merino sheep, then a novelty, which provided rams
for farmers all over France. Josephine eventually brought a
shepherd and shepherdess from Switzerland to look after them ;
they married and were housed in a Swiss chalet at Malmaison,
which then covered over two thousand acres – they are now
reduced to four.

Josephine was surrounded by attractive young ladies and Bonaparte by handsome, eligible young men in his consular guard. Matches were inevitable. Flamboyant, twenty-nine-year-old Murat had fallen in love with Bonaparte's ambitious, quick-witted sister Caroline. After the coup of 18 Brumaire, in which he had taken an active part, Murat dispatched four guards to announce the news to his beloved, who was still a boarder at Madame Campan's. Hortense related in her memoirs what a stir the event caused in that decorous establishment: 'Murat sent us four grenadiers of the guard, of which he was Commander, to tell us of what had taken place at Saint-Cloud and the appointment of General Bonaparte to the Consulate. Imagine the effect of four grenadiers knocking on the doors of a convent in the middle of the night! Every one got a terrible shock. Madame Campan was incensed at this military method of sending news. But Caroline read it as a proof of love. . . .'

When Murat formally asked for Caroline's hand Bonaparte hesitated and told him that he could not give him a positive reply. He informed the womenfolk of his household and that evening there was an animated discussion, with Josephine, Hortense and Bourrienne pleading Murat's cause. Bonaparte objected: 'Murat is the son of an innkeeper. In the lofty rank in which fortune and glory have placed me, I cannot mingle his blood with mine. Besides, there's no hurry. I'll see about it later.' Murat's supporters spoke of his love for Caroline, reminding Bonaparte of his devotion to him and of his fine conduct in Egypt. 'Yes,' Bonaparte agreed reluctantly. 'I acknowledge that Murat was superb at Aboukir.' At last he gave in and, turning to Bourrienne, said: 'Well, you should now be satisfied, and I am too. On the whole Murat suits my sister and then people won't say that I'm proud and seeking grand marriages. If I had given my sister to a nobleman all your Jacobins would have shrieked: "Counter-Revolution!"'

The Faubourg-Saint-Germain was full of returned *émigrés*. Sunday took the place of *décadi* and the old festivities began to be celebrated again: Christmas, New Year, Carnival, Lent,

Shrove Tuesday masquerades, Easter eggs found their way back into the cycle of the year.

The great actor Talma, who helped the amateurs of Malmaison, was Bonaparte's protégé at the popular Théâtre-Français. Josephine admired him too. 'He had the fierce inspiration, the savageness of the Revolution through which he had passed,' the author Chateaubriand wrote. 'The terrible sights he had seen were repeated in the remote and mournful accents of the choruses of Sophocles and Euripides. His mere entrance on the stage, the mere sound of his voice, were intensely tragic.' The Théâtre Feydeau was also popular, while boxes at the opera were as much a spectacle as the stage, with their brilliantly dressed and prominent patrons. Josephine attended every first night attired in new gowns and resplendent with jewels. The simple white muslin gowns that Bonaparte had once favoured (except when Indian muslin was forbidden as being of British provenance) gave way to more sumptuous creations: a white tulle dress, for instance, sprinkled with tiny feathers of exotic birds, each one fastened by a pearl; a white crêpe dress showered with rose leaves and, on her head, garlands of flowers woven by Duplan, her 'artist coiffeur', whom she kindly lent to her friends. He made a fortune.

Although Bonaparte frequently complained that his wife spent too much on clothes, she soon became France's number-one model, thereby encouraging the textile industry. The manufacturers of Lyons, Saint-Quentin, Caen and Chantilly increased their trade.

Outside the palace, the Opéra and the Théâtre-Français Josephine was seen at a very few private houses. In addition to the receptions at the houses of the Bonaparte circle her severe husband allowed her to attend only Madame de Montesson's breakfasts. This lady, the morganatic wife of the Duc d'Orléans, another adviser on court etiquette, also gave celebrated Wednesday dinners; during Lent her religious friends, and ecclesiastics, were served meatless dishes. Bonaparte, who was soon to sign the Concordat, overlooked her temerity. But he was more severe to Josephine's old friends; Madame

Tallien had been forbidden entrance to the Tuileries. Yet Josephine must have continued to see her in secret because in later years Madame Tallien, who had married the Prince de Caraman-Chimay, approached Hortense on the subject of the marriage of her daughter (another of Josephine's goddaughters). She would surely not have done so had the relationship not been maintained.

Bonaparte wanted Paris to become renowned as a centre of culture and civilization and Josephine supported him enthusiastically. On 14 June 1801 the victory of Marengo was celebrated and the minister of war, Berthier, gave a splendid supper in the gardens of his mansion under tents; bivouac fires were lit in the grottoes; trophies were hung in the ballroom; officers in uniform acted as the ladies' cupbearers. A balloon ascended bearing the word 'Marengo'. Also present were the King and Queen of Etruria (travelling under the name of the Count and Countess of Leghorn) to whom Bonaparte had given the kingdom of Tuscany. The new Queen of Etruria was the daughter of the Spanish kings, with whom Bonaparte wished to be on friendly terms because of their possible usefulness in his campaigns against Portugal and her ally England. He was to make use of them, then cast them away when they had served their purpose.

Monarchs – Bourbons – at the Tuileries! It would have been inconceivable even a year before. Josephine welcomed the timid little pair with her usual affability and the Queen of Etruria wrote to her mother in Madrid singing the praises of the elegant woman who had made her feel so much at home.

The festival of 18 Brumaire was celebrated in November and a 'Festival of Peace' heralded the Peace of Amiens signed with England in March 1802. Lord Cornwallis, the English plenipotentiary, took part in the festivities. The Place de la Revolution was renamed Place de la Concorde, decorated with porticoes and covered with dance halls. A temporary theatre showed panoramic scenes of bombardments – the 'terrors of war' – followed by others depicting the peaceful joys of arts, crafts and trade. A 'temple of commerce' was built on a bridge over the Seine and a fleet of barges representing the different nations of Europe plied between the Pont Royal and the Pont Neuf, decorated with flags and bunting.

Meanwhile poor Hortense had fallen in love with her father's aide-de-camp, Duroc, and the sentiment was reciprocated. Bourrienne was used as a go-between for the young couple when Duroc was sent to St Petersburg with a message of congratulations from Bonaparte to the new Tsar Alexander. The pair exchanged letters and very probably a marriage would have taken place if Josephine had not opposed it. This is the only recorded instance in which she placed her own happiness and security above those of her children, for she was determined to strengthen her hold on Bonaparte by marrying Hortense into his family. Her choice fell on her husband's younger brother Louis.

Louis was then twenty-three years old. He had served on his brother's staff since the age of fourteen and fought creditably in Italy and Egypt. He had been made colonel of the Fifth Dragoons, had distinguished himself at Marengo and had taken part in an expedition to Portugal. He seemed gentle and modest, though very different from the handsome, vivacious Duroc. Bourrienne was now used as a go-between by the opposite camp. He asked for an audience and informed Hortense that her mother and stepfather wished her to marry Louis. 'Your mother's misfortune, as you know, is that she can no longer hope for children. You can remedy this and perhaps ward off a still greater misfortune. I can assure you that intrigues are constantly afoot to persuade the consul to a divorce. Only your marriage can tighten and strengthen these bonds on which your mother's happiness depends. Can you hesitate?'

Hortense, horror struck, asked for a week in which to consider her reply. Her confidant, Eugène, was at Lyons. Had he been with her, she suggested in her memoirs, he might have dissuaded her from entering into an alliance that was repellent to her. Josephine wept continually and stole sorrowful glances at her that seemed to imply: 'I know that you are about to sacrifice your life for me.' Cynics could argue that she was putting on an unforgivable act to achieve her purpose. Madame Campan, no doubt prodded by Josephine, appealed to Hortense's reason in schoolmarmish terms:

The illusion of love [she wrote to her former pupil] passes away and the indissoluble tie remains; the husband is seen as he is and he is not to blame, for he is not changed. It is wrong to find fault with him; the fault lies in your eye and the prepossession of the wife's heart. . . . Act in such a way that your conduct and Eugène's shall please the First Consul and suit his views about establishing you both. You are one of the closest ties between him and your mother, and if you fall into disgrace you must not think that you would readily find consolation. One may live in a humble position, or even feel that it is pleasant to be obscure, but it is painful to descend and this, I assure you, is true. . . .

Yet had it not been for Josephine's entreaties, Duroc might have been successful in his suit. Bonaparte liked him. He once told Bourrienne: 'I like Duroc; he is of good birth. I gave Caroline to Murat and Pauline to Leclerc and I can give Hortense to Duroc, who is a capital fellow.' But Bourrienne says that Josephine used all her wiles and cajolery to dissuade him, and Duroc was too modest to insist. On the other hand, as Comte Saint-Imbert pointed out, he would have been given a command away from Bonaparte had he married Hortense. Bonaparte had declared openly: 'I don't want any in-laws about the house,' and Duroc was greatly attached to his master.

Eventually, in order to console her mother, Hortense 'tried to appear content' and gave her consent to the marriage. 'I renounced my romantic notions for my mother's happiness,' she wrote sadly in her memoirs. Bonaparte, obviously embarrassed, said to her hypocritically: 'Well, well, so Louis is courting you? That suits me, as well as your mother. I shall therefore give my consent.'

The date of the wedding was fixed for 4 January 1802. Josephine shed more tears and Madame Campan wrote to Hortense hopefully:

You are about to form a tie that all Europe will applaud, as I do. I have some slight knowledge of character and of similarities. . . . I have noticed in you both a conformity of tastes that assures your domestic happiness. . . . You will unite two families that ought to form one and both are dear to France. I am sure that you will love each other much and always. The First Consul, who knows how to remedy every evil, has chosen for him the woman who cannot fail to make him happy by the qualities he admires and one can only praise the man who desires such qualities in his wife. Soon, my dear friend, I shall cease to write to you letters of advice. You will have a competent guide. Now the teacher can only rejoice in her work. A marriage based on a similarity of position, education and tastes, such as all the world sees here, must be the happiest union possible.

But Madame Campan was utterly wrong. The marriage was disastrous.

If only Hortense had spoken her mind to Bonaparte! But she was 'respectfully timid towards Bonaparte, and she trembled when she spoke to him', according to Bourrienne, through whom she had indirectly submitted her requests. 'Little goose! Why doesn't she ask me herself? Is she afraid of me?' Bonaparte cried.

On his side Louis felt that he could not oppose his brother, although he had little feeling for Hortense. At one time he had paid court to Emilie de Beauharnais. He described his marriage in his memoirs: 'Never was there so gloomy a ceremony, never did man and wife have a stronger presentiment of a forced and ill-assorted marriage.' And to his wife he wrote later: 'There are those still living who can bear witness that our consent was never freely given and that ... we were both equally victims of an unjust and false policy. It is known that I loved your cousin Emilie long before my departure for Egypt and for this reason, even at that time, rejected your mother's proposals for our union.'

The civil ceremony took place at the Tuileries and the religious one in the house in the rue de la Victoire where the young couple were to live before they acquired the Hôtel

Saint-Julien in the rue Cerutti and, the Château de Saint-Leu on the outskirts of Paris. Mass could not be said at the palace and before the Concordat church ceremonies were celebrated in private houses, with unsworn priests officiating. Cardinal Caprara, the papal legate, who was negotiating the terms of the Concordat with the French government, gave the nuptial blessing. It was decided that Caroline and Murat should take advantage of his holy presence to be blessed at the same time. Caroline, who must have known that her ex-schoolfriend Hortense had taken her side when Murat's suitability as a groom was being discussed, was nevertheless furious that Louis had become her husband ; she believed, and her belief was shared by all the Bonapartes, that Hortense's children would have precedence over hers for the succession. They knew how much their brother loved Hortense.

Hortense did make one little gesture to show her disapproval of her mother's choice. Instead of the magnificent wedding gown given to her by her mother she put on a simple white crêpe dress and wore no ornaments. Thereafter she did the honours at Malmaison and Saint-Cloud whenever Josephine went to Plombières to take the waters and was, as Bonaparte wrote to his wife, an excellent hostess – so tolerant that she allowed one of Bonaparte's current mistresses, the singer Louise Rolandeau, to sup at Malmaison. Josephine rebuked her daughter. Was Hortense taking her revenge ?

Louis's character soon began to reveal itself as brooding, moody and pathologically jealous. He was even jealous of his brother :

The Bonapartes [wrote Madame de Rémusat], and especially Madame Murat, who had opposed this marriage with some violence, because since Joseph's children were girls it was evident that if Louis had a son, who would be Josephine's grandson, he would at once be a very important child, spread abroad the detestable rumour of the intimacy of the First Consul with his stepdaughter. The public heard it with delight. Madame Murat confided it to Louis who, whether he believed it or not, only redoubled his precautions. Servants were taught to spy, letters and notes were opened, all acquaintances were frowned on, even Eugène was regarded with jealously. There was a series of violent scenes; the poor woman knew no rest.

Hortense herself could be difficult and aloof, as her former teacher was aware. When a son was born on 18 October 1802 and Louis showed his pleasure at the event, Madame Campan wrote to Hortense: 'You were moved by it ; your tender heart must have been moved. But – I know you well – did you *show* it ? I am well aware that simple, pure souls that have been well trained despise all demonstrations, but sometimes with the best motives errors are made.'

The rumour that the child was Bonaparte's spread abroad. 'Is there no way of escaping this vile gossip?' Bourrienne lamented. 'The whole disgusting story is a lie and yet it spread not only throughout France but into every corner of Europe.' Josephine was horrified.

Poor Josephine paid a high price for her glory [wrote Madame de Rémusat]. Knowing the groundlessness of these reports I tried to console her by telling her how I tried to show their wickedness and falsity. But Bonaparte, under the influence of the affection of which he was the object, only augmented his wife's grief. He was deluded enough to imagine that the whole thing was due to the desire of the country to see an heir ; consequently, when he tried to console her as a mother, he pained her as a wife and the vision of a divorce returned. In his wild illusion Bonaparte imagined that France wanted to be governed by a bastard, which is a curious way of establishing a new legitimacy.

Writing on St Helena, he said: 'Louis knew what value to set on such rumours, but his vain capricious character was shocked and he made use of them as pretexts.'

Hortense's son was named Napoleon-Charles, the solemn christening ceremony being held at Saint-Cloud. Six months later Bonaparte and Josephine paid a formal visit to the parents and Bonaparte asked his brother to allow him to adopt the infant. Louis firmly refused and he subsequently wrote a rude letter advising his brother to get a divorce and have a child of his own. He also forbade Hortense to spend more time than was strictly necessary at Saint-Cloud and never to spend a night there. 'I shall make a law that will render me master of my family,' Bonaparte was to declare angrily in 1803. First, however, he had to become the recognized master of France.

Lucien Bonaparte, as minister of the interior, was alleged to be the author of a pamphlet comparing Bonaparte to Caesar and Cromwell. Josephine sat on her husband's knees, ran her fingers through his hair and murmured: 'Bonaparte, don't be king; wretched Lucien is giving you ideas.' He had his own ideas on the subject, but he thought that his brother had acted prematurely and tactlessly. So he banished him to Spain as ambassador to the court of Charles IV. Josephine had tried to make the peace between the two brothers. Lucien did not regret his ambassadorship as it allowed him to make a handsome profit out of the comic opera 'War of the Oranges' between Spain and Portugal, in which France intervened. But he did not like Josephine; and nor did Bonaparte's sisters.

The Concordat was celebrated on Easter Sunday 1802. It was alleged that the sound of the church bell at Rueil near Malmaison had influenced Bonaparte who, according to Bourrienne, would stop to listen to it when he was walking in the gardens and exclaim: 'That reminds me of my early years at the military academy of Brienne. I was happy at that time.' He decided to mark the occasion by a religious ceremony in Notre Dame. Josephine accompanied him to the cathedral, where they were solemnly received at the door by the Archbishop of Paris, who presented Bonaparte with holy water and led him under a canopy to his place in the choir near the high altar. Behind him stood a row of generals in uniform, members of the Senate, the legislative body and the Tribunate. Josephine assisted at the unusual spectacle from the Gothic rood-loft (since removed), surrounded by eighty of her ladies and friends. The Duchesse d'Abrantès observed that Caroline Murat looked becoming in pink with a pink satin hat surmounted by a tuft of feathers of the same colour, while Josephine was in white

and ablaze with diamonds. 'No worldly festival was more magnificent than this religious one,' she wrote maliciously, 'and
while the thoughts of the pious turned to their Creator, it was
in His creatures that the free-thinking Generals most interested
themselves and many of them, standing behind the First Consul,
and so in no dread of his eyes, acted unbecomingly. . . .'

They left the cathedral in fine carriages. What a change from
the shabby, patched-up hansom cabs of only two years before!
Members of the diplomatic corps dined at the home of
Talleyrand, the minister for foreign affairs ; the archbishop,
cardinals and high-ranking ecclesiastics dined with Bonaparte.
'Noble mummery!' were the words of an eyewitness.

From then on the archbishop celebrated mass at Saint-Cloud
on Sundays. People dressed up to the nines for these occasions,
which were compared to 'very fine concerts', and Josephine
was observed to genuflect beautifully. A bishop consecrated the
chapel of the academy of Saint-Cyr. Holy water was in great
demand. But Bonaparte's ambition was to be anointed.

Josephine confided to Secretary of State Roederer in May
1802 :

I do not approve of all the plans that are projected. I said as
much to Bonaparte, who listened attentively to me, but his flatter-
ers soon made him change his mind. The Generals say that they
did not fight against the Bourbons to set up the family of Bonaparte
in their place. I do not regret that I have given no children to my
husband, for I should tremble for their fate. I shall remain devoted
to Bonaparte's destiny, however perilous it may be, so long as he
has the regard and friendship for me that he has always shown
until now. But the day he changes I shall withdraw from the
Tuileries.

Thibaudeau wrote in his memoirs :

In France and in Europe everything conspired for the sacrifice
of the rights of the people in favour of the First Consul. At court
one woman resisted the mighty current ; she alone was not blinded
by all the illusions of greatness. She was incessantly pursued by the
wildest alarm and the gloomiest forebodings Indeed, Madame
Bonaparte perhaps foresaw her fall in her husband's elevation to

the throne; but a delicate instinct, which in women often takes the place of perspicacity, prevented her seeing without horror a man reigning over the ruins of the Republic who owed to the Republic his greatness and glory.

'Bonaparte's true enemies are those who fill him with ideas of a dynasty, of hereditary succession, of divorce and a second marriage,' Josephine said to Roederer, and to Bonaparte she pleaded: 'Don't be king.' 'You are absurd, Josephine. It's all those old dowagers of the Faubourg-Saint-Germain, and especially Madame de la Rochefoucauld, who have concocted these stories; you tire me, leave me alone,' he replied testily. She was beginning to nag. Fouché, the minister of police, wisely advised her: 'Madame, keep quiet. You will only annoy your husband to no purpose. He will be life consul, king or emperor – whatever anyone can be. Your timidity wearies him; your advice wounds him. Let us stay in our place, let things happen that neither you nor I can prevent.'

Bonaparte was elected consul for life on 2 August 1802 by a plebiscite that produced 3,568,885 votes in favour out of 3,577,259 votes cast. He celebrated his birthday on the Feast of the Assumption of the Virgin Mary, 15 August. A great pasteboard star was hoisted above the towers of Notre Dame and illuminated at night; in the centre shone the sign of the zodiac under which this predestined man (as he firmly believed) was born.

Saint-Cloud had become the summer residence of Bonaparte and Josephine. It was magnificent if rather severe, situated high above the Seine, and surrounded by woods and parkland dotted with fountains and cascades. There was a grand staircase in the centre as one entered from the main court, adorned with marble columns, built by Mique, Marie Antoinette's architect. Up one flight was the main hall with its painted ceiling; a door to the right led to the Hall of Mars, and an anteroom to the Gallery of Apollo. The roof, covings and spaces over the doors in the Hall of Mars were decorated by the famous artist Mignard, as was the Gallery of Apollo. At the end of the gallery was the Room of Diana, in which Mignard had painted the goddess at her toilette, in her bath, hunting and asleep. Other rooms were dedicated to Venus, Truth, Mercury and Aurora – the allusions appealed to Bonaparte's southern imagination and they remind us of his familiarity with the gods of pagan antiquity. Josephine took up residence in the former apartments of Marie Antoinette in the left wing. So once again she was liable to be haunted by the ghost of her predecessor.

Visitors were received from all over Europe and a rigid etiquette evolved. One of the problems heatedly debated was whether or not men should wear powder, as they had in the old days. Most foreigners, and especially the British who wore their hair short, attended receptions with whitened hair and a bag of powder fastened to their coat collar. But in the end it was decided that each person should be free to do as he pleased.

At that time Bonaparte was described by his new secretary, Méneval, as being 'like a father in the midst of his family, full of a sportive and sometimes boisterous gaiety and sometimes really delightful'. But Madame de Rémusat found him heartless:

If it is possible to believe that a being, in other respects like ourselves, could yet be without this part of our system that makes us require to love and to be loved, I should say that at his creation his heart was forgotten, or else that he succeeded in entirely silencing it. He always takes too much interest in himself to be controlled by any feeling or affection whatsoever. He almost ignores the ties of blood, the rights of nature.

Madame de Rémusat, it must be remembered, was an ardent royalist. General Rapp did not agree with her views on Bonaparte: 'No one was more constant in his affections than Napoleon. He loved his mother tenderly, he adored his wife, he was very fond of his brothers and sisters and of all his relatives.'

Most contemporaries, however, agreed with Madame de Rémusat when she wrote: 'He was never quite at ease with women and since this lack of ease put him somewhat out of temper, he always approached them awkwardly, not knowing how to talk to them. . . . He cared for a woman only if she was handsome, or at least young. He may perhaps have thought that in a well-organized society we should be put to death, as certain insects die naturally, the work of maturity once accomplished.' Prince Metternich, the Austrian ambassador, confirmed:

Never did [Napoleon] address a gracious or even a polite phrase to a woman, although one could perceive by his expression or the sound of his voice that he tried to do so. He spoke to women only about their dress, of which he boasted that he was a severe judge; or else about the number of their children, and one of his favourite questions was whether they had nursed them themselves – a question he often asked in language unusual in good society. His voice could not adopt soft modulations.

Bonaparte's first love letters to Josephine, as Comte Saint-Imbert observed, were written in the style of Rousseau's *La Nouvelle Héloïse*, which he soon abandoned. He detested sentimentality; whenever he fell in love, 'it was with a sort of wild fury'. It was said that he conquered a woman like a province. There were often stormy scenes at the Tuileries when Josephine, inflamed by jealousy, accused her husband of his infidelities. When he spoke too long and with too much obvious interest to Madame de Rémusat she even became jealous of that decorous lady.

Claire, Comtesse de Rémusat, was born in 1780. Both her father and her grandfather had been guillotined three days before the fall of Robespierre. At the age of sixteen she married a Provençal nobleman who had been a magistrate at Aix before the Revolution. Her mother had known Josephine when she was Vicomtesse de Beauharnais, and her husband was appointed prefect of the palace. She was one of the few women with whom the first consul enjoyed talking. She was twenty-three when she assumed her duties at the palace, vivacious and intelligent, with black hair and eyes. Talleyrand too admired her intellect: 'It is broad and cultivated. I know no one who talks better,' he said. When Bonaparte went to Boulogne in 1803 to inspect the camp at Boulogne opposite the English coast he took the Comte de Rémusat with him. The Comte fell ill

Josephine painted by Gros; her belt is decorated with portraits of
Napoleon, Eugène and Hortense.

Alexandre de Beauharnais, Josephine's first husband.

A watercolour portrait of Josephine by Jean Baptiste Isabey painted shortly after her marriage to Bonaparte.

Josephine's house in the rue Chantereine.

Napoleon by Isabey; an early portrait miniature painted on ivory.

Eugène de Beauharnais in the robes designed for the emperor's coronation.

An accomplished self-portrait by Hortense de Beauharnais.

The garden front of
Malmaison; a contemporary
engraving.

Bonaparte at Malmaison,
painted by Gérard in 1804.

Josephine's bedroom at Malmaison.

The Temple of Swans in
the gardens of Malmaison.

A detail from 'The
Coronation' by Jacques Louis
David. Napoleon gave the
artist instructions to paint in
the figure of his absent
mother.

Rosa gallica regalis from
Pierre-Joseph Redouté's
Les Roses.

Hortense, when Queen of Holland, painted by Gérard.

Eugène was appointed Viceroy of Italy in 1805; a portrait by an unknown artist.

'The Divorce of Napoleon and Josephine' by H. F. Schopin (1804–1880).

Napoleon on the eve of the invasion of Russia; a
portrait by Girodet.

Josephine in 1814, the year of her death, painted by
Ferdinando Quaglia.

and his wife was summoned to look after him. Bonaparte invited her to lunch with him every day. She told him bluntly that his affairs distressed Josephine. Bonaparte replied crossly : 'She upsets herself a lot more than she need ; she is always afraid that I shall fall seriously in love. Doesn't she realize that I am not made for love ? What is love ? A passion that sets all the universe in one scale and the loved one in the other. It is certainly not in my nature to surrender to any such engrossing feeling. Why then does she worry about these fancies in which my affections are not engaged' In these words we hear man's eternal complaint about woman's possessive nature and her desire to be his exclusive and dominant absorption.

Josephine had heard that her lady-in-waiting had been seeing her husband every day and received her coldly upon her return to Paris. Madame de Rémusat exclaimed tearfully: 'What, Madame, is it I whom you now suspect ?' Josephine, 'as she was kind and open to every passing emotion, kissed me and was as friendly wth me as in the past'. When Bonaparte wrote to her from Boulogne: 'I am longing to see you, to tell you of all that you inspire in me, and to cover you with kisses. This bachelor life is wretched and nothing can equal the worth of a wife who is good, beautiful, tender . . .', she replied ecstatically :

All my sorrows have disappeared in reading the good, sympathetic letter that contains such loving expressions of your feelings for me. How grateful I am to you for giving so much time to your Josephine. If you could know, you would applaud yourself for being the means of causing so much joy to the wife whom you love. . . . A letter is the portrait of a soul and I press this one to my heart. It does me so much good. I wish to keep it always. It will be my consolation during your absence, my guide when I am near you. I wish to be always in your eyes the good, the tender Josephine, concerned only with your happiness. . . . Adieu, Bonaparte. I shall never forget the last sentence of your letter. I keep it in my heart. How deeply it is engraved there! With what emotion mine has responded. Yes, my wish is to please you, to love you – rather, to adore you.

This letter displays a pathetic, dog-like devotion on the part

E

of a woman and subject eager not to displease her master and grateful for any crumbs of affection thrown her way. There is a note of servility about it. Moreover, it shows signs of having been carefully drafted. It does not sound spontaneous. The style bears a close resemblance to the tone of the petitions that Josephine had written to the authorities in the revolutionary days.

Josephine had many occasions to be jealous and her husband did not spare her feelings. His affair with the actress Mademoiselle George was notorious. Josephine could not restrain herself when she found out, through her spies, that he was making love to her one evening in his apartments; 'I can't stand it any longer,' she told Madame de Rémusat. Follow me. We'll go upstairs together.' Madame de Rémusat tried vainly to remonstrate but Josephine 'who was very agitated' made her take the candlestick and led her to the secret staircase up to Bonaparte's bedroom. Suddenly they heard a noise and Josephine whispered: 'Maybe it is Roustau [Bonaparte's Mameluk who guarded his door]. He is capable of cutting our throats.'

'When I heard this,' wrote Madame de Rémusat, 'I was so frightened that without waiting to hear more I rushed downstairs, candle in hand, leaving Madame Bonaparte in the dark. . . . She followed a few minutes later, surprised at my sudden departure. When she saw my scared face she began to laugh. So did I and we gave up our original plan.'

But Madame de Rémusat was forced to become Josephine's accomplice on another occasion when she (rightly) suspected that her husband was in bed with her reader, Madame Duchâtel. He had left the drawing-room surreptitiously and so had Madame Duchâtel. Josephine turned to Madame de Rémusat and whispered: 'I am going to find out whether they are together.' Madame de Rémusat tried to dissuade her but it was useless. She waited, trembling, in Josephine's bedroom while her mistress tiptoed up the private staircase leading to Bonaparte's room. She returned soon after, wild with jealousy, to report that she had knocked on the door but had received no reply; then she had looked through the keyhole, heard familiar voices and knocked again, giving her name and demanding that the door be opened to her. This was done and she had found the guilty pair 'in a disorderly state'. She had poured out abuse, Madame Duchâtel had cried and Bonaparte had flown into such a violent temper that she had run away. 'When I think that only ten days ago Bonaparte came to my bedroom and we had a wonderful night – he was as ardent as a young lieutenant,' she exclaimed tearfully. 'What shall I do?' 'Go back to him,' Madame de Rémusat advised her, 'be as sweet as you can and try to calm him down.'

The consequence was pandemonium, the sound of slaps and broken china.

Bonaparte carried on with the lady until she became domineering, when he decided to put an end to the affair – but how? She was still his wife's reader, so in a cowardly fashion he appealed to Josephine to perform the disagreeable task for him. 'I confess that I have been very much in love with her, but now it is all over. She wants to get me under her thumb. I won't have it. Tell her,' he commanded.

Josephine was anything but vindictive.

As soon as she knew that she no longer had anything to fear, her anger melted away. She sent for Madame Duchâtel and informed her according to Madame Rémusat: 'The First Consul has asked me to tell you that he would be very displeased by any display of affection you might think yourself authorized to give him.' Madame Duchâtel listened coolly and made no reply. Bonaparte avoided her thereafter but she remained in Josephine's service. 'You must put up with my whims,' Bonaparte scolded. 'Accept that it is natural. I must have distractions. I am a man apart and no one is going to tell me what to do.'

Hortense tried to enlist the help of Murat of all people (he was under his wife's thumb and anti-Josephine) to persuade Bonaparte to consider her mother's feelings. Her stepfather walked up to her one day and said: 'Your mother's jealousy makes me appear ridiculous. She talks to all and sundry about my passing fancies.' 'You make her suffer.' Hortense countered. He reflected. 'Perhaps you're right. I'm magnanimous whenever important matters are concerned and small-minded about little ones.' Then he laughed and said ; 'Louis and Josephine would have made an ideal pair : one would have spied through the keyhole while the other was spying behind the curtains!'

Rumours of Bonaparte's infidelities or of his complaints about the lack of an heir may have reached Martinique. Josephine wrote to her mother in 1803 : 'I do not write to you as often as I should like, dear mama, because I have little time to myself. . . . I imagine that you feel some occasional concern about me, but there is no need for this, so I beg you not to give way to such feelings and believe only the news I send you. . . .' The year before she had asked her mother to come to France, and had added : 'Bonaparte is making your daughter very happy. He is . . . in every way a charming man and he truly loves your Yeyette. . . .' On the conclusion of the Concordat she sent her mother a diamond-studded box and a chaplet blessed by the Pope.

Madame Tascher de La Pagerie never went to France ; she stayed in her house at Trois-Ilets surrounded by her slaves, living quietly, helped by the yearly allowance of 100,000 francs sent to her by Josephine, but without feeling any urge to cross the sea and see her daughter again. Josephine had always wanted to go to France ; she was the only one of the three daughters who had been eager to leave home and seek her fortune over-seas, as her father had told Aunt Edmée years before. (A few months after the Marquis de Beauharnais's death in 1801, Aunt Edmée married the mayor of Saint-Germain, Monsieur Pierre Danès de Montardat. She died in 1803.) Madame Tascher appears to have been afraid of what could yet come out of turbulent France and she was perhaps not very sanguine about her daughter's future. Also, as a fervent royalist she probably considered Bonaparte to be an upstart and preferred to keep out of his way. If letters from her had survived it would have been interesting to compare their tone with those sent when Marie-Rose was about to be separated from Alexandre. It would seem that Madame Tascher lacked her daughter's flexibility and preferred to be mistress of her own small domain rather than appear in a minor role at the court of Madame Bonaparte and have to be polite to a son-in-law of whom she disapproved. She must have realized, when Marie-Rose returned to Martinique in 1788, that her daughter had become a *grande dame* with very different tastes and interests from her own. Mother and daughter could not have been very close. It does seem extraordinary, however, that Madame Tascher should not have paid her daughter a visit even for the sake of seeing her grandchildren. She never set eyes on Eugène. She remained until her death in 1807 in the tropical climate that Josephine was emulating on a small scale in her hothouses at Malmaison.

In June 1803 Bonaparte decided to make a progress through northern France and Belgium, to show himself, and Josephine, who was ordered to wear the crown jewels that had not been seen since the death of Marie Antoinette.

A family dinner party was held at Joseph Bonaparte's domain at Mortefontaine on the eve of the departure. Instead of being a friendly occasion it turned out to be yet another Bonaparte–Beauharnais confrontation, through no fault of Josephine's. When dinner was announced Joseph crossed over to escort his mother, Madame Letizia, and lead her to sit on his right-hand side at table. Napoleon quickly outmanoeuvred him by seizing Josephine's arm and propelling her to the head of the table to seat her to the right of Joseph. The meal took place in chilly silence, with Josephine looking pained and uncomfortable.

The next day she put on a smile and a diamond tiara as the triumphant progress began. At Amiens, where the enthusiastic populace wanted to unharness their horses and drag their carriage through the streets, four swans were presented to the couple and Bonaparte arranged for them to be transported to the basins of the Tuileries Gardens. The swan – symbol of marital devotion, being a monogamous bird – had been adopted by Josephine as her emblem.

Boulogne, Dunkirk, Lille. . . . By 9 July Josephine had had enough and she wrote to Hortense, as she had written from Italy during her tour of that country:

I have been receiving compliments ever since I left Paris. You know me and you may judge for yourself whether I should not prefer a quieter life. Fortunately the society of my ladies consoles me for the noisy life I lead. I receive every morning, and often every evening, and then I have to go to a ball. This I would enjoy if you could be with me as I could see you enjoying yourself. What I miss more than anything is my dear Hortense, and my little grandson, whom I love almost as much as I do his mother.

Ostend, Bruges, Ghent – where the populace was a little less enthusiastic. The people were very devout and Bonaparte, shrewdly observing their mood, behaved in consequence. He paid a long visit to the church, where he heard mass with an air of profound devotion. The clergy was won over and people cheered him and Josephine that night at the city ball.

On to Antwerp, where six bay horses were presented to Bonaparte and an ambiguous address was made to Josephine by the archbishop:

Madame, after being united to the first consul by the sacred bonds of a holy alliance, you now find yourself surrounded by his glory. This situation adds to the charm of your intelligence, to the sweetness of your character and the fascination of your company. Continue, *madame*, to exercise those amiable qualities that you have received from the Author of every perfect gift; they will be for your husband a pleasant relaxation from the immense and painful tasks to which he devotes himself every day out of love for his country. If our prayers and our vows determine our mutual destinies, you will both be happy and your happiness will secure ours.

The 'sacred' bonds of a holy alliance'? The archbishop must surely have known that the bonds that united the couple were the secular ones of a civil marriage. Or was he obliquely inviting them to make them 'sacred' as soon as possible?

Flowers, triumphal arches, ovations. . . . Josephine may have been exhausted but she did not show it. She bowed and smiled and was a model of charm. Bonaparte was thoroughly enjoying himself. In Brussels, at the church of Sainte-Gudule, where the clergy were lined up waiting to receive him, he entered through a side door, having read that that was what Charles v had done

on a similar occasion. He was beginning to model himself
closely on the kings of the great dynasties. Josephine and her
ladies were relegated to a tribune, from which she watched
her husband's little comedy enacted below.

Liège, Maastricht ... then home at last after an absence of
forty-eight days and visits to eighty towns – a good pace for
a horse-powered era.

Josephine now devoted more and more of her time to
Malmaison. In 1803 the botanist Ventenat dedicated the first
volume of his book on the gardens to his patroness, accompanied
by a fulsome letter of praise:

Madame, you have thought that the taste for flowers should not
be a sterile study; you have brought together the rarest French plants
and many that had never left the deserts of Arabia and the burning
sands of Egypt have been naturalized by your orders and now,
carefully classified, they present to our eyes, in the gardens of
Malmaison, the most charming memory of the conquests of your
illustrious husband and a most expressive token of your studious
leisure. You have been kind enough to choose me to describe these
different plants and to inform the public of the wealth of a garden
that already equals the best that England, Germany and Spain can
boast of. Deign to accept the homage of a task undertaken by your
command.

He ended on a compliment after the fashion of the day: 'If
in the course of this work I have described any one of the
modest and beneficent plants that seem to exist only to spread
round them an influence as sweet as it is salutary, I shall have,
madame, great difficulty to avoid making a comparison that
doubtless will not escape my readers.'

Madame de Rémusat described Josephine as she was at that
time as follows:

Without being exactly pretty, her whole appearance had a peculiar charm. Her features were delicate ; her expression was gentle ;
her mouth, which was very small, did not disclose her teeth, which
were not good ; she disguised the brownness of her complexion
with the aid of rouge and powder ; her figure was perfect, her limbs

were delicate and graceful and of no one could it be said more truthfully than of her that grace was more beautiful than beauty. She dressed with great taste and graced what she wore ; and, thanks to these advantages and her constant attention to dress, she escaped being effaced by the beauty and youth of the many women who surrounded her.

Bourrienne's valet Constant agreed with this opinion of Josephine, whom he described in his memoirs as being

... of medium height, and very well made. All her movements were light and graceful so that her walk was almost flitting, yet without losing the majesty expected of a queen. Her expressive countenance varied with her emotions, and yet it always retained the charming sweetness that was its main characteristic. Happy or unhappy, she was a beautiful object. No woman ever more thoroughly proved the statement that the eyes are the mirror of the soul. Her own were dark blue [most people described them as brown] and almost always half hidden by her long lids, which were slighty arched and bordered by the most beautiful lashes in the world, so that they had an irresistible charm. Her hair was long and silky. In the morning she liked to wear a red turban, which gave her a most piquant Creole air.

Referring to her voice, he exclaimed : 'How often it happened that I, like a good many others, would stop on hearing this voice, simply for the pleasure of listening to it.' Bonaparte preferred his wife's voice to that of all his readers. Here is Constant again : 'Kindness was as much part of her character as grace of her person. Being extremely kind, tender almost to excess, generous to profusion, she made all who were near her happy, so no woman was better loved or more deserved to be loved.'

Too many similar opinions were expressed about Josephine by her contemporaries for us to dismiss them as courtiers' flattery. But a myth-making process was undeniably taking place. *La bonne Joséphine ... la douce Joséphine....* No doubt the many satisfied tradespeople who swarmed in her private apartments and sold her so many of their wares were only too eager to spread the myth of the beneficent, generous, utterly charming woman. As she herself confessed to Bourrienne, Bonaparte's first secretary: 'People bring me beautiful things, they tell me how precious they are, and I buy them. They don't ask me to pay them at the time, but send me the bill when I have money. You know what I do with it; I give most of it to suffering people who come to beg, and to penniless *émigrés*.' Prince Metternich judged her more severely: 'She had frivolous tastes, empty conversation and no influence over her husband in important matters. . . . Her mind was not a powerful one, but it was of an excellent sort so far as it went . . .' an ambiguous statement if ever there was one!

No political party was against Josephine. The Republicans were grateful to her for her friendship with Fouché, who represented the republican element in Bonaparte's entourage, while members of the *ancien régime* considered her to be their ally.

Bonaparte continued to appreciate her talents as a hostess who added to his popularity. She remembered faces, dates, the trivia of previous encounters, and this delighted the people she received at the Tuileries, Saint-Cloud and Malmaison. Her conversation may not have been profound but she knew how to make people speak about themselves, which is what they want most. As time went by she became more fluent and accumulated a large stock of anecdotes and memories, which she related very well. But Bonaparte wanted more from her than that.

'It is a great misfortune that I have given no son to Bonaparte,' she told Madame de Rémusat in 1803. 'It will always be a means made use of by hatred to disturb my peace.' 'But, *madame*, it seems to me that your daughter's son does much to repair this misfortune. The first consul loves him; he may end by adopting him.' Josephine confessed that she had already envisaged that solution, but Louis Bonaparte's jealousy and stormy character would always oppose it: 'In their malice, his family have repeated to him the outrageous reports about my daughter. Hatred attributes the child to Bonaparte and that would be enough to prevent Louis from consenting to any such arrangement. You see how he keeps himself apart and how my

E*

daughter is forced to be on her guard as to the least of her actions.'

The question of the succession came to the fore again in 1804, the year of the royalist conspiracy against Bonaparte, which prompted him to take the last step in his triumphant career: his elevation to the throne as emperor.

In August 1803 Georges Cadoudal, the leader of the anti-republican forces, mounted a plot against Bonaparte with the aid of General Pichegru. The latter tried to win the support of General Moreau who, after disagreement with Bonaparte, had retired to his property near Paris with his wife, formerly Mademoiselle Hulot, a Creole friend of Josephine. There were rumours that *émigrés* across the border in Germany were planning an invasion of France. General Moreau had nothing to do with the alleged plot, but as he was believed to be involved with the conspirators, he was arrested. Bonaparte informed Josephine curtly: 'Do you know what I've done? I've given orders to arrest Moreau.' She began to cry. 'You are weeping. Why? Are you afraid?' 'No,' she replied, 'but I don't like what people will say.'

She was even more afraid when she heard of the arrest of Duc d'Enghien. There are conflicting accounts as to how and when she learnt about the young duke's death but all agree that she was deeply affected.

On Passion Sunday, 14 March 1804, General Ordener led a troop of cavalry across the Rhine to kidnap the Duc d'Enghien, the only son of the Prince de Condé, who was living in the castle of Ettenheim near Baden. He was accused of plotting against Bonaparte, taken to the ancient fortress of Vincennes outside Paris, given a mock trial and shot ; immediately afterwards his body was thrown into a prepared grave within the fortress.

'I did what I could to save him,' Josephine told Madame de Rémusat. 'But Bonaparte's mind was made up. "Go away, you are a child, you don't understand such matters," he said.' On St Helena, Napoleon said that the Duc d'Enghien confessed that he was planning an invasion of France, but there is absolutely no evidence of this. General Pichegru was found strangled in his cell, Cadoudal was executed, but General Moreau and several others, including the Prince de Polignac, had their sentences commuted to exile, thanks to the intervention of Josephine and Caroline Murat. When Josephine heard that it had been discovered that the late duke's visits across the border, which the police had mistaken for political plotting, were in fact to see a lady, Madame de Rohan, she collected a few souvenirs to send to her including the duke's pet dog, who had refused to leave his master's graveside.

But Eugène, Bonaparte's most loyal supporter, was dismayed by the affair. 'It seemed to me that Bonaparte's glory was thereby tarnished,' he wrote in his memoirs. A few days after the execution of the duke, Bonaparte went to the opera accompanied by Josephine. He was paler than usual. He gave a quick look round to gauge the atmosphere of the house. He need not have feared. Both he and Josephine were welcomed with a tumultuous applause. Josephine was trembling as she sat beside her husband in their box, but his mouth was set in a tight line. He could go ahead with his plans. The people were with him, they bore him no grudge.

He made a fresh approach to Louis. Would his brother allow him to adopt his son, Napoleon-Charles? Louis stubbornly refused. Josephine's heart sank. Hortense's sacrifice had been in vain. Her marriage to the melancholy, hypochondriac Louis had not helped her mother after all.

On 27 March the Senate approached the first consul and appealed to him to become their permanent ruler: 'You have brought us out of the chaos of the past. You have made us bless the benefits of the present. Guarantee for us the future. . . .' On 18 May the Senate proposed to ask the people of France whether the imperial dignity should be conferred on 'the direct, natural, legitimate and adoptive descent of Napoleon, and in the direct, natural, legitimate descent of Joseph and Louis Bonaparte'. After an affirmative vote the senators rushed to Saint-Cloud to congratulate the first consul on his appointment as emperor. Cambacérès addressed Josephine in flattering terms as she stood by the side of her husband on the wide terrace overlooking the Seine:

The Senate still has a pleasant duty to perform, that of offering to Your Imperial Majesty the homage of its respect and the expression of the gratitude of the French people. Yes, *madame*, France makes known the good you are never tired of doing. It says that, always associated to the unfortunate, you never exercise your influence over the head of the State save to console their misery and that to the pleasure of obliging them Your Majesty adds that amiable delicacy that makes gratitude sweeter and the benefit more precious. This happy disposition is a sure token that the name of the Empress Josephine will be the signal of consolation and hope, and as the virtues of Napoleon will always serve as an example to his successors to teach them the art of governing nations, so the undying memory of drying tears is the surest way of ruling over men's hearts. . . .

As Josephine graciously acknowledged the compliments, she must have reflected that the prophecy made to her when she was a girl in Martinique had come true. She was to be queen – more than a queen, an empress. 'But not for long,' the prophetess had warned. To be precise: five years and seven months.

III

EMPRESS OF FRANCE

On 18 May 1804, according to Constant, 'Everyone was filled with joy at the palace of Saint-Cloud. Everyone imagined that he had risen a step, like General Bonaparte, who from First Consul had become a monarch. Men were embracing and complimenting one another, confiding their share of hopes and plans for the future ; there was no official so humble that he was not filled with ambition.'

Only the members of the Bonaparte family were discontented. Two of the brothers were absent and on bad terms with Napoleon : Lucien because of his marriage to his former mistress Madame Jouberthon (widow of a Martinique merchant who had been a stockbroker in Paris) ; and Jérôme for having married Miss Elizabeth Patterson without his brother's consent.

Madame Mère had sided with her beloved Lucien and followed him to Rome. To avoid gossip it was explained that they had gone there for reasons of health, although the air of Rome has never been known to possess curative properties. Meanwhile Elisa, Caroline and Pauline were furious at being placed below their sister-in-law and at not having been appointed princesses of the blood, as were the wives of Joseph and Louis.

At the first official dinner at Saint-Cloud on 18 May General Duroc, now grand marshal of the Palace, informed all the guests in succession that the titles of prince and princess were to be given to Joseph, Louis and their wives, but not to the emperor's sisters or their husbands. All were embarrassed, except Napoleon, who was 'in a merry mood'. Next day, at a reception at the Tuileries, there was a great bandying of titles : Emperor, Empress, My Lord, Prince, Princess, Imperial Highness, Most Serene Highness.

That evening at a family dinner, the sisters poured their recriminations into their brother's ears. 'Why condemn me and my sisters to contempt and obscurity, while covering strangers with honours and dignities?' Caroline protested. 'Judging by your pretensions,' he answered gruffly, 'one would suppose that we had inherited the throne from the king our father.' Caroline considered that this was an opportune moment to faint, and Napoleon still susceptible to these feminine stratagems, gave way. A few days later a notice appeared in *Le Moniteur* that henceforth the emperor's sisters should be called princesses and imperial highnesses.

Everybody put on airs. The Comte de Ségur confided to Josephine what it had cost him to enlist under the tricolour and then to enter the first consul's military household: 'The Empress understood me so well that she made me a similar confidence, confessing her own struggles, her almost invincible repugnance at the end of 1795, in spite of her feeling for Bonaparte, before she could make up her mind to marry the man whom at that time she herself used to call 'the little general'. Josephine was straining to persuade her entourage of her noble origins, while Napoleon, as Prince Metternich recorded, was eager 'to invoke legitimacy as the foundation of his power'.

At the festival of 14 July there was no mention of the Bastille, but a formal distribution was made of crosses of the newly founded Legion of Honour. The emperor and empress made a public appearance in full imperial pomp. They drove through the broad Tuileries Gardens in a carriage drawn by eight horses and repaired to the chapel (no longer called the Temple) of the Invalides, where they listened attentively to mass.

Josephine [wrote Madame de Rémusat], stood in the full light of the setting sun, wearing a dress of pink tulle adorned with silver stars, cut very low after the fashion of the time, and crowned by a great many diamond clusters; this fresh and brilliant dress, her graceful bearing, her delightful smile, her gentle expression, produced such an effect that I heard a number of persons who had been present at the ceremony say that she eclipsed all her suite.

Four days later Napoleon started for Boulogne, while Josephine went to Aix-la-Chapelle to take the waters. He wrote to her from Calais: 'My dear, I have been here since midnight. I am thinking of leaving this evening for Dunkirk. I am satisfied with what I see and I am tolerably well. I hope that you will get as much good from the waters as I got from going about and seeing the camps and the sea. Eugène has left for Blois. Hortense is well. Louis is at Plombières. I am very anxious to see you. You are always essential to my happiness. A thousand kind messages.' Josephine was still a bad correspondent. A few days later Napoleon wrote from Ostend reproaching her:

My dear, I have not heard from you for several days, though I should have been glad to hear that the waters have done you good and how you spend your time. I have been here a week. Tomorrow I shall be at Boulogne for a rather brilliant festival. Send me word by messenger of what you intend to do and when you will have finished your cure.

I am much satisfied with the army and the fleet. Eugène is still at Blois. I hear no more from Hortense than if she were in the Congo. I am writing to scold her. Many kind wishes for all.

At the beginning of September Napoleon joined Josephine at Aix-la-Chapelle, where they visited the cathedral and were shown the relics of Charlemagne. Josephine was even offered Charlemagne's arm, which she tactfully declined, saying that she 'did not wish to deprive Aix-la-Chapelle of so precious a memorial, especially when she had the arm of a man as great as Charlemagne to support her'. This reply must have delighted her husband as he contemplated the crown and sword, no doubt with his forthcoming coronation in mind.

A visit to the cities along the Rhine followed, husband and wife travelling separately. Josephine was invited to sail down the river in the yacht of the Prince of Nassau-Weilburg, a splendid craft with a gilded Neptune in the bows, while Napoleon showed himself at Cologne, Coblenz and Mainz, where, on 21 September, the imperial couple were fêted by a court of German princes from Hesse and Bavaria. The Théâtre-

Français company were summoned from Paris to perform classical plays from their repertoire and the town spent a great deal of money on illuminations and fireworks.

When they returned to Saint-Cloud Napoleon called a meeting of the special council set up to arrange the formalities for his coronation. Bickerings began almost at once. Joseph Bonaparte declared emphatically:

Since it had been recognized that, with the exception of the head of state, no one else, whatever his rank, can be regarded as partaking of the honours of sovereignty and that we especially are not treated as princes but only as high dignitaries, it would not be right that our wives, who are only wives of high dignitaries, should as princesses carry the train of the empress's robe, which consequently must be carried by ladies-in-waiting or of the palace.

This remark displeased Napoleon; members of the Council quoted examples to refute it, notably that of Marie de Médicis. Joseph, who had done his homework, immediately retorted:

Marie de Médicis was accompanied only by Queen Marguerite, the first wife of Henri IV, and by Madame [Catherine of Bourbon, the king's sister]. The train was carried by a very distant relative. Queen Marguerite had indeed offered a fine example of generosity by being present at the coronation of a woman who took her place and who, more fortunate than herself, had borne heirs to Henri IV. But she was not asked to carry the train of Marie de Médicis and yet Marie had a right to every honour, because she was a mother.

This transparent allusion to Josephine's barrenness exasperated Napoleon, who flew into a temper. But he was too fond of Joseph for it to last. A few days later he entreated him: 'Take your position in a hereditary monarchy; be the first of my subjects.' Joseph yielded, but a concession was made to feminine susceptibilities: in the rules drawn up for the coronation the phrase 'bear the cloak' was substituted for 'carry the train'.

For the coronation to be valid in the eyes of the world it was essential that the Pope should officiate, so sixty-four-year-old Pope Pius VII was cajoled into coming to Paris for the ceremony. Napoleon hastily prepared the palace of Fontaine-bleau for his stay. Questions of precedence were avoided by organizing a hunt at the moment when the Pope was due to arrive, and in the course of it Napoleon came across his guest's carriage 'by accident'. The Pope stepped delicately on to the muddy ground in his white satin slippers; the two men embraced – and continued the journey to the palace in the same carriage.

At the palace Josephine stood in the centre of a reception circle of generals and dignitaries. As the Pope proceeded to bless her, she bowed to hide her embarrassment. Curiously enough the benevolent prelate did not know that she was not married to Napoleon according to the rites of the Church. Josephine was seriously alarmed. Her sisters-in-law were in open revolt at her being crowned and Napoleon had had to remind them that 'Josephine has every right to be crowned in my hour of triumph'. Their persistence produced the opposite effect to what they had hoped. In conversation with Roederer Napoleon remarked:

They are jealous of my wife, of Eugène, of Hortense, of all who surround me. *Eh bien*, my wife has diamonds and debts – nothing else. Eugène does not possess an income of twenty thousand *livres*. I love these children because they have always been anxious to please me. If there is a cannon shot, it is Eugène who goes to see what it is; if I have to cross a trench, it is he who gives me his hand. . . . They say that my wife is false, that her children's atten-tions are interested. Well, be it so. They treat me like an old uncle – it none the less gives all the sweetness to my life. . . . If I had been thrown into prison instead of mounting a throne, Josephine would have shared my misfortune. It is right for her to share my success.

But the danger remained – the danger that Josephine could be repudiated on the grounds of her barrenness; she was therefore determined that a religious marriage ceremony should take place before the coronation and that a certificate should be issued to prove that it had done so. This was her last chance and she summoned her courage to face the Pope in a private audience and tell him that in the eyes of the Church she was

Napoleon's concubine and as such could not be crowned except in a state of mortal sin. Napoleon finally agreed and the secret marriage service was held in the chapel of the Tuileries on the eve of the coronation, in the presence of Cardinal Fesch (Napoleon's uncle) and Talleyrand.

In the meantime more frivolous matters occupied the minds of husband and wife as they took part in endless deliberations over ceremonial details and dress. Extravagance was the order of the day. No expense was to be spared to make the occasion a truly historic one. Josephine's chief milliner, Monsieur Leroy, undertook dressmaking for the occasion, with the help of his partner, Madame Raimbault, a well-known *couturière*. The crown, diadems and girdles to be worn by the imperial pair were ordered from the jeweller Margueritte. Napoleon's crown consisted of eight branches meeting under a golden globe surmounted by a cross, set in diamonds, four branches in the shape of a palm leaf, the others in the shape of a myrtle leaf. Round the curve was a ribbon inlaid with eight large emeralds. Josephine's diadem was formed of four rows of pearls interlaced with diamond leaves and brilliants. All the ladies were to be in ball dress with a train and a collar of blond lace called a *chérusque*, fastened on both shoulders and rising high above the head – as in the time of Catherine de Médicis.

As the interior of Notre Dame was being hung with tapestries, fitted with platforms, extra steps and pews and so on it was impossible to rehearse the ceremony there. The painter Isabey (who had designed Napoleon's coronation dress and was in his element acting as stage director of a show that would surpass any of the masquerades he had produced at Versailles) hit upon the device of making a model of the cathedral interior, which he filled with dolls to represent the various personages. This improvised puppet show took the place of rehearsals.

Napoleon and Josephine went to the cathedral every day to watch the crimson, gold-fringed hangings being put in place, the arms of the empire fixed in the corners, the nave and choir fitted with rows of galleries decorated with crimson silk and flags placed round the pillars like trophies. Above them winged and gilt victories held candelabra and twenty-four chandeliers were suspended from the roof. The interior would be dark, as the main door would be shut and concealed by wooden steps leading to the platform on which were placed the two thrones to be occupied by Napoleon and Josephine at the conclusion of the ceremony. The pontifical throne was placed to the right of the high altar on a platform above which was a golden dome adorned with the arms of the Catholic Church. In front and on the sides were benches provided with backs for the cardinals. Both large and small thrones were provided for Napoleon and Josephine. The 'small thrones' consisted of an armchair, one for Napoleon and another for Josephine, on a platform with steps facing the high altar. These were to be occupied during the first part of the ceremony. The 'large throne' at the far end of the cathedral, with its back against the great door, was placed on a semicircular platform reached by twenty-four steps under a canopy in the form of a triumphal arch. This was to be occupied after the coronation.

The day before the great event Madame Junot breakfasted with Josephine at the Tuileries. She was excited and radiantly happy and told her friend how amiably the emperor had talked with her that morning and how he had tried on her head the crown she was to wear. She also spoke to her of the pain she had felt when Napoleon refused her request for his brother Lucien to be allowed to return from Rome for the occasion : 'I wanted him to be with us on this great day, but Bonaparte spoke so harshly that I had to keep silent.' Lucien had never been friendly to Josephine, but she was always ready to forgive past slights.

On the eve of the coronation salvoes of artillery were fired every hour from six in the evening until midnight and towers and all public buildings were illuminated by Bengal lights. The sword of Charlemagne, which had been ceremoniously brought from Aix-la-Chapelle, was watched over throughout the night in Notre Dame by Comte Ségur, who caught two young officers engaging in a mock duel with the revered trophy and admonished them severely.

Coronation day dawned cloudy and very cold. The streets had been liberally sprinkled with sand to prevent the processional horses from slipping. At 9 am the Pope left the Pavillon de Flore, where he had been temporarily housed ; he was preceded by the traditional mule bearing a large wooden cross, in accordance with Roman custom, which made the mocking Parisians smile ; but on the whole they behaved with admirable restraint, considering that they had only just emerged from a period of revolutionary atheism. Many spectators kneeled as the Pope went by ; he looked pale, wise and benevolent and the masses took to him.

At 10.30 am, half an hour later than scheduled, Napoleon and Josephine started out from the Tuileries. On the roof of their coach was a golden crown upheld by four eagles with outstretched wings ; the sides were of glass set in slender carved uprights so as to give the crowds a good view of them in all their splendour. They were, however, in 'undress' attire, though even this was impressive. Napoleon wore a crimson velvet jacket lined with white velvet and a short crimson cloak lined with white satin, and on his head a black velvet cap surmounted by two aigrettes and the celebrated crown jewel called 'the Regent'. Josephine wore a satin, silver-fringed dress embroidered with golden bees. (Napoleon had recently adopted this emblem of the Merovingian dynasty, which had caught his imagination.) Her shoulders were bare (she must have been frozen) but on her arms were tight sleeves embroidered in gold, the upper part adorned with diamonds. Fastened to them was a lace ruff worked in gold, which rose half way up her head. On her carefully curled head was a diadem of four rows of pearls and she displayed a profusion of diamond bracelets, necklaces and earrings. Everybody agreed that she looked positively youthful – twenty-five rather than nearly forty.

Napoleon and Josephine sat at the back of the coach, with Joseph and Louis opposite. They were escorted by twenty squadrons of cavalry headed by Murat. Eighteen carriages each drawn by six horses followed, carrying courtiers and dignitaries – fine carriages, every one of them, and a far cry from the hackney cabs with pasted-over numbers that had had to be used when the first consul had set foot in the Tuileries four years earlier.

The procession, which had started from the Carrousel, made its way along the rue Saint-Honoré to the rue des Lombards, crossed the Pont-au-Change, followed the quay to the rue du Parvis-Notre-Dame and stopped in front of the archbishop's palace, where Napoleon was to change into his coronation robes. The moment he stepped out of his carriage the mist cleared and the sun came out – royal weather for a royal occasion, as the superstitious crowds were quick to observe.

Inside the palace he put on his tight-fitting coronation gown of white satin with gold-embroidered seams and a crimson velvet mantle was placed on his shoulders ; it was adorned with golden bees, with a border of olive branches, laurel and oak leaves in circles enclosing the letter N, with a crown above each one. The cape was lined and trimmed with ermine ; it weighed eighty pounds and had to be held by four men: Joseph, Louis, Arch-chancellor Cambacérès and Arch-treasurer Lebrun. A garland of golden leaves was placed on his head, a diamond necklace of the Legion of Honour round his neck ; he wore a sword in a blue enamel scabbard on his left, adorned with golden eagles and bees. In his right hand he carried the 'hand of justice'. He presented a magnificent figure ('rather like an antique medallion,' Madame de Rémusat observed), which would look well not only in the cathedral but later on canvas, for David had been commissioned to paint the coronation scene. Napoleon gave David instructions to paint in the figure of his absent mother, Madame Mère, who was still in self-imposed exile in Rome with Lucien.

Did Josephine think of her own mother (thereafter known as the 'Empress-Mother') at this moment ? This was her greatest moment, the apogee of her extraordinary career. She would never know greater personal or public happiness, surrounded as she was by the three people she loved most: her husband, who was about to crown her, Eugène, her son, and her daughter Hortense.

Josephine did not undergo such a complete transformation as her spouse. She was merely covered with a long red velvet cloak sprinkled with golden bees and lined with ermine.

A cold collation was thoughtfully provided for the chief participants in the archbishop's palace before the procession walked slowly through the wooden gallery connecting the palace to the interior of Notre Dame, with an interval of ten paces between each group. First came the ushers, heralds-at-arms, the chief herald-at-arms, pages, aides of the master of ceremonies, the grand master of ceremonies (the Comte de Ségur), Marshal Sérurier, carrying a cushion upon which the emperor's ring looked rather small, Marshal Moncey, with the basket that was to receive the empress's cloak and Marshal Murat, carrying the imperial crown on a cushion. Josephine followed, with the first equerry on her right and her first chamberlain on her left. The imperial cloak was 'supported' by the princesses and Hortense, and their trains were carried by an officer of their respective households. Marshal Kellermann carried the crown of Charlemagne, Marshal Pérignon the sceptre, at the end of which was a ball representing the world and a small figure of the Carolingian emperor. Marshal Lefebvre carried Charlemagne's sword, Marshal Bernadotte Napoleon's necklace, Colonel-General Eugène de Beauharnais the empress's ring, Marshal Berthier the imperial globe, Monsieur de Talleyrand the basket destined to receive the emperor's cloak.

Then Napoleon himself appeared, holding a silver sceptre topped by an eagle encircled by a golden serpent. He was followed by ministers, grand equerries and army officers, walking three abreast. Shouts of 'Long live the Emperor!' rose, a little prematurely, from the twenty thousand spectators in the cathedral. A cardinal presented Josephine with holy water; the Archbishop of Paris sprinkled Napoleon and then conducted the pair under a canopy held by canons to the thrones in the choir.

As the Pope rose and came down from his chair the choir intoned the 'Veni Creator'. The six royal ornaments (sceptre, crown, sword, hand of justice, cloak and ring) were taken from

Napoleon and placed on the altar, while Josephine's attendants followed a similar procedure with hers. There was an awkward moment when the ring slipped from Josephine's fingers and had to be retrieved by Isabey and Eugène, who dived under the throne. Isabey recalled later that 'this made a great impression on Josephine's sensitive and somewhat superstitious mind'. As for Eugène, the ceremony made so little impression upon him that years afterwards he could not even remember which of the royal ornaments he had been asked to carry.

The litany was chanted. Napoleon and Josephine knelt on a blue velvet cushion on the first steps of the altar to be anointed and were then conducted to their two chairs while mass proceeded, with music by Pasiello, the Abbé Rose and Lesueur. There were three hundred performers at the mass, including the celebrated singer Lais and the two famous violinists Kreutzer and Baillot. At the 'Gradual' the royal ornaments were blessed before being given back to Napoleon and Josephine, who then advanced and ascended the steps to the Pope's throne. He blessed the crowns, then Napoleon stretched out his arms and placed his own on his head before turning to crown Josephine. This had been planned in advance. Onlookers were amused to see how playfully he placed the crown upon his wife's head, picking it up and replacing it gently as if it had been a bauble being tried on at a jewellers.

After this culminating point of the ceremony the imperial pair were led to the great throne near the door by the Pope and cardinals. The princesses hesitated before lifting the empress's cloak and for a second it looked as though she would fall under its weight. A few angrily rapped-out words from Napoleon brought them to their senses and they dutifully lifted the cloak and escorted Josephine to her throne, placed one step below the emperor's. On yet a lower step the princesses were obliged to sit on simple seats. Even Napoleon stumbled slightly at one point and almost fell backwards under the weight of his cloak, but he quickly recovered himself.

The Pope ascended and blessed the pair: 'May God establish you on your throne, and may Christ allow you to reign with him in his eternal kingdom,' he chanted. Then he kissed Napoleon's cheek and turned to the people who took up the refrain: 'May the Emperor live for ever!' These same words had been used ten centuries before in St Peter's in Rome when Charlemagne was proclaimed 'Emperor of the West'. The whole ceremony was more like a deification than a coronation.

The three hundred musicians struck up the 'Vivat Imperator' a hymn composed by the Abbé Rose, and the Pope began the 'Te Deum' which was taken up by four choirs and two orchestras. At the offertory Napoleon and Josephine laid their gifts before the Pope: a silver gilt vase, a lump of gold, a lump of silver, a candle round which were inlaid thirteen pieces of money. At the elevation their crowns were removed (by Joseph Bonaparte and Madame de La Rochefoucauld respectively), then put on again. After mass Napoleon took the political oath prescribed by the constitution: with one hand held over the gospels, he swore to maintain the principles of the Revolution, to preserve the integrity of the territory and to uphold the interest and glory of the French people.

The first herald-at-arms now called out: 'The most glorious and august Emperor Napoleon, Emperor of the French, is crowned and enthroned. Long live the Emperor!' Salvoes of artillery mingled with the applause of the crowds.

It had been a great success (at a cost that Napoleon estimated at 3 million francs, though others have calculated that it was nearer 10 million). Napoleon and Josephine re-entered the Tuileries at 6.30 pm, where Napoleon changed with relief into his uniform of a *chasseur* of the guard; he was, understandably in an excellent mood and praised the ladies-in-waiting, adding childishly: 'It is I who deserve the credit for your charming appearance.' He dined alone with Josephine, obliging her to keep on her diadem because, he said, it became her so well.

For days afterwards Paris was the centre of festivities. Flags were distributed to old soldiers at the Champ de Mars in pouring rain (Josephine and Hortense were obliged to leave before the end of the ceremony). Wooden booths and temporary dance halls were put up in the Place de la Concorde. There was a state dinner in the Gallery of Diana at the Tuileries, with Napoleon and Josephine seated under a canopy on a platform and the Pope seated on Josephine's left. There were public concerts, ballets and theatrical performances, fireworks and illuminations. Luxury was compulsory, trade flourished, but the City of Paris was in debt after offering a lavish dinner to the imperial couple on 16 December at the Hôtel de Ville ; a gold toilet set was presented to Josephine and a silver-gilt table service to Napoleon. Each of the marshals of the empire contributed 10,000 francs to a joint entertainment at the Opéra.

The imperial court was formed at the beginning of 1805. 'Ceremony is born,' wrote Isabey. 'I seem to be recalling a dream,' said Madame de Rémusat, 'a dream resembling an oriental tale, when I describe the lavish luxury of that period, the disputes for precedence, the claims of rank, the demands of everyone.'

Splendidly accoutred palace officers were appointed : a grand almoner, a grand master of ceremonies, a grand equerry, a grand chamberlain. Handsome boys were sent as pages to the palace to be 'polished', as at medieval courts. Madame de Rémusat wrote : 'They have good figures and wear a new and becoming uniform. In full dress they wear, like footmen, a green coat with seams laced with gold, gold shoe buckles, a hat with a white feather. All are sons of generals of divisions or of high dignitaries.' Josephine's household was increased. She was given a first almoner, Bishop Ferdinand de Rohan, five chamberlains, six ladies of the bedchamber, a new reader, four valets, two footmen, two pages to carry her train and two more to walk before her in her closely guarded apartments. These were divided into the apartments of honour, consisting of an antechamber, a first drawing-room, a second drawing-room, a music-room ; and the inner apartments, which consisted of a bedroom, library, dressing-room, boudoir and bathroom. The entrance to these apartments was controlled by a strict etiquette, and by female ushers, rather like an oriental purdah.

Thirteen young and pretty ladies were added to the original four ladies-in-waiting.

Josephine stepped into her new role with her customary ease. The Duchess d'Abrantès observes: 'One of her charms was not merely her graceful figure but the way she held her head and the gracious dignity with which she walked and turned. I have had the honour of being presented to many real princesses, as they are called in the Faubourg-Saint-Germain, and I can truly say that I have never seen one more imposing than Josephine. She combined elegance and majesty. Never did any queen so grace a throne without having been trained to it.' Madame de Rémusat remarked, less flatteringly:

> The Empress is enchanted to be surrounded by a large suite and it gratifies her vanity. Her success in attaching Madame de La Rochefoucauld to her person, her pleasure in counting Messieurs d'Aubusson and de Lafeuillade among Chamberlains, Madame d'Arberg, Madame de Ségur and the wives of the Marshals among the ladies of the palace, turned her head a little, but even this feminine joy did not lessen her usual graciousness; she always succeeded in maintaining her rank, even when most deferential to those men and women who lent it a new lustre by their brilliant names.

Josephine's reader, Mademoiselle Avrillon, wrote: 'I do not believe that there ever lived a woman with a better character, or with a less changeable disposition.'

Anxious not to make *faux pas* in her new position, Josephine attached to her service the Abbé Nicolas Halna, who instructed her in history and in the background of the high-ranking people received at court. Monsieur de Rémusat had discovered the *abbé* when he was a teacher in Fontainebleau. He had had a varied background as medical student, priest, tutor, professor and headmaster of the College at Sedan. Josephine engaged him officially as her librarian, at a salary of 4,200 francs a year. She took her lessons seriously and wept after she had made the mistake of asking a minister for news of a *'prince régnant'* instead of a *'prince régent'* and been scolded afterwards by her mentor.

Another gentleman, Monsieur Deschamps, was appointed to deal with the endless petitions she received and to forward her recommendations through the right ministerial channels. He wrote either at her dictation or in accordance with her expressed wishes. She also wrote many letters of recommendation by hand. They would fill several volumes. Deschamps had been chosen by Napoleon ; he had written the libretto of an opera on the Celtic Bards and had a passion – shared by the Emperor – for the poems of Ossian. Otherwise he was dry and stern. Napoleon probably hoped that he would restrain Josephine's generosity.

Hortense's second son, Napoleon-Louis, had been born in October 1804. Louis was moodier than ever, although his brother had tried to woo him by offering him successively the titles of prince, constable of France, colonel-general, grand officer of the empire, member of the Privy Council, of the Senate and of the Council of State.

Josephine had written to her daughter early in February 1804 to tell her that she had asked Louis to keep his promise and bring her to Paris from Compiègne for the carnival. 'We are awaiting your arrival to fix the days for the balls.' Hortense's character had changed since her unhappy marriage. Everybody noticed it ; even Josephine lamented that she was no longer the cheerful, dancing creature she had once been. Madame Campan wrote to her former pupil, perhaps after a conversation with Josephine : 'Since you have left childhood behind you your character has become very serious and strikingly cold. Try to temper this disposition.'

Napoleon liked to play with Hortense's elder son Napoleon-Charles rather roughly, as was his manner, sometimes smearing the infant's face with jam and cream. He also had the habit of lifting him on to a table by seizing him on each side of the head until Josephine implored him to desist from such 'a dangerous way of holding a child'. One day in the presence of Murat he said to the child : 'Do you know, little baby, that you are in danger of one day becoming a king'? 'And Achille?'

said Murat quickly, referring to his eldest boy. 'Ah, Achille – he will be a good soldier,' Napoleon replied and, turning to Napoleon-Charles, added: 'In any case I advise you, my poor child, if you wish to live, to accept no meals that may be offered to you by your cousins.'

The Pope stayed on in Paris and was asked to baptize Napoleon-Louis at Saint-Cloud on 24 March 1805. The gallery was turned into a chapel for the occasion, and a bed was placed in one of Josephine's drawing-rooms with a large ermine-lined cloak at the foot in which to wrap the baby. Two tables were brought in for the candle, chrisom-cap, saltcellar – the child's *honneurs*, as they were called – and for the basin, ewer and napkin, called the godparents' *honneurs*. Napoleon was god-father and Madame Mère, now back from Rome, the godmother. The gardens of Saint-Cloud were opened to the public during the day and there was a performance of Racine's *Athalie* in the court theatre, followed by a ball and fireworks.

Napoleon wished to be crowned King of Italy and when the Pope left Paris on 2 April he and Josephine accompanied him as far as Alessandria. The arrangements for the departure of the two cortèges had been protracted and the constant delays irritated the emperor, who exclaimed angrily to his entourage: 'The devil take you all! Are we never to leave? Each day's delay costs me twenty-four thousand francs. I can't afford to throw all that money away!'

At Marengo, the scene of his famous victory, Napoleon took Josephine over the battlefield to explain to her exactly what had happened. He had even brought the hat he had worn on that occasion. She listened patiently, pleased to be treated with such confidence, although she was not interested in warfare or military strategy. Napoleon was in a good mood, but when his youngest brother, Jérôme, came to see him in Milan to be forgiven, he was made to give up his wife, the ex-Miss Patterson, in return for the kingdom of Westphalia and a marriage to a German princess that his brother was planning for him.

Eugène went to Milan in advance to help with the prepar-ations. He had recently been on bad terms with his stepfather, as they had both fallen for the same woman (Madame Duchâtel) but the incident had now been forgotten – so had the woman – and Napoleon was about to make Eugène Viceroy of Italy. He was also to be formally adopted as Napoleon's son. All this infuriated the Bonaparte clan.

In Milan Eugène supervised the building of a gallery connecting the palace with the cathedral, which was decorated with hangings of silk and gauze. A few days before the coronation he accompanied a detachment of the National Guard who had been sent on Napoleon's orders to fetch the cross of Lombardy from the sacristy of Monza, nine miles from Milan ; Milan had been the traditional coronation town of the kings of Lombardy since the eleventh century. The crown consisted of a circle of iron with a metal band inside that was said to have been brought from Jerusalem by the Empress Helena and to contain a nail from the cross.

Napoleon placed it on his head during the ceremony, as he had done with the crown of France three months before, exclaiming loudly in Italian: 'God has given it to me ; woe to him who touches it !' On this occasion Josephine was not crowned; she merely watched the proceedings from the gallery.

After the ceremony Napoleon, in high spirits, visited her and her ladies in their palace apartments. 'Did you hear what I said?' he asked them, repeating the formula and tapping Josephine on the shoulder. He did this, her lady-in-waiting Mademoiselle Avrillon observed, whenever he was in a good mood, often hurting his wife to the point of bringing tears to her eyes. 'Leave off, Bonaparte, leave off,' she would implore him, exasperated, but he paid no attention to her remonstrances.

The festivities included a visit to an art exhibition at Brera, where the imperial couple saw Canova's sculpture of *Hebe* and a colossal statue of Clement XIII. The crowds jostled each other to catch a closer view and an old man was knocked down some steps ; Josephine, seeing the incident, rushed down to help him up. This warm, spontaneous gesture endeared her to the people.

Three days later Napoleon left for the Austrian frontier. At Bologna he received a deputation from Lucca asking him to take the town under his protection. He decided to give it to his sister Elisa, who was already Duchess of Piombino. He went on to Modena and Parma.

In his absence Josephine visited Lake Como where, free from the trammels of etiquette, she became light-hearted and took childish pleasure in playing pranks. 'She was always happy to be absolved from the rigidity of ceremonial,' Mademoiselle Avrillon wrote in her memoirs. She and her ladies were accompanied by a chamberlain, Monsieur de Beaumont, a vain little man who was convinced that he aroused great passions in women. Josephine and her ladies made him believe that he had made an Italian conquest and that his admirer wished to visit him on a certain night. A mock rendezvous was arranged. Then another chamberlain, Monsieur de Brassac, was dressed up as a woman and led by Josephine to Monsieur de Beaumont's room, where his play-acting, watched through the keyhole, caused great merriment.

Life with Napoleon, who had little sense of humour, had made Josephine outwardly rather solemn ; she was for ever at his beck and call, never daring to move from her room in case he was to summon her for a drive, to read to him or just to talk. Although she was more at ease with him than most people, according to Hortense, she was nevertheless a little overawed in his presence. After the coronation she even began to call him 'Sire'. Yet she could laugh and enjoy bawdy tales. When the notorious Madame la Maréchale Lefebvre (popularly known as 'Madame Sans-Gêne' thanks to her freedom of speech and manners) was going about relating a spicy story about a valet who had stolen one of her diamonds, Josephine called her, dismissed her ladies and asked the maréchale to tell the story without mincing her words. Apparently the maréchale, who suspected her valet of the robbery, had made him undress in her presence – still no diamond ; then she had continued her search on his person – she omitted no details – until she discovered the missing jewel. Josephine laughed heartily at her earthy description of the scene.

On another occasion, at Strasbourg, she received a former

member of Napoleon's staff, a Monsieur Pfister, who had become very odd and was being taken to a hospital in Paris ; Josephine asked him, in the presence of Mademoiselle Avrillon, whether he had met any handsome ladies on his journey, at which he 'broke into a string of obscenities that were so grotesque that the Empress burst into peals of laughter'.

On 30 June Napoleon arrived in Genoa, where Josephine met him and both were given a splendid *fête* by the municipality to celebrate its incorporation into the French empire. As the imperial couple descended the steps from the terrace of the Palazzo Doria they were led to a round, floating temple on a raft ; the raft was rowed to the middle of the harbour and was surrounded by four others covered with shrubs and flowers, from which proceeded music and singing. Hundreds of tiny boats lit by coloured lanterns plied between the rafts like glow-worms.

When the time came to leave Italy and Eugène (who had been given a sheaf of detailed instructions by Napoleon, as he was naturally a little dubious about the ruling capacities of the twenty-three-year-old man), Josephine could not conceal her chagrin. Her dear boy was to be left in a foreign land, far from his family and friends. Napoleon confided to his wife that Eugène would soon have a delightful companion to share his life, but this was to be kept secret until he had completed certain delicate negotiations.

Eugène had been such an intimate confidant, such a good friend as well as loved son, that his mother shed bitter tears on the eve of her departure from Milan. Napoleon addressed her brusquely : 'Why are you crying, Josephine ? Is it because you are leaving one of your children ? You are fortunate to have them. Imagine what I must feel. The affection you show for your children makes me feel sorely the unhappiness of having none myself.' She dried her tears and turned pale. The eternal shadow in the background of her life moved forward again.

Fortunately Napoleon was soon immersed in politics. At Genoa he heard about the coalition being prepared against him and he left suddenly for France with Josephine who, ever accommodating, could be relied upon to be ready at a moment's notice. Her punctuality was proverbial. They travelled full speed back to Fontainebleau, arriving unannounced on the night of 11 July, after an absence from Paris of a hundred days. The porter, Guillot, who had been Napoleon's cook in Egypt, threw up his hands in dismay. 'Nothing is ready – we did not expect you!' he cried. 'Well, you must go back to your old trade and cook us some supper,' Napoleon replied. The imperial pair dined cheerfully off mutton chops and eggs. Next day they visited Napoleon's mother on their way back to Saint-Cloud. On the eighteenth they made an appearance at the Opéra, as they always did on their return from abroad – to show themselves to the public and receive their applause. The Opéra was used by Napoleon as a tribune and popular opinion poll.

In September Austria invaded Bavaria and drove away the elector, France's ally. Napoleon told the Senate that he was going to his aid. Josephine accompanied him as far as Strasbourg.

In Strasbourg Josephine was burgled for the first recorded time in her life. Her jewel casket was broken into and a diamond necklace stolen. The culprit was soon discovered. She was the daughter of one of Josephine's valets who had fallen in with a local ne'er-do-well. They had taken the necklace, worth 4000 francs, to a jeweller, whose suspicions were immediately aroused. The girl was sent to Paris to be tried and was condemned to prison. Josephine was deeply affected as she was fond of the girl's father and she wrote to Paris to try to prevent the case from being taken to court. The letter arrived too late. The valet felt he could not continue in the empress's service so she accepted his dismissal but granted him a generous pension.

From Strasbourg she was authorized by her husband to proceed to Munich via Baden and Stuttgart and to buy presents for 'the wedding' that he had planned for Eugène. On 5 December Napoleon wrote to her about his victory at Austerlitz: 'The Battle of Austerlitz is the grandest of all I have fought. . . . The Emperor Alexander is in despair and is on his way back to Russia.... I look forward with much pleasure to the moment when I can once more be near you....' From Brunn on 10 December he wrote: 'It is a long time since I had news of you. Have the grand *fêtes* at Baden, Stuttgart and Munich made you forget the poor soldiers who live covered with mud, rain and blood? I am very anxious to be with you. Adieu, dear. My bad eyes are cured.' On 19 December: 'Great Empress, not a single letter from you since your departure from Strasbourg. You have gone to Baden, Stuttgart, Munich, without writing a word. This is neither very kind nor very affectionate. Deign from the height of your grandeur to concern yourself a little with your slaves. The Russians have gone. I expect a truce....' 20 December: 'I got your letter of the 16th. I am sorry to learn you feel unwell. Stay in Munich. Enjoy yourself....'

Josephine had written to Eugène from Plombières where she had taken another cure in August:

The Emperor is always amiable towards me and I on my part do all that I can to please him. No more jealousy, my dear Eugène, this is absolutely true. This makes him happy and me even happier.... I can't give you any up-to-date political news. The situation is a mystery that the Emperor allows no one to penetrate.... You have no doubt heard that the marriage of the Prince of Baden is broken off, which gives me great hopes of the lady (you know who I mean). I have seen her portrait; she could not be more beautiful. Your sister is well also and her children. I had the second one at Saint-Cloud. He is absolutely sweet. Louis is the same as ever....

Josephine was referring here to the projected marriage of Eugène to Princess Augusta, daughter of the Elector of Bavaria, whom Napoleon was to elevate to a kingship in return for his help against the Austrians. Augusta had been engaged to her cousin, Prince Carl of Baden, and the Electress Caroline of Bavaria had been prejudiced against Napoleon since his violation of Bavarian territory to seize the late Duc d'Enghien, but these obstacles were to be airily waived. Napoleon was planning three marriages: Eugène to Augusta of Bavaria; Stéphanie de Beauharnais (his niece by marriage) to the jilted Prince Carl of Baden; and his brother Jérôme to Princess Catherine of Württemberg.

Josephine had not written to Hortense about the plan for Eugène, which seems strange in view of their closeness. Perhaps she feared an outburst that would have irritated Napoleon. Eugène had not set eyes on his proposed bride and Hortense might have been indignant – she was not as diplomatic as her mother. She had, however, heard rumours and she wrote to Josephine for confirmation. The reply was guarded and devious: 'Surely if there had been a question of your brother's marriage you would have been the first person whom I would have told. In Strasbourg I did hear the German papers were speaking about it.... The Emperor would not marry off Eugène without telling me. I accept the public rumours.... I should like Princess Augusta as a daughter-in-law. She has a charming character and is as lovely as an angel.'

Eugène, too, was officially kept in the dark until the last moment, although his mother had dropped broad hints. Prepared as he was for an arranged marriage – and, in his easy-going way, he did not seem to be alarmed at the prospect, perhaps because he had so much confidence in his stepfather – he must have been taken aback to receive, on 31 December 1805, the following curt message from Napoleon, delivered by an imperial courier together with a porcelain coffee cup bearing a portrait of Augusta from the Royal Nymphenburg factory: 'My Cousin, I have arrived in Munich. I have arranged your marriage with the Princess Augusta. It has been announced this morning. The Princess paid me a visit and we had quite a long conversation. She is very pretty. I am enclosing a coffee cup with her portrait, but it does not do her justice.' Eugène replied almost as briefly: 'The picture on the coffee cup is wonderfully beautiful. I shall do my best to make the original happy.' On 3 January 1806 he received orders to go to Munich immediately for the wedding, which had been planned for the fourteenth.

In Munich Josephine had exercised her charm to win over the princess's family and Napoleon contributed by flirting outrageously with the Electress Caroline, who now beamed upon him. (Josephine was in danger of forgetting her promise to Eugène and was showing signs of jealousy.) Hortense was prevented from attending the wedding by her morose husband Louis. 'Be happy for both of us,' she wrote to her brother. 'Tell your wife how sad it makes me not to be able to see her.' Caroline was in Munich but was so offended to see Augusta, as the viceroy's wife, taking precedence over her that she feigned illness, took to her bed and did not attend the wedding service.

Eugène's marriage, unlike poor Hortense's, was blissfully happy. (Napoleon was unhappy about his beloved stepdaughter. 'The marriage', he confided to Bourrienne, 'has not turned out as I wished. Their union is not happy. It grieves me because I love them both.') He now returned to Italy with Augusta and Napoleon and Josephine returned to the Tuileries.

Almost immediately after they arrived Josephine chose a magnificent basket to send to her new daughter-in-law in Italy, full of expensive gowns, shawls, hats, even shoes. She loved giving presents. On New Year's Day her apartments resembled a toyshop, full of gifts for her grandchildren and the children of her ladies. During her travels she lavishly distributed necklaces, earrings, diamond pins, snuff boxes, shawls. She gave a *parure* in gold and pearls worth 1,400 francs to a Madame Doublat at Epinal, who had been her hostess for one night. She remembered people's names from previous visits. She distributed rosaries to old ladies ; once she stopped at a peasant's house while her carriage was being repaired and, hearing that the couple were celebrating their golden wedding anniversary, gave the husband a gold-chased snuffbox and the wife a gold watch. Numerous relatives were given regular financial help, including her uncle, Baron Tascher de La Pagerie, who had settled in France with his six children.

As soon as they heard that the empress was back in residence tradespeople began to lure her with their tempting merchandise. And, as usual, she overspent. Napoleon drew up a palace decree on 28 February 1806: 'All persons belonging to the Chamber of the Empress are forbidden to receive into her apartments any articles of furniture, pictures, jewels or other effects brought by tradespeople or private individuals. These are to be sent back to the steward.' One day, however, an enterprising milliner, Mademoiselle Despeaux, hearing that the empress had been indisposed, decided to try to liven her up, and do herself some good at the same time, by presenting her with some of her latest creations. Through an oversight on the part of the staff she was admitted to Josephine's anteroom and, by a piece of unfortunate timing, Napoleon himself happened to walk into the dressing-room while Mademoiselle Despeaux was waiting. He eyed her and her array of bandboxes balefully. 'Who are you?' he asked angrily. Mademoiselle Despeaux declined to give her name. She was speechless with fear. Napoleon strode into Josephine's dressing-room. 'Who has called that woman here?' he barked. 'Who has let her in? I must know!' As Mademoiselle Despeaux had come of her own accord nobody was to blame, but the empress's ladies dispersed in fright, fearing an imperial outburst. Poor Josephine was in an awkward position: her coiffeur Duplan was attending to her hair, so that her head was immobilized, and her feet were plunged in a hot footbath. Napoleon paced up and down shouting: 'I'll have them all put into prison. Oh yes, I will!' Duplan and the ladies in attendance fled in terror, except for plucky Mademoiselle Avrillon.

Napoleon rushed out of the room as quickly as he had entered it, asking for General Savary, the Duc de Rovigo. When that gentleman appeared he gave orders for Mademoiselle Despeaux to be arrested and sent to the prison of La Force. Poor Mademoiselle Despeaux was stopped as she was leaving the palace grounds and obliged to spend a night in prison. As soon as she had recovered from her husband's irruption, Josephine went to him to intercede on behalf of the milliner and Napoleon gave orders for her release. Josephine sent the lady a present and note of apology and she also apologized to her ladies for Napoleon's tirade. Two days later he himself laughed at the incident, treating it as a joke. It had not been so amusing for the victim.

Josephine interceded on two other occasions when the staff complained about Napoleon's parsimony. One day he suddenly decided that the laundry bills were too high and decreed that henceforth the sheets of the palace household were to be changed once a month only and, moreover, each person was to be allowed only two towels. Josephine's ladies were indignant ; their mistress had to inform her husband that even in bourgeois households sheets were changed once a week before he could be persuaded to revoke the order. Then he found that too much food was being consumed, and probably, he thought, sent out of the palace to relatives of the personnel, so he devised a complex system of coupons to be exchanged even for simple items like a cup of coffee. This, too, was hotly resented and again Josephine had to intervene, pointing out that the system was unworkable as well as ridiculous. Napoleon reluctantly gave in.

He still continued to pay her visits when she was dressing to comment on her *toilettes* ; if he did not like a dress and she still insisted on wearing it he was capable of tearing it or even, on one occasion, spilling ink over it so that she was obliged to take it off.

Josephine loved clothes and her wardrobes were crammed with an average of five hundred chemises (she changed three times a day) and seven hundred pairs of shoes (made of kid, silk or satin ; plus sandals for walking and travelling boots of leather or velvet lined with fur). She also possessed dozens of pairs of stockings, white silk ones, flesh-coloured and pink ones, lace and openwork ones. Until her later years she wore light corsets of lined cambric or muslin trimmed with Valenciennes lace, or of piqué lined with muslin, a petticoat, and nothing else. She had only two pairs of drawers – for riding which she gave up after her coronation. Her ordinary gowns cost from 500 to 2000 francs, her court dresses from 3000 to 4000 francs. In one year alone she bought 23 bales of lace, 7 court dresses, 136 gowns, 20 cashmere shawls, 73 corsets,

71 pairs of stockings, 980 pairs of gloves, 520 pairs of shoes and 87 hats. Hats! It is difficult to picture Josephine in a hat. One tends so much to think of her wearing a tiara, a diadem or one of the flower garlands that Monsieur Duplan was so adept at entwining in her nut-brown hair ; but she always wore a hat in the morning. Napoleon examined her bills closely and usually knocked 20 per cent off the prices quoted before paying them, after angry and tearful scenes between husband and wife.

It was noticeable that the emperor slept more and more infrequently with his empress from the day of their coronation. His rooms were now further away from hers and to reach her bedroom he had to walk down a long passage in his dressing-gown, preceded by his valet Constant bearing a torch, a conspicuous procedure that was embarrassing for all concerned. His political duties obliged him to work by night as well as by day, he explained, although he usually went to bed early. Josephine preferred to go to bed late, although she rose before 9 am. She would ring as soon as she woke up to ask for a drink of lemon or an *infusion* before breakfast. Like her husband she ate and drank sparingly. Those biographers who have alleged that she spent three hours at her toilet have palpably exaggerated. When we read in the memoirs of her ladies that she had a light breakfast at 9 am and lunched at 11 am it is obvious that she could not have taken three hours to bath and dress.

She still continued to read to Napoleon when he was in bed. He would call her through a chamberlain and she would leave her ladies to go up to her husband's bedroom to read to him from some new book. When he was on the point of falling asleep she would gently tiptoe out of the room and rejoin her ladies until 1 am or later. It would be unkind to suggest that he liked her voice because it had a soporific effect and acted like a sleeping draught.

Josephine was inclined to be a *malade imaginaire* at times and she often consulted Napoleon's doctor, Corvisart, a thickset, broad-shouldered little man with a no-nonsense attitude towards his august employers that appealed to Napoleon, though

Josephine complained that he consistently refused to give her the medicines she wanted. He would not even allow her to take a laxative, although, as Mademoiselle Avrillon remarked, 'she tried to coax him into giving her one like a child asking for a sweet'. Corvisart sensibly believed that nature was the best and most reliable repairer of the body's ailments ; he also believed in fasting, before the era of nature-cure practitioners. Whenever she felt below par Josephine followed a strict diet in accordance with Corvisart's pet theory, and it usually worked.

Another of Josephine's *protégées* had come to live at the Tuileries until her marriage in April 1806. This was Aunt Fanny's granddaughter Stéphanie de Beauharnais, a pretty, fair-haired, blue-eyed girl who had, like so many of the empress's other *protégées*, been sent to Madame Campan's to be educated. She was delicate and had a skin complaint when she arrived at the palace ; according to Mademoiselle Avrillon, Josephine looked after her as tenderly as a mother. Napoleon had adopted her, although her father, Comte Claude de Beauharnais, was still living, and there were the usual rumours that he was half in love with Stéphanie himself. He subsequently arranged for her to marry Prince Carl of Baden, the young man who had once been engaged to Augusta of Bavaria ; and the wedding took place at the Tuileries with much pomp on 7 April 1806.

Napoleon had begun to distribute honours and crowns to the various members of his family : Joseph became King of Naples, Murat, his brother-in-law, Grand Duke of Berg and Cleves ; Pauline, the Princess of Guastella (she was already Princess Borghese through her second marriage) ; and Louis, King of Holland — a prospect that did not please him at all. He pleaded ill-health and the bad effect that the damp climate would have upon it, but all to no avail. He left for Holland with Hortense on 15 June 1806. Josephine was broken-hearted to be separated from the daughter she had been so accustomed to have near her, and also from her little grandsons.

Since you left [she wrote to Hortense on 15 July] I have often been ill, sad and unhappy. I have even been feverish and have had to keep to my bed. I am now well again, but my sorrow remains.

How could it be otherwise when I am separated from a daughter like you, loving, gentle and amiable, who was the charm of my life? . . . How is your husband? Are my grandchildren well? Heavens, how sad it makes me not to see them! And how is your health, dear Hortense? If you are ever ill, let me know and I will hasten to you at once. . . . Goodbye, my dear Hortense, think often of your mother and be sure that never was a daughter more loved than you are. Many kind messages to your husband ; kiss the children for me. It would be kind of you to send me one of your latest songs.

Later that year Napoleon engaged in a war against Prussia and Russia. He wanted to go alone but Josephine wept and implored him to let her accompany him ; in the end he relented and allowed her into his carriage. They stayed together for a few days in Mainz, from where Josephine wrote to Hortense: 'I am very happy, for I am with the Emperor. . . . The more I am near him the less I fear. Another reason for my joy is at seeing you again. The Emperor bids me tell you that he has just given an army of 80,000 men to the King of Holland and that his command will extend to quite close to Mainz. Every day we shall get news from the Emperor and your husband, and we shall rejoice over it together.'

When Napoleon left Mainz and Josephine he was so upset that he nearly had an attack of the convulsions to which he was prone. He had to sit down for a few minutes before getting into his carriage to drink a glass of his favourite orange-flower water. 'It is painful to leave the two people one loves most', he told Monsieur de Rémusat referring to Josephine and to Hortense. But this did not prevent him from keeping them on a tight rein. Hortense took the opportunity of visiting her cousin Stéphanie in Baden. When Napoleon heard about it, for everything was relayed to him, he wrote to her sternly: 'I am greatly displeased that you have left Mainz without my permission. Within one hour of your receiving this letter send my two nephews to Mainz to the Empress. This is the first time you have given me cause for displeasure. You must not dispose of my nephews without my permission.' No wonder Hortense was timid in her stepfather's presence! Josephine enclosed this missive with one of hers in which she had dictated a suggested reply. Hortense was to tell Napoleon that she had foreseen his wishes, that the boys were now with the empress, that she had had them with her in Baden for a few days only to give them the benefit of a change of air. This answer seems to have appeased the great man, who conducted himself towards his family like an oriental despot.

Josephine was depressed ; perhaps she sensed that this time she really was going to lose Napoleon. In a letter dated 1 November 1806 he reproached her because he had heard from Talleyrand that she was crying nearly all the time. 'I do not know why you weep. Courage and gaiety: that is the prescription.' Yet for once she was justified in weeping. She appears to have had a presentiment about Napoleon's infidelity and she was right. But she began to complain before he had set eyes on her serious rival : the Polish countess, Marie Walewska.

Napoleon met her on 1 January 1807. Josephine had been tormenting him for over a month with her allusions to 'Polish belles', but he replied that she 'was imagining things'. Back in Paris, on 31 January 1807, she wrote to Hortense :

I got here, dear Hortense, on the evening of the 30th as I expected. My journey was pleasant, if I can call it so when it separates me from the Emperor. I have received five letters from him since my departure. I need to hear from you now that you are no longer with me to console me. . . . Although I see more people here than in Mainz I am quite as lonely, and you will seem to be with me if you write. Goodbye my dear. I love you tenderly.

Occupied though he was in Poland, Napoleon found time to admonish his brother Louis because 'his quarrels with the queen [Hortense] have become public. Show then in private life some of the paternal and effeminate character that you display in matters of government. . . . You treat a young woman as we treat a regiment. . . . You have an excellent and most virtuous wife and you make her unhappy. Let her dance as much as she pleases. She is young. My wife is forty yet I wrote to her from the battlefield to go to a ball.'

He was always ready to preach to members of his family on their domestic affairs while he pursued his own untrammelled amorous course. Eugène had been overworking and finding his duties onerous. Napoleon heard that Augusta was a little bored so he wrote to Eugène urging him to devote more time to his young wife who needed diversion and her husband's company. 'Spend more evenings with your wife,' he counselled. 'Organize some social life. I lead the same life as you do but I have an older wife who does not need me to amuse her and, alas, I have more responsibilities. Even so, it is true that I take more diversions and amusements than you do. . . . A young wife needs to be entertained. . . .'

At that time Napoleon was sending affectionate letters to his wife. In November 1806 he had written: 'I am used to kind, gentle, persuasive women; those are the sort I like. If I have been spoiled, it is not my fault, but yours. . . .' On 7 January 1807 he wrote from Warsaw: 'Go to the Tuileries, receive people and lead the same life as you are accustomed to when I am there; that is my wish. Perhaps I shall not be long in rejoining you but it is absolutely necessary to give up the idea of making the journey here; 750 kilometres at this time of the year through enemy country is unthinkable. Be cheerful and show character. . . .' (In fact he had no desire to see his wife, involved as he was with the Countess Walewska.) On the eighteenth he wrote again from Warsaw: 'I hear that you are always weeping. Fie! How unbecoming it is! Be worthy of me. Be brave. I am very well . . . and I love you very much, but if you are always crying I shall think you lack courage and character. An empress ought to have fortitude. . . .' The next day he harped on the same theme: 'I want you to be cheerful, lovable, happy. . . .'

On 21 February he had received a letter from Josephine and was pleased to hear that she had been to the opera. 'I see with pleasure that you propose holding receptions weekly. Go occasionally to the theatre and always in the royal box. I notice also with pleasure the banquets you are giving. . . . Never be doleful, love me, and believe in my entire affection. . . .'

Informed of all that was going on in Paris, he learned with dis-approval that Josephine had been visiting the smaller theatres of the capital. He upbraided her on 17 March: 'It is not necessary for you to go to the small plays and into a private box. It ill befits your rank. You should go only to the four big theatres and always in the royal box. Live as you would do if I were in Paris. My health is very good. The cold weather has begun again. . . .'

From the castle of Finckenstein, where he was dallying with Countess Walewska, he wrote on 10 May:

I have received your letter. I don't understand what you say about ladies in correspondence with me. I love only my little Josephine, sweet, pouting and capricious, who can quarrel with grace as she does everything else, for she is always lovable except when she is jealous; then she becomes a real she-devil. . . . Only invite to dinner those who have dined with me; never make intimates at Malmaison of ambassadors and foreigners. . . .

On 5 May 1807 a great domestic tragedy occurred: little Napoleon-Charles, the grandson on whom Josephine had pinned such hopes and of whom she was so fond, died of the croup in The Hague, at the age of four years and seven months. At the first sign of the illness taking a serious turn Hortense had summoned Dr Corvisart, but he arrived too late and there was little he could have done.

Caroline, herself a doting mother, set out for Holland to console Hortense, although she had never felt much friendship for her ex-school companion. In Napoleon's absence, Josephine had to ask permission from the Regency Council before she could leave Paris to see her daughter, whom she eventually met halfway at the castle of Laeken near Brussels. She was alarmed by Hortense's behaviour. Incapable of shedding tears, she looked vacant and dry-eyed, but she spoke constantly of her dead son, recalling incident after incident in the child's short life. Josephine herself was almost constantly in tears. She finally persuaded Hortense to go to Bagnières in the Pyrenees to take the waters and have a change of air, while she looked after

Napoleon-Louis. Hortense's husband decided to accompany her and Josephine wrote to her after she had left Paris: 'It will be a consolation for you both to meet again. All the letters I have received from Louis since his departure are filled with affection for you. Your heart is too sensitive not to be touched by it. . . .'

Both Josephine and Hortense sent heart-rending letters to Napoleon, who was deeply affected by the child's death. 'Never did I see Napoleon the prey of a more concentrated and profound sorrow,' wrote Fouché in his memoirs. 'Never did I see Josephine and her daughter in more bitter affliction. They appeared to look forward thenceforth to a future without joy and without hope. Even the courtiers had pity on so great a sorrow. I thought I saw the chain of imperial perpetuity severed.'

But Napoleon believed that his wife and stepdaughter were allowing their grief to overwhelm them. He wrote severely to Josephine: 'I can understand the grief that the death of poor little Napoleon-Charles has caused you. You can understand, too, how grieved I am myself. I should like to be near you to moderate and lessen your sadness. You have had the happiness never to lose a child but that is one of the pains and conditions inseparable from our human condition. Let me hear that you are sensible and well. Do not increase my own unhappiness.' In a further letter he referred to Hortense's excessive grief: 'She is unreasonable. She loves only her children. She must have more courage.' To Hortense herself he wrote: 'I fear you are not sensible and that you are making yourself too wretched over the misfortune that has come to us. . . . Grief has limits.'

Hortense was offended and thought that her stepfather was heartless. Josephine, always anxious to smooth relations between the members of her family, tried to explain his attitude: 'You don't understand the Emperor,' she wrote to her daughter at Bagnières. 'He believes that you have increased your grief by giving way to it immoderately. He warned me that he was going to write to you in a severe tone, with the conviction that it was the only way to cure you, but do believe that he shares our grief. He has often spoken of it to me.' She

tried to interest Hortense in her second son, Napoleon-Louis:
'He amuses me very much ; he is so sweet. I find he has all the
ways of the poor child whom we mourn.'

In July she wrote to Hortense from Saint-Cloud: 'I often
hear from the Emperor, who speaks a great deal about the Tsar
Alexander, with whom he seems well satisfied.... What
interests me most in all this good news is my hope of soon seeing
the Emperor again.' He had just concluded the Peace of Tilsit
with the tsar. After an absence of nearly a year he returned
to Saint-Cloud on 27 July 1807, at 6 am. He looked changed and
he was more distant.

Soon after his return he tackled Josephine on the possibility
of a divorce. He begged her 'if, in the interest of his dynasty,
he should be forced to separate himself from her in order to
have an heir, she should have the courage to make things easy
for him and take the initiative herself'. Josephine stood her
ground and was surprisingly firm. She would, she replied, never
take the initiative of a break. It must come from her husband,
who had crowned her himself.

In a letter to Eugène written soon after this interview she
asked him whether there were rumours of a divorce abroad.
'As for myself,' she added, 'you know that I aspire for nothing
but his love. If they should succeed in separating me from him
it is not the loss of rank I should regret.... Sooner or later
he would find that all those who surround him think more of
themselves than of him, and he would realize that he had been
deceived.' Eugène replied frankly: 'Yes, there is much talk
of divorce. I have heard of it both from Paris and from Munich,
but I am reassured by your conversation with the Emperor, if
it was such as you have described it.' He evidently put little
trust in his mother's accuracy or perhaps, to interpret his
remark in a more charitable light, he was inclined to believe
that wishful thinking had made her omit parts of the conversation that might have been damaging to her.

You must always speak frankly to His Majesty [he went on] ; to
do otherwise would be to love him no more.... He must treat you
well, give you an adequate settlement and let you live in Italy with

your children. The Emperor will then be able to make the marriage that his policy and his happiness demand. Don't pester the Emperor and do make an effort to regulate your private expenses. Don't be too friendly with those around you or you will soon be their dupe. Forgive me, dear mother, I am eager to give you good advice because I have need of it myself.

Eugène's letter to his mother contained excellent advice from a loving son who saw his mother's failings very clearly, but it was too late for her to mend her ways and in any event Napoleon was determined to ally himself with a European dynasty and begin one of his own. Murat had been strongly urging him to divorce for a long time. He and his wife Caroline, the most ambitious of Napoleon's sisters, had resented his partiality for Josephine, Eugène and Hortense for years. Napoleon had once expressed doubts in Caroline's presence as to whether he was capable of producing children. He had had none from his many mistresses. Caroline had decided to arrange a foolproof 'test'.

In 1805 Madame Campan had paid her a visit to ask her to help one of her ex-pupils, an attractive young lady called Eléonore de la Plaigne. She had been married to a man who had been brought to the school by her parents and who claimed to be a captain in the Fifteenth Dragoons. After the wedding he had been arrested for forgery and Eléonore had been left without money or a home, for her parents had disappeared. Caroline asked Madame Campan to bring the girl to her Parisian home, the lovely Hôtel Thelusson near the rue de la Victoire. As soon as she set eyes on pretty but submissive Eléonore, Caroline began to scheme. Supposing she were to introduce the girl, whom she could employ as a reader, to her brother, and supposing, as was most likely, for she was his type, he were to fall for her? Eléonore would be strictly chaperoned, so there would be no doubt, if she became pregnant, that the father was Napoleon. The plan worked and Eléonore was delivered of a son, Léon, in 1806. After this proof of his virility, Napoleon pensioned off Eléonore and began to think seriously about a divorce.

In September 1807 the court moved to Fontainebleau, where important negotiations were to take place on the subject of Spain. Napoleon was plotting to lure the effete Catholic kings and their heir, Prince Ferdinand, to Bayonne in order to dispossess them and put one of his brothers on the throne. He first offered the crown to sullen Louis, who refused it, so he thought of appealing to Joseph and offering the crown of Naples to his brother-in-law Murat, now the Grand Duke of Berg. Joseph, however, was not eager to accept the proposition.

In the meantime Louis and Hortense had been temporarily reconciled. Hortense was pregnant for the third time. When Napoleon saw his stepdaughter's condition he remarked bitterly: 'It hurts me to see you like that. How I should love your mother if she was in your state!'

Napoleon had invited a large number of guests to Fontainebleau and wanted them to enjoy themselves but then he went about it in such a heavy-handed way that nobody felt at ease. Seeing the long faces round him he complained to Talleyrand, himself a perfect host, who truthfully replied: 'You cannot amuse people, Sire, by ordering them to a roll of drums as if they were on marching orders.' Hunting costumes were devised for the ladies. Josephine ordered an elegant outfit in amaranth-coloured velvet embroidered in gold, with a toque of the same colour as her costume, surmounted by white feathers. Hortense, who had joined the court having again quarrelled with Louis, chose a blue and gold costume; Caroline wore pink and silver; Pauline, lilac and silver. All these ladies took turns in giving receptions. Italian singers and actors from the Théâtre-Français were invited to perform; very often Napoleon would change his mind about the play just before it was due to be performed and couriers would be dispatched post-haste to Paris to instruct the company, who had to memorize their new parts in a few hours.

Napoleon was moody and often taciturn. His attitude to Josephine was so marked that Metternich reported that there were rumours of a divorce: 'Since his return, the Emperor's bearing towards his wife had been cold and embarrassed. He no longer lives in the same apartments with her and many of his daily habits have undergone a change.'

Fouché, the minister of police, who had been on close terms with Josephine for years, took it upon himself (or so he alleged) to write a letter to her, invoking his devotion as a pretext, to acquaint her of her position and that of the emperor. 'You must not have any illusions, Madame,' he wrote. 'The political future of France is compromised by the lack of an heir for the Emperor. As Minister of Police I am in a position to be well informed about public opinion and I am made aware that people are worried about the succession of the empire.' He advised Josephine to make a brave effort and take the first step towards a divorce, assuring her that Napoleon knew nothing about his letter – a statement that sounds very unconvincing.

Josephine received the letter late one night when she was preparing to retire and became hysterical. She sent a valet to call Madame de Rémusat, who was already in bed; her husband was still dressed and he went to Josephine's room, where he found her half-undressed, with her hair down, wild with grief and terror. He sent away her ladies and she put the letter into his hands, exclaiming that she was lost. After having read it carefully Monsieur de Rémusat advised her to show it to Napoleon and to reaffirm that she would obey only an order emanating from him, and him alone. Josephine asked him to inform Talleyrand and to ask him to tell her what to reply to Fouché. Talleyrand and de Rémusat composed a dignified letter the following day, to the effect that Fouché had no right to meddle in such a private matter. Josephine signed this letter.

When Josephine confronted Napoleon he affected to be very angry with Fouché, saying that he would dismiss him from his post if Josephine so willed it. 'You must believe that I could not live without you,' he told her, taking her into his arms; but she was not entirely reassured. Comte de Bausset, governor of the imperial palace, thought that Napoleon began by play-acting in scenes like these, but entered so thoroughly into his assumed role that he ended by believing in it.

Napoleon confided to Talleyrand: 'If I separated myself from my wife, I should thereby renounce all the charm she lends to my domestic life. I should have to study the tastes and habits of a new and younger wife. Josephine adapts herself to everything and knows me perfectly. In brief, I should show myself to be ungrateful for all she has done for me. I am not liked. She is a link between me and many people.' Talleyrand listened, but he was convinced that Napoleon's hesitations would vanish when his policy dictated that he should put away his wife. 'Josephine is good and gentle,' Talleyrand observed to Monsieur de Rémusat. 'She knows how to pacify Napoleon. She has been a refuge to us on many occasions; if a foreign princess were to be installed here we would soon see a complete change at court and we should all be affected, maybe crushed.' He advised Josephine to show her husband the letter she was sending to Fouché, guessing that he would not dare to disapprove of it. Fouché returned to Fontainebleau a few days later and Napoleon treated him coldly in the presence of his wife, though the minister feigned not to notice it. In November Napoleon was to write to him from Venice: 'Stop interfering in an affair that does not concern you in the least.' Perhaps he thought he had gone too far and was regretting the instructions he had given to his minister.

The night after his talk with Talleyrand Napoleon suffered another of his nervous attacks. He had dined at six o'clock, as usual, but appeared sad and unusually silent. Then he threw himself onto his bed, gripped by stomach spasms, and clasped Josephine to him, exclaiming: 'My poor Josephine! I shall never be able to leave you.' 'Be calm, Sire,' she replied. 'Make up your mind. Tell me what you want and let us not have any more of these painful scenes.' He insisted that she should lie down beside him. 'They torment me, they make me unhappy,' he sobbed.

Josephine's nerves were in a frayed state, for she did not know who or what to believe. One day she said to Madame de Rémusat: 'I shan't give in. I shall certainly not behave like his victim but if I am too much in his way, goodness knows what he may be capable of doing – he might even have me poisoned!' 'Oh, *madame*,' cried Madame de Rémusat, shocked and alarmed, 'he would never be capable of doing such a thing.'

Hortense was weary of so many ups and downs and tearful confidences. 'Is a throne so much to be regretted?' she asked crossly. Josephine repeated what she had written to Eugène: 'For me the affection of the Emperor is everything. How unhappy thrones make people! If I should lose that [Napoleon's affection] I should have few regrets about anything else.' 'There are wives who are even more unhappy than you,' Hortense retorted. 'If Napoleon divorces you, so much the better. We'll be at peace.' There was a domestic lull when Napoleon went to Italy at the end of 1807 to sound out Joseph on the issue of Spain. In March 1808 he was back and went to Bayonne to receive the Spanish sovereigns and force them to abdicate. They had left Madrid hurriedly and the queen, Maria Luisa, arrived in France with hardly any servants or clothes. They had to be entertained; the situation was delicate. Napoleon wanted this side of affairs to be taken off his hands, so he sent for Josephine. Delighted to feel wanted and useful she went to the little château of Marrac outside Bayonne, which had been hastily redecorated and refurnished for the emperor's short stay. Josephine was accustomed to sudden summons and cramped quarters, often in chilly provincial prefectures or cold castles. Had not her life with Napoleon been a constant whirl, moving from town to town in France, Belgium, Italy and Germany? And 'at home' in their various palaces, how often had she been obliged to wait for him at mealtimes when he was too busy to think of eating and kept everybody waiting! On one occasion no less than twenty-three birds had to be roasted before Napoleon appeared at 11pm, asking jocularly: 'Am I late? I thought I had already dined!' These were some of the customs he may have been thinking of when he spoke to Talleyrand about having to adapt to the habits of a new, younger wife. Josephine had been moulded and she never complained.

The King and Queen of Spain were invited to dine at Marrac. Hearing in what state the queen had arrived, Josephine sent Duplan to arrange her hair. He did his best, as he said afterwards but even his artistry could not transform Maria Luisa into a beauty. The sovereigns' French was abominable but Josephine pretended to understand it and, to Napoleon's relief, made light conversation at table. Later she sent some of her dresses to the queen, before the Spanish royal family separated and went into exile.

While Napoleon waited for the arrival of Joseph, who was to ascend their throne, he took a little relaxation in Bayonne. Josephine was delighted to see him in such a good, even playful mood. One afternoon they went driving along the coast. The sea was very blue, it was early May, the scents of spring were in the air, the hedgerows a mosaic of wild flowers. Suddenly Napoleon ordered the coachman to stop, seized his wife by the hand and cried: 'Come, Josephine, let's go and paddle – the sea looks so enticing!' They ran down to the beach hand in hand, laughing like children. After they had paddled for a few minutes Napoleon turned, raced back to the beach, picked up Josephine's shoes, and made off with them to the carriage, obliging her to rejoin it barefoot. She was radiant. Perhaps this prank was a good omen? It seemed to prove that Napoleon was still fond of her, could treat her still like a young, newly wedded wife, would not part from her. But it was only a passing mood.

They eventually made a slow progress back to Paris, fêted everywhere, Josephine as always warmly applauded. She distributed presents, again as always, and many little portraits, of which she took a large supply on her travels. They were for the most part copies of Isabey's exquisite little miniatures; he excelled in painting her as Napoleon had described her in the early days of their marriage: 'all gauze and lace', with a sweet expression and a mysterious, tight-lipped smile.

No sooner were they back in Paris than news came that the Austrians had again violated Bavarian territory. Napoleon hurried off to the Rhine. Josephine accompanied him as far as Strasbourg before going on to Plombières for her annual cure, then Napoleon went on to Vienna. At Schönbrunn he was met by Countess Walewska and they resumed their love affair.

Meanwhile Josephine returned to Malmaison to inspect her plants and her pictures. The hundred-foot-long picture gallery opening from the music-room was filled with a valuable collection of paintings by artists ranging from Memling to David. Napoleon had a penchant for romantic and epic subjects ; he had commissioned a picture from Gérard depicting Ossian evoking ghosts and from Girodet a huge 'Apotheosis of French Heroes who had given up their lives for their country'. Both of these hung in the drawing-room. Josephine, who preferred pastoral scenes and painters of troubadour subjects such as Paul Potter, Duperreux or Forbin, replaced them with landscape paintings and Redouté's flower pictures.

From Schönbrunn Napoleon wrote: 'I shall celebrate our reunion and I impatiently await that moment. . . .' Later: 'No letter from you for several days ; the pleasures of Malmaison, the beautiful greenhouses, the gardens, cause the absent to be forgotten.' He gave the erroneous impression that he was pining.

But when, on 26 October 1809, he arrived back in Fontaine-bleau, preceding Josephine, who rushed to meet him from Malmaison, he greeted her coldly. Worse, Josephine discovered that he had ordered the communicating door between their apartments to be sealed up. She summoned Comte de Bausset.

'Monsieur de Bausset, I have every confidence in you and in your devotion to me. I hope that you will answer the question I am about to put to you frankly. Tell me, do you know why the door between my apartment and that of the emperor has been sealed up?'

'I was unaware of the fact, *madame*,' he replied uneasily.

'Believe me, Monsieur de Bausset, there is some mystery behind this. I do not like it.'

Napoleon now took Hortense aside and told her that he had taken the irrevocable decision, and he hoped that she would warn her mother. It is not clear whether she summoned up her courage to do so, but everybody noticed the tension between

Napoleon and Josephine during the next few days. At meal-times Josephine wore wide-brimmed hats tied under her chin with enormous bows to hide her face and red-rimmed eyes. Napoleon opened his mouth only to ask what the weather was like.

Comte de Bausset described the scene that took place after dinner at the Tuileries on 30 November 1809, when Napoleon braced himself to tell Josephine that the end had come.

I had been on duty since Monday 27 November. During that day and the following two days I observed a great change in the Empress and a marked coldness in the Emperor. At dinner on the 30th they toyed with the food put before them. The only words uttered were Napoleon's to me : 'What's the time?'

He got up and Josephine slowly followed. Coffee was brought in and Napoleon took his cup from the page, nodding that he wanted to be left alone. Josephine usually took his cup for him and passed it to him. She took hers silently.

I left and sat down on a chair close to the door of the Emperor's drawing-room. I was watching the servants clearing the table when I suddenly heard loud cries from the Empress Josephine coming from the Emperor's room.

The usher on duty, thinking she must be ill, made for the door, but I stopped him, saying that the Emperor would call for help if it was required. I was standing by the door when he opened it himself and, seeing me there, called out : 'Bausset, come in and close the door behind you.'

I went into the room and found the Empress on the floor sobbing and crying : 'I shall never survive, never!'

'Are you strong enough,' Napoleon asked, 'to pick up the Empress and carry her down to her room by the private stairs so that she may be looked after by her ladies?'

I obeyed and lifted up the Empress. I thought she was in a faint. With Napoleon's help I raised her while he took a candle from the table, lighted the way for me and opened the door of the room leading into a dark passage and the little staircase.

When I reached the bottom step I told him that it was too narrow for me to go down without danger of falling. He then called the guard who was stationed day and night at one of the doors of the study adjoining the stairs. Napoleon handed him the candle, which we did not need for these passages were well lit, and ordered him to walk in front. He himself took hold of Josephine's legs. On the way down I got entangled in my sword and we nearly fell. Finally we laid the Empress on a sofa in her bedroom.

Napoleon pulled a bellrope and sent for her ladies.

When I had picked her up in the drawing-room she had stopped crying. I thought she was ill but when I was having trouble with my sword on our way downstairs I was obliged to hold her tighter ; her back was against my chest and her head touching my right shoulder. When I was struggling to prevent myself from falling, she whispered: 'You are holding me too tight.' I then realized that I need not worry too much about her ; she had never been unconscious at all.

When the Empress's ladies came in, Napoleon went into the anteroom outside the bedroom. I followed him. He was very agitated and in his distressed state he told me what had happened. These were his very words :

'The interests of France and of my dynasty have played havoc with my feelings. . . . Divorce has become an inescapable duty for me. I particularly regret the scene Josephine has just made because three days ago she must have learned from Hortense of the sad obligation that compels me to leave her. . . . I pity her with all my heart. . . . I thought she was stronger and I was not prepared for this outburst of grief.'

His voice was trembling and his eyes were full of tears. He must have been really beside himself to give me, a man in no way in his confidence or counsels, such details.

Napoleon sent for Dr Corvisart, Hortense, Cambacérès, and Fouché ; before returning to his own room he looked in to see Josephine, who was by then calmer and more resigned. Bausset told the servants that the empress had had a nervous collapse.

A family council was now called to ratify the divorce. While the speeches were being prepared and the members of the family assembled, Madame Letizia and Napoleon's sisters did the honours, for Paris was full of monarchs come to celebrate the Treaty of Vienna.

On the occasion of the 'Te Deum' sung at Notre Dame to

mark the fifth anniversary of the coronation Josephine was ordered to drive through Paris in a carriage by herself. Then everybody knew that the divorce was imminent.

Hortense set out to meet Eugène. 'Bad news?' he asked when her carriage drew up alongside his at Nemours and he jumped in to join her. 'Yes, very bad news. It is all over,' she replied. When they arrived at the Tuileries they went to see Napoleon, who began to talk agitatedly. 'I have made up my mind. I cannot resist the country's appeal. Nothing will make me change my mind now, neither tears nor supplications.' Hortense said quietly:

You are the master, Sire, and free to do as you please. Nobody will oppose you. Since your happiness depends upon it, we shall make the necessary sacrifice. Do not be surprised if our mother is in tears. You should be surprised were she not to shed any, after a union that has lasted fifteen years. I am convinced she will submit and we shall all go, taking with us the memory of your great kindnesses.

Napoleon's face contracted and he burst out:

'What? Would you all leave me? Would you abandon me? Then you do not love me any more. If only my personal happiness were concerned I should sacrifice it, but it is a question of what France desires. Be sorry for me to be forced to give up my dearest affections.'

'Be brave, Sire; we too shall need courage to become accustomed to the idea that we shall no longer be your children; but, by leaving you, we shall no longer be an obstacle to your hopes and plans.'

Napoleon assured them that nothing would be changed in their relationship, and that their mother would lose none of her prerogatives or possessions. Eugène, however, insisted that the separation should be complete and final: 'Should it not be so, our position would be false. My mother may end by being in your way. It is best for us to part. Tell us where we may go, far from the court and its intrigues so that we may help our mother to bear her misfortune.'

Napoleon cried bitterly:

Eugène, what a bad opinion you have of me! I have been useful to you, I have taken the place of your father, do not abandon me now. I need you and your sister. She must not leave ; she owes it to her children, my nephews. You too must think of your posterity. Stay, unless you want people to say : 'The Empress was sent away and repudiated – perhaps she deserved it.' Will it not be better for her to be near me and to keep her rank and titles, proofs that the separation has been prompted by political motives only?

He was continuing in this vein when Josephine entered the room. Although she was crying she rallied sufficiently to exclaim, pointing to Eugène: 'Make him King of Italy!' In the middle of her woes her first thought, as always, was for her children and their future. 'Mother, let me be! Your son does not want a crown that would be, so to speak, the price of your separation,' Eugène reproved her gently.

Napoleon was moved. 'There is Eugène's good heart speaking,' he exclaimed.

It was finally decided that Hortense should remain at court (under the still-unchosen new empress) and that Eugène should remain Viceroy of Italy. Josephine was to keep Malmaison for herself, and to have an annual allowance of 2 million francs, plus an extra 1 million with which to pay off her debts.

The family council assembled at 9 pm on 14 December 1809. Josephine's lady-in-waiting observed while she was dressing that her mistress was scanning a sheet of paper. It was the prepared speech of renunciation that Napoleon had asked her to learn by heart.

As usual on important occasions she wore a simple white dress and no ornaments. She entered the throne-room adjoining the emperor's study on Eugène's arm. He had kept her company for several hours beforehand to give her courage to go through with the ordeal. She walked slowly, with her head held high, to face the triumphant members of the Bonaparte clan, who could scarcely conceal their exultation: Madame Mère ; Caroline and her husband, the King of Naples ; Jérôme, the King of Westphalia, and Queen Catherine; Louis, King of Holland, and Hortense; Pauline, Princess Borghese and

Guastella (she had been giving parties all week and openly declared that she had a beautiful new mistress ready for her brother, a Piedmontese) ; Julie, wife of Joseph, King of Spain (her husband had been detained in that country).

All rose as Napoleon entered and began to read the speech setting out his reasons for his wish to divorce. At the end he paused and added, with a tremor in his voice : 'My wife has graced fifteen years of my life ; the memory will remain for ever stamped on my heart. She was crowned by my hand. I want her to keep her rank and title of crowned Empress, but above all that she will never doubt my feelings for her and that she shall always consider me as her best and dearest friend.' Then he sat down, visibly moved.

Talleyrand handed Josephine her speech and she began to read: 'With the permission of our august and dear husband, I declare that having no further hope of children who would satisfy the needs of his policy and the interests of France, I am pleased to offer him the greatest proof of attachment and devotion which was ever given on earth. . . .' She choked on the phrase 'I therefore consent to end a marriage that henceforth is an obstacle to the well-being of France' and, dissolving into tears, handed the paper to the secretary of state, Regnault de Saint-Jean d'Angely, to finish reading it for her. Then she left the room on Eugène's arm, as she had entered, with Hortense following close behind.

Napoleon's histrionic sense had not deserted him. 'What a splendid picture it would make!' he exclaimed, and he commissioned David to paint the scene that had just taken place, allocating 20,000 francs for the purpose. But it was never executed.

The agreement for the civil dissolution of the marriage was signed and witnessed by all those who had taken part in the family council and Eugène, with a heavy heart, took it to the Senate the following day for ratification.

The divorce proceedings were illegal. They went counter to article number seven of the Civil Code, which stipulated that no members of the imperial family could divorce, whatever their sex or age. As for the religious ceremony, the scrap of paper so carefully preserved by Josephine proved to be of little use to her. Pope Pius VII was incarcerated and had excommunicated Napoleon. Cardinal Fesch, Napoleon's uncle, and the Catholic hierarchy of Paris could be relied upon to be accommodating and find a loophole. They declared that witnesses should have been present at the ceremony for it to have been valid.

Napoleon's valet, Constant, described how, the night after the family council, just as Napoleon had got into bed and he was waiting for his last orders,

. . . the door suddenly opened and the Empress came in, her hair in disorder and looking distracted with grief. She tottered towards the Emperor's bed, stopped, and began to cry in the most heart-rending way. Then she fell on the bed, flung her arms round His Majesty's neck and smothered him with the most tender caresses.

The Emperor too began to cry. He sat up, pressed her to his breast, and murmured: 'Come, little Josephine, be reasonable. Cheer up. I shall always be your friend.'

She was half-suffocated by sobs and could not answer. There was no sound for several minutes, during which they mingled tears and sobbing far more eloquent than any words. At last the Emperor noticed that I was still there and he said unsteadily: 'Go away, Constant.'

I obeyed and went into the next room. Perhaps, who knows, they enjoyed one last night of lovemaking.

At 2 pm on 15 December 1809 Josephine left the Tuileries for Malmaison in pouring rain. She had said goodbye to Napoleon in his study in the presence of his secretary Méneval. She clung to her husband in a torrent of tears and would have fallen in a faint (probably genuine for once) had he not gently placed her in Méneval's arms and hurried out of the room. 'Tell him not to forget me – tell him to come and see me,' she implored Méneval.

Then she went downstairs, passed through the salon full of silent ladies-in-waiting and out into the forecourt, where she was assisted into the gilded carriage nicknamed by Napoleon

'The Opal' ; it can still be seen at Malmaison. Hortense climbed in beside her, then Mademoiselle Avrillon, carrying a cage in which the parrot that spoke Spanish was crouched, mute from cold ; a servant handed in a basket containing Josephine's latest pet, a bitch, and a footman brought another basket containing the puppies to which she had recently given birth. Then the coachman whipped up the dripping horses.

Josephine could not bear to look back at the Tuileries, which she was leaving after nearly ten years. How well she must have remembered her feelings when she had first set foot in the palace. 'I shall not be happy here,' she had written to Hortense, 'I have misgivings. . . .'

Eugène sat at Napoleon's writing-desk and wrote to his wife Augusta: 'Everything has passed off quietly. The Empress displayed the greatest courage and resignation. Tomorrow or the next day the papers will publish everything and you will have copies. The Emperor has gone to Trianon and the Empress to Malmaison ; I am at this moment leaving to join her there. . . .'

IV

EMPRESS IN RETIREMENT

The long ordeal of protracted suspense, suspicions, fears was over.

Insistent though Napoleon had been throughout the divorce proceedings that it was not to be considered as a repudiation, the stark reality was that the ex-empress had lost him. Like a death that has been foreseen, it was still a great shock when it came. From now on she was to have no husband to love, to fear, to chide, to wait for, to depend upon, to quarrel with ; even quarrels and jealous scenes can be missed when they have become a part of one's life.

Her consolation, as always, was her children. 'The Viceroy is gay and does what he can to give her strength. Both he and the Queen of Holland are a real help to her,' wrote Mademoiselle Avrillon. Eugène wrote to his wife the day after they had left the Tuileries : '. . . the Empress is well. Her sorrow revived this morning when she went through the rooms where she had so long lived with the Emperor, but she recovered her courage and is resigned to her new position. Personally, I think she will become calmer and more settled in time. We had several visitors this morning. . . .' 'The Empress was gentle and affectionate ; she uttered not a word too much, gave vent to no bitterness and displayed the sweetness of an angel,' remarked Madame de Rémusat.

Napoleon drove over to Malmaison from Trianon the next day, but he was careful not to see Josephine alone ; he was determined to avoid scenes and tears. For nearly two weeks afterwards he sent her daily notes. For a time he seemed to feel the separation keenly, and perhaps he had guilt feelings too. Although he had seldom lived with his wife for long periods at a time, she had always 'been there', ready to welcome him

G

back from the battlefield in the Paris they both loved, the heart of France, the scene of their joint ascension to the throne. Her poise had given him self-confidence at the start of his career ; she had smoothed his path into society ; she had graced the throne and helped to make him popular. More than that she could not have accomplished ; he would not have allowed her, or any woman, to influence his decisions on major issues.

Napoleon paid a brief visit to Malmaison on 16 December and wrote to Josephine that evening : 'My dear, today I found you weaker than you should be. You have shown courage ; you should maintain it and not give way to a doleful melancholy. You must be contented and take special care of your health, which is so precious to me. . . . Do not doubt my constant and tender friendship. . . .'

Friendship ! Over the stormy years Josephine had learned to love him. Who can analyze the depth of her sentiments for him ? Could she have analyzed it herself, gentle Josephine who was not given to profound thoughts or self-examination ? Napoleon had made her shed many tears ; he had often been unfaithful ; his manners were brusque ; he had constantly reproached her for her extravagance ; he had ordered her about ; he had meddled in every detail of her life ; he had lied and written love letters to her while making love to other women ; the Countess Walewska was on the point of presenting him with a son. And yet there seems to be no doubt that Josephine loved him as well as fearing him ; she had become his willing, obedient, unquestioning slave, accustomed to do whatever he commanded. And Napoleon, on his side, had become so accustomed to dictating to her that he continued to do so even after their divorce.

Napoleon invited Josephine and Hortense to Trianon for a Christmas dinner. Josephine could not help recalling the days when she had been mistress where she was now but a guest. It was a mournful occasion, never to be repeated.

As time went on Josephine allowed herself and her entourage to relax in the matter of clothes and etiquette ; when the emperor heard of it he requested her sternly to 'keep up her position' and live like an empress. She was to restore the livery she had momentarily abandoned, she was to be served at meal-times with full ceremonial. In brief, she was not to 'let herself go' and lead the existence of a squiress in her *gentilhommière* of Malmaison. Yet this, ideally, is what Josephine had always wanted to do – she had never aspired to more.

Napoleon tried to soften the blow of the separation by a display of financial generosity:

'I was very glad to see you yesterday. . . . I feel what charms your company has for me. Today I talked with Estève [general treasurer to the Crown]. I have allowed four thousand *livres* for 1810 for the extra expenditure at Malmaison. You can therefore do as much planting as you like. I have ordered the Maison Julien to pay for your *parure* of rubies, which will be valued by the Treasury, for I do not wish to be robbed by jewellers. This may cost me 16,000 *livres*. I have given orders to keep the million *livres* that the Civil List allows you for 1810 at the disposal of your financial advisor so that you can pay your debts. You should find 20,000 to 25,000 *livres* in the coffers of Malmaison, which you can use to buy plate and linen. I have given instructions to the Sèvres manufactory to make you a fine new porcelain service. . . .

Some time before the divorce Napoleon had sounded out the Tsar Alexander about the possibility of a marriage to one of his sisters, but he had been rebuffed. He now turned to Austria and actually enlisted the help of Josephine. Could he have believed that it would flatter her to play the role of match-maker for her ex-husband?

This is what Madame de Metternich, the Austrian ambas-sador's wife, reported to her husband while he was in Vienna, after she had been summoned to Malmaison on 3 January 1810:

When I arrived, only the Viceroy was in the salon; he is the best of human beings – he is the Queen of Holland as a man. He spoke much of you and, in the middle of our conversation, the Queen came in, rejoicing that we had so soon renewed our acquaintance. Then, taking me aside, she said: 'You know we are all Austrians at heart, but you would never guess that my mother has had the courage to advise the Emperor to ask for your Archduchess.' I had not recovered from my astonishment when the Empress entered and, after talking to me of all that had happened and of all she had suffered, said to me: 'I have a project that occupies me exclusively and of which the success alone makes me hope that the sacrifice I have just made will not be an entire loss. It is that the Emperor should marry your Archduchess. I spoke of it to him yesterday and he said that his choice was not yet made. But I think that were he certain of being accepted by you, it would be. . . . She said that the Emperor was to lunch with her today and that she would then tell me something more positive.

Napoleon and Josephine must obviously have come to an agreement, but how and when is not known.

With the new marriage project proceeding smoothly, Napoleon began to recover from the temporary sadness of parting from Josephine and look forward to a new life and sexual experience with fresh, eighteen-year-old Marie Louise of Austria. He began to go out and enjoy himself. He went to the theatre and the Opéra Comique; he invited Feydeau's company to perform in Josephine's former apartments, insisting that they should present one of Molière's comedies; he hunted at Saint-Germain and rode in the Bois de Boulogne; he attended balls given by Prince von Schwarzenberg, Talleyrand (now Prince of Benevento), Pauline Borghese and the Prince de Neuchâtel. Feeling elated himself, he wrote insensitively to Josephine: 'Be gay – believe that that is the way to please me', while General Berthier was on his way to Vienna to ask for the hand of the archduchess.

The public had to be prepared for the new marriage and the festivities that would accompany it. All mention of Josephine was deleted from the newspapers by order of the emperor, who objected when he read that all her movements to and from Malmaison to the Elysée were reported in detail. There were rumours that 'the masses' had reacted with chagrin to Josephine's dismissal. People had been heard to say: 'He shouldn't have sent away *la vieille* – she brought him luck.' Josephine went to the races at Longchamp, where she was loudly applauded. 'It is pleasant not to be forgotten,' she told her entourage afterwards. That was precisely what Napoleon wanted her to be.

Nor did he want her to be around during the marriage festivities. He had given her the Elysée Palace which he now regretted, and he forbade her to visit the capital until the wedding was over ; he thought he had found the ideal solution by buying a third residence for her well away from the city : the dilapidated château of Navarre (so named because it had once belonged to the kings of Navarre) near Evreux, about sixty miles from Paris. It was a two-storied square block topped by a dome on which a statue was to have been placed ; it looked like an overturned casserole and was locally known as '*la marmite*'. '*Mon amie,*' Napoleon wrote hypocritically, 'I hope that you will be pleased with what I have done about Navarre. You will see in this fresh proof of my desire to please you. Take possession of it ; you can go there on 25 March and spend April there.'

Josephine, however, lingered on at Malmaison. She was still in residence when Marie Louise reached the forest of Compiègne and was met by her ardent wooer, who leaped into her carriage and insisted on sleeping with her that very night. (They had been married by proxy.) At last, and very probably on firm orders from her ex-husband, Josephine reached Navarre on 29 March and was fêted by the local inhabitants. 'Their display of festivities looked a little like complimentary condolences,' she wrote sadly to Hortense.

The château was situated in a wooded valley and the rooms were terribly damp ; the roof leaked, the chimneys smoked, and the windows would not close. Josephine appealed to Napoleon for money to effect the necessary repairs. She had no intention of paying for them from her own purse. She then asked for permission to return to Malmaison while Navarre was being made habitable. He had not written to her for some time but he now sent a letter through Eugène, to which Josephine replied with pathetic gratitude :

Sire, I have received by my son the assurance that Your Majesty consents to my return to Malmaison and grants to me the advance asked for in order to make the château of Navarre habitable. This double favour, Sire, dispels to a great extent the uneasiness, nay even the fears that Your Majesty's long silence has inspired. I was afraid that I might be entirely banished from your memory. I see that I am not. I am therefore less wretched. . . .

I have made a great sacrifice, Sire, and every day I realize more its full extent. Yet that sacrifice will be as it ought to be, a complete one on my part. Your Majesty, amid your happiness, shall be troubled by no expression of my regrets.

I shall pray unceasingly for Your Majesty's happiness. Perhaps even I shall pray that I may see you again.

This is the first time that Josephine had ever alluded to prayers in her correspondence. Maybe the almost daily presence of the Bishop of Evreux, who played trick-track with her at Navarre after dinner, had prompted her to take a transient refuge in the consolations of the Church. 'I shall go to Malmaison at the end of the month,' she added, 'since Your Majesty sees no objection to this. . . . I shall soon take my departure to go to the waters but during my stay at Malmaison Your Majesty may be sure I shall live there as if I were a thousand leagues away from Paris. . . .'

The tone of this letter displeased Napoleon. He would always be her friend, he assured her, and he implored her not to 'listen to the babble of Paris ; they are idle and far from knowing the truth'. He was evidently referring to current gossip about Marie Louise's jealousy of Josephine, that Malmaison was to be bought back and Josephine made Duchess of Navarre or exiled to the duchy of Berg.

It was true that the new empress was jealous of her husband's former wife. Napoleon confided to Hortense :

Things haven't worked out as I had hoped. Marie Louise is scared of your mother's charm and the ascendancy that it is well known she still has over me. Recently I wanted to drive her to Malmaison. I don't know whether she thought your mother was in residence there but she began to cry and I was forced to turn back. I shall never go against Josephine's wishes. I shall always remember the sacrifice she has made. If she wants to settle in Rome I would appoint her Governor. She could hold a court in Brussels and even do good to the country. She would be even happier near her son and her grandchildren. But tell her that if she prefers to live at Malmaison she can do so.

Hortense replied that that was what her mother wanted.

'My sole desire is to fulfil your slightest inclination,' Napoleon wrote to Josephine in April. She hung on to every one of his words: 'With what impetuosity I read your letter, yet I took a long time over it for there was not a word which did not make me weep, but these tears were very pleasant ones. I have found my whole heart again, such as it will always be ; there are affections that are life itself and can only end with it.' She confided to Hortense: 'It seems to me that I am dead and there remains in me nothing but a vague sensation that I no longer exist. If the Emperor asks for news of me, tell him the truth : that my only occupation is to think of him.'

That, of course was the main reason for her moping. She had not got enough to do. She thought of taking up the harp, but so many years had elapsed since she had played an instrument that she soon gave up the effort. It was the same with sketching. That left tapestry work ; one of her ladies outlined the designs for her to fill in. 'She really believed,' wrote Madame de Rémusat sarcastically, 'that she had made the tapestry covers for the chairs at Malmaison all by herself. . . .' Josephine's indolence made it impossible for her to concentrate for any length of time and she did not like using her hands. So she busied herself by rearranging the interior of Malmaison, redecorated her bedroom and ordered a splendid gilt carved bed with a canopy adorned with cornucopias and her emblem, the Swan. She ordered a carpet from Aubusson with a swan motif in the centre. With widow-like nostalgia she turned Napoleon's study and library into a museum, preserving it just as he had left it. The Comtesse de Kielmansegge, who visited Malmaison in 1810, noted in her diary: 'The Empress took me to the library, where she had left every single object as it was when he had occupied the room. She pointed every one of them out to me. The last object she showed me was a very worn black leather armchair that he had riddled with penknife thrusts, as was his custom. . . .'

Josephine was pleased, she told Hortense, to be at Malmaison in the tulip season ; she had never yet seen the gorgeous double tulips sent to her from Holland in blossom. Later in the year she enjoyed the sight of the two hundred and fifty species of roses in her rose garden, some of which had been given romantic names like 'Beautiful without Flattery', 'Incomparable Beauty', 'Emotional Nymph's Thigh' or 'Amorous Flame'. Even so, as she wrote to Hortense, who had gone back to Holland with Louis: 'Time passes slowly ; it will seem less so when you are here again. I await you with impatience. I have had your lodging prepared. It is not a handsome one ; you will only camp here [at Navarre] but you know with what tenderness you will be welcomed.'

Napoleon paid Josephine a visit a few days before her departure for Savoy and Switzerland ; they sat on a bench in the garden and spoke mainly about Hortense and her domestic troubles. On 13 June Josephine wrote to her daughter, who was then at Plombières :

I had a day of happiness yesterday : the Emperor came to see me. His presence made me happy, although it renewed my sorrows. Such emotion one would willingly go through often. All the time he stayed with me I had sufficient courage to keep back the tears I felt were ready to flow, but after he was gone I could not keep them back and I became very unhappy. He was kind and friendly to me as usual and I hope that he read in my heart all the affection and all the devotion for him which fills me.

I spoke to him about your position. He thinks you should not go back to Holland, the king not having behaved as he ought to have done. . . . Take the waters, then go on to Italy ; tell Louis it is on your doctor's advice.

She herself soon set out for Aix-les-Bains. 'My health requires distraction,' she told Hortense, 'and I hope to find more of that in a place I have not seen and whose situation is picturesque. The waters are especially renowned for the nerves.'

She travelled more or less incognito as the Comtesse d'Arberg and rented two small houses for herself and her suite, but the news soon spread that the Empress Josephine was in residence. Visitors flocked from Geneva, Chambéry, Grenoble and northern Italy. Festivities were organized for her by the municipality of Geneva, including a regatta during which swans drew lightweight gilded toy boats in honour of her well-known predilection for those graceful birds. She was enchanted. 'It is so gratifying to be loved,' she wrote to Hortense.

Louis abdicated in July and went to Graz in Austria. Holland was annexed to France and Napoleon declared: 'That unfortunate girl [Hortense] must come to Paris with her sons; that will make her perfectly happy.' At last he agreed to her separation from Louis and gave her the guardianship of their sons. Hortense opened a salon in her Paris mansion and in the château de Saint-Leu, to which she invited the *literati*. She became more cheerful, more like her former self, interested in music and the arts. Her separation from Louis was not the only reason for this transformation. Two years before, when she had accompanied Napoleon to Boulogne with the Murats, she had met and fallen in love with a handsome talented young hussar, Charles de Flahaut (Talleyrand's natural son) and they had become lovers. The son born to her was later known as the Duc de Morny; he was brought up by Madame de Souza, his father's mother. Did Josephine know? She must have done. Perhaps she reflected that the same thing might have happened to her when she too had fallen for a young hussar – Hippolyte Charles – before she had become deeply attached to Napoleon. At that time she had written her husband letters that he had found cold. He had complained that they were like those written during 'the winter of love, after fifteen years of marriage'. These were the kind of letters he was writing to her now, thirteen years later, when she was so much in need of the love he had once craved from her.

Hortense became the go-between through whom Josephine learnt what was going on at court. Marie Louise had taken to

Hortense and Josephine was delighted to hear it. The new empress even read extracts from Napoleon's letters to Hortense when he was away, which were passed on to Josephine ; she was grateful for these secondhand crumbs of information as her ex-husband wrote to her more and more infrequently.

There had been defections in her staff. She was particularly hurt when the Maréchale Ney, Madame Campan's niece, whom she had befriended and married off, forsook her for the court of Marie Louise on the pretext that her husband had commanded her to do so. But little by little her ladies found that Marie Louise was stiff, haughty and rather dull. Josephine's court had been more informal and amusing and the ex-empress more easy-going

Is it true [Josephine asked Madame de Canisy, one of Marie Louise's ladies of honour who visited Malmaison] that the Empress is so serious? She has no cause to be dissatisfied. I should be delighted to hear of her possessing a cheerful disposition, for the Emperor would not be happy if she were of a dejected turn of mind. We might both have met if she had felt inclined for the interview. Napoleon proposed it to her but she rejected the proposal with so much ill-humour that he never repeated it. I am sorry; her presence would not have caused me any mortification and I should have advised her on the course she ought to pursue in order to please the emperor. I should deeply deplore his experiencing any domestic troubles. When I was at the Tuileries I often found him deploring some petty family quarrels that he did not always succeed in appeasing, and I have so often been the means of restoring harmony. . . . Let her above all things endeavour to be on good terms with the Queen of Naples, whose temper is not easily managed. . . .

Josephine was probably sincere when she said that she would not have felt any mortification in Marie Louise's presence. She had forgiven her first husband's mistress and had even had a pension granted to her. She had forgiven and retained in her service Mesdames Duchâtel and Gazzani, both of whom had been Napoleon's mistresses, and she would no doubt have treated his new young wife with maternal affection. They could have formed a *ménage à trois* as in a harem, where the first and eldest wife assumes the role of guide and mentor to the younger ones, still retaining a place in her husband's affections, if not sharing his bed. This would have been compatible with Napoleon's nature and sentiments, but of course Marie Louise would have none of it ; she had no desire to be advised by her husband's former wife, whose grace everybody extolled.

At Aix-les-Bains Josephine held a little court. She visited the nearby abbey of Hautecombe by boat and a storm nearly wrecked the vessel. Napoleon heard of the near-accident and wrote, with one of his rare attempts at humour: 'For an inhabitant of the Isles of the Ocean to die in a lake would have been an inappropriate catastrophe!'

At Geneva Josephine heard that Marie Louise was pregnant ; 'Marie Louise is well and much attached to me,' Napoleon informed her tactlessly. She wrote to congratulate Napoleon on the event for which she had been cast aside, but it made her melancholy, and she wrote to Hortense: 'Alone, forsaken, far from all who belong to me, judge how great is my sadness and how much I need your presence.' She went on to Berne and Neuchâtel. Napoleon advised her to go to Milan to see her grandchildren ; he probably thought that it would take her mind off the impending event, but she seems to have been afraid of being exiled and commanded to live permanently in Italy, as Napoleon had suggested earlier. 'I should die of grief if I had to live outside France,' she told Hortense. Although she bought the little château of Prégny-la-Tour on the edge of Lake Geneva, facing Mont Blanc, she rarely stayed in it ; she had acquired it much as one would buy a toy, as a passing whim.

Josephine was back at Navarre when Napoleon's son, the King of Rome, was born on 20 March 1811. Napoleon was too excited to write a lengthy letter but he sent a page to announce the news. 'A message from the Emperor!' Josephine's chamberlain boomed at 11 pm on the night of 20 March. The tired young page was ushered into her presence ; he had difficulty in finding the letter, which he had thrust into a side-pocket for fear of losing it. Josephine, with her usual delicacy, observed his embarrassment and conversed with him easily on personal matters, remembering that he had lost an uncle in Spain. At last the letter was produced and Josephine withdrew to read it and then reply to it, after ordering supper for the page. 'This child,' Napoleon had written, 'conjointly with our Eugène, will secure my happiness and that of France. . . .'

'It is impossible to be more amiable,' Josephine told her ladies, 'or to make greater efforts to soften the bitterness that this event would impart to my mind if I were not so sincerely attached to the Emperor. The connection of my son with his is worthy of the man who, when he pleases, is the most engaging of all.' *'When he pleases. . . .'* The parenthesis was significant. She gave the page a diamond pin worth 5000 francs before he left ; only a slight contraction of her face betrayed her inner emotion. Then she gave orders for a celebration ball to be given in the château.

Eugène had arrived in Paris and Napoleon told him, before he set off for Navarre : 'Eugène, you are going to see your mother. Tell her that I am certain she will rejoice more than anyone else at my happiness. I should have written to her before had I not been wrapped up in the delight of looking at my son. I cannot be moved from his side except by indispensable duties. I shall this night perform the most pleasing of all by writing to Josephine.' On 22 March he wrote to her : 'My son is fat and in excellent health. He has my chest, my mouth and my eyes. I hope he may fulfil his destiny. I am always pleased with Eugène ; he has never given me the least anxiety.' Again he had the tact to couple the two names – those of his own son and of his stepson, for whom he preserved a deep attachment to the end of his life.

Eugène cheered everybody up at Navarre with his high spirits. He was as averse to etiquette as his mother. The only people who grumbled during his visits were the cooks, who had to fry vast quantities of fish, which he and his friends caught in the local streams and ponds. He gave prizes for the best catches and everybody ate fish for days on end. Hortense was less popular ; she was delicate, tended to look after herself and was more of a stickler for etiquette than her mother and brother.

Josephine told her ladies: 'Napoleon fell in with court etiquette quite naturally; it was a mere matter of amusement to him and certainly nobody at court understood it better. He believed that court ceremonies gave the sovereign dignity and ascendancy. I submitted to them although I did not entirely approve of them.' She had devised a kind of green uniform for her household. Napoleon considered it unsuitable and asked her to revert to the stiff court costumes reminiscent of the Tuileries. She had replied: 'The only thing that distresses me is that you should require a rigid etiquette in dress, which is a drawback to the charms of country life. . . .'

She was really taking to country life, not merely playing at it. Mademoiselle Avrillon relates in her memoirs that the empress went for a one-hour or two-hour walk every day unless the weather was very bad and that she found clogs the most suitable form of footwear for these occasions. Soon her entire feminine entourage began wearing them.

Her interest in plants increased, as a letter to Hortense proves:

In the woods of Fontainebleau you will find, dear Hortense, a plant of the *Chenopdio-Morus* family called *blète effilée* [strawberry spinach]. You will distinguish it by the peculiarity of its fruit, being precisely of the form and colour of the strawberry. Being one of those plants which do not easily thrive on being transplanted, you must take care to carry away a good portion of the grassy turf that surrounds it, along with the light earth with which it is nurtured. The whole must be well packed and forwarded by Phédart's coach. Spire, my gardener, tells me that he has transplanted *blète* from its native soil into earth suited to it, and that on being cultivated it will produce the common strawberry. I think this must be a mistake but as the experiment will cost but little trouble I should like to try it.

Other items cost more and, as usual, Josephine soon found herself in the red. Napoleon admonished her in August 1811: 'Put some order into your affairs. Spend only 1,500,000 francs and save as much every year. That will make a reserve fund of 15 million livres in ten years for your grandchildren.... Instead of that I hear you have debts. Don't give to everyone who wants to help himself.... Nevertheless, never doubt my affection for you and don't worry any more about the present embarrassment.' (Josephine's comptroller, Monsieur Pierlot, had reported a tearful scene and Napoleon, still susceptible to her tears, had protested: 'Oh, but you must not make her cry!') A few months later, when Josephine was again insolvent, he bought back the Elysée Palace from her in exchange for the château of Laeken near Brussels, which she never stayed in. He was mean enough to inform her that Marie Louise settled her bills every week and deprived herself of clothes and luxuries so as never to have any debts – and to lure Josephine's *coiffeur* Duplan for his new wife by offering him double the salary he was receiving from Josephine!

As for Josephine's not 'giving to everyone', this command went too much against her nature for her to be able to comply. Every evening her first valet, Monsieur Frère, left a sheaf of petitions on her dressing-table and she read them before going to bed. The following morning Frère was sent to visit those people who were near enough to find out the best means of assisting them. Other petitions were forwarded to people in high places. Josephine sent Dr Horeau, her personal physician, to look after the man who delivered coal and had fallen sick. He had a wife and six children to support. The man was insane and flung himself out of his window. Josephine gave the widow a pension and money to educate the children. She opened a school for orphan girls in Evreux, where they were taught reading and writing, arithmetic, sewing and lacemaking. She ordered a road to be built between the grounds of Malmaison and Boispréau and asked that poor workmen be employed on the task. Her steward, Monsieur Montlivet, wrote to chief gardener Bonpland: 'This plan will have the dual advantage of fulfilling Her Majesty's wishes for the beautification of her gardens and her charitable intensions for the *commune* of Rueil by giving bread and work to the poor. You are to choose the workmen from the poor inhabitants of the *commune*. Their number can be increased to a maximum of thirty.'

Josephine also sent Mademoiselle de Castellane, one of her ladies-in-waiting and an orphan, to be educated at her expense at Madame Campan's school which was still flourishing. (Dr Corvisart had known the girl's mother.) Later she gave her a trousseau worth 100,000 francs and married her to Monsieur Pourtalès, her equerry and the son of a wealthy merchant. He was a Protestant and so the marriage was conducted at Malmaison according to both Catholic and Protestant rites. Another young lady-in-waiting, Mademoiselle Mackau, was married to General Vallier de Saint-Alphonse. A Creole domestic married a negro footman ; for this, it is curious to observe, permission had to be obtained from Napoleon.

In the evenings the younger members of Josephine's little court played the piano and the harp. They were sometimes boisterous and Madame d'Arberg, the severe first lady-in-waiting, wished to restrain them. Josephine forbade it, saying that they amused her and lifted her spirits. To her ladies she was as kind as ever. Mademoiselle Ducrest, a singer and new-comer, who stayed only five months at Navarre, was so afraid of making a *faux pas* at mealtimes that at first she didn't eat ; Josephine noticed this and ordered chicken and Malaga wine to be sent up to her room every night until she gained self-confidence.

On rising, each guest and member of staff was presented with a glass of lukewarm water with which to rinse out his or her mouth. (A guest from Evreux thought that he was supposed to drink the water.) Breakfast was served at 10 am in the *salon* and lasted forty-five minutes. Then Josephine picked up her tapestry frame, while the chamberlain on duty read aloud novels, travel stories and memoirs. Chateaubriand's *Itinéraire de Paris à Jérusalem* was read twice over. Lunch was served at twelve and all the dishes were placed on the table at the same time, following the Tuileries custom : soup, roast meat and, on the sideboards, pastries and jellies. Two valets, a footman and the chief steward stood behind Josephine at table. She named the two people who were to sit near her and the rest of the company seated themselves 'as they thought proper'. On ceremonial days the magnificent Sèvres porcelain service given to her by Napoleon after the divorce was used.

At 2 pm she went for a drive, accompanied by two carriages containing her ladies-in-waiting and escorted by a picket of cuirassiers. (Josephine had suppressed them but Napoleon insisted they should be reinstated.) At 4 pm they returned to the château and supper was served at six, attended by visitors from Evreux – rather dull company on the whole. After supper Josephine played backgammon, piquet or casino. She did not play for money when strangers were of the party, but otherwise she held the bank and took great delight in winning from her comptroller, Monsieur Pierlot, who was a wretched player and could not conceal his temper when he lost. At 11 pm a table was laid in the small *salon* and after a light collation the visitors left, while Josephine continued to chat with her ladies. She would tell them anecdotes of her past life and occasionally bring out her caskets of jewels for them to touch and examine. Mademoiselle Ducrest was present on one of these occasions. She recounted in her memoirs that Josephine told them:

I have had no other motive in ordering my jewels to be opened before you than to spoil your fancy for such ornaments. After having seen such splendid sets you can never wish for inferior ones, the less so when you reflect how unhappy I have been, although with such a rare collection at my command. At the beginning of my extraordinary life I delighted in these trifles, many of which were presented to me in Italy. I grew by degrees so tired of them that I no longer wear any except when I am in some respects compelled to do so by my rank in the world. A thousand accidents may contribute to deprive me of these brilliant though useless objects. Do I not possess the pendants of Queen Marie Antoinette? And yet am I quite sure of retaining them? Believe me, ladies, do not envy a splendour that does not constitute happiness. I shall probably surprise you when I relate that I felt more pleasure at receiving an old pair of shoes than at being presented with all the diamonds that are spread out before you.

As her ladies smiled, unconvinced, Josephine proceeded to tell them the story of her crossing from Martinique to Toulon in 1790 with Hortense and about Jacques, the old sailor who had made her little girl a pair of sandals when her feet bled from dancing on deck in her worn-out shoes.

Winters were cold at Navarre (twenty-one loads of wood were consumed daily, besides twelve cauldrons of coal) and the ponds froze, to the delight of the younger ladies, who learnt how to skate or were pulled over the ice in sleighs by the gentlemen. On one such occasion Mademoiselle Avrillon toppled over and broke her leg. Josephine sent to Paris for a newly invented invalid bed she had read about, and visited her lady-in-waiting every day for two months, although her room was situated at the top of a narrow and steep staircase.

Mademoiselle Avrillon married a Monsieur Parquin and was soon to leave Josephine's service. One day the lacemaker Mademoiselle Lesueur came to Malmaison to show Josephine some of her latest work and offered to take Mademoiselle Avrillon back with her to Paris in her carriage to see her husband, who was dining at the Lesueurs' house that night. Mademoiselle Avrillon was on duty and she asked for permission to go to Paris. Josephine refused and Mademoiselle Avrillon was bitterly disappointed. That evening Josephine beckoned her over and said kindly: 'Mademoiselle Avrillon, I upset you this morning. I noticed it at once and I am sorry, because I do not like to upset people. But when you want to go to Paris, try to arrange for your visits to coincide with the times you are not on duty. Tomorrow, for instance, you are free, and I shall ask M. Pourtalès to give orders for a carriage to be at your disposal. You can leave as early as you like.'

Josephine made an effort to reduce her expenses but her household was not helpful. As Mademoiselle Ducrest observed: 'The graduation of rank in the lower-class household was more remarkable than in Her Majesty's *salon*. The chief steward insisted that it was impossible to have less than twenty-two tables separately laid for them.' 'Can you imagine, ladies,' Josephine exclaimed, 'anything equal to the wasteful ex-

H

travagance to which I am thus exposed? Is it possible that the cooks should refuse to eat with the kitchenmaids and scullions, the servants who scrub the floors with those who light the fires? All this must be set to rights. . . .' In the end sixteen tables were laid instead of twenty-two.

In 1812 Josephine wrote jubilantly to Eugène: 'I have some news that will please you. My affairs are in order and all my debts paid. Such is my New Year's gift for you. . . .' (He had borrowed money to come to his mothers rescue the year before.)

It was to be a bad year for her ex-husband, who was engaged in the fatal Russian campaign. 'The Emperor has forgotten me; I am a stranger to everything,' she complained to Eugène. Before leaving for Russia, however, Napoleon did allow her to see his little son. The rendezvous in the Bois de Boulogne, where the child was taken every day by his governess, Madame de Montesquiou, was kept secret from the ever-jealous Marie Louise. 'Dear child,' Josephine is alleged to have murmured, 'you cannot know what pain you have unwittingly caused me.' She asked for a portrait of the child, a copy of a picture of him astride a stuffed lamb by the portraitist Madame Thibaut. It is not certain whether Napoleon was present at the meeting. If he was, then it was the last time he saw Josephine.

The year before Josephine had seen the son born to Napoleon by Countess Walewska; he was later to become Count Walewski. The Countess had come to Paris on a political mission when it was thought that Napoleon might marry a Russian princess and the position of Poland would therefore be endangered. Josephine had invited her and her little son to Malmaison. Now that her jealousy was spent she clutched at anyone connected with Napoleon; anyone whom he had loved or still loved she too was prepared to love. The relics in the library to which he would never return in her lifetime were the lifeless cult objects of an invisible god.

When Josephine expressed the wish to visit her grandchildren in Milan she had to obtain permission from Napoleon. 'I see no objection,' he replied, 'but you would do well to travel incognito.

It will be very hot. My health is good. Eugène is doing very well. Never doubt my interest and affection.' She would have liked to take with her the gold toilet set, the coronation gift of the City of Paris, as a present for her daughter-in-law, but Eugène restrained her; it was too personal a memento to give away in her lifetime. While Josephine was in Milan, Eugène was fighting at his stepfather's side in the Battle of Borodino; 35,000 Russians were killed or wounded and 28,000 French, but he made no mention of this when he wrote to his mother afterwards: 'The Emperor has won a great victory over the Russians. We fought for thirteen hours. I commanded the left wing. We have all done our duty and hope that the Emperor will be satisfied.... I hear that you are adored in Milan, as you are everywhere. People have written charming things about you, and you have turned the heads of everyone you have approached.'

After her stay in Milan Josephine had gone to Aix-les-Bains; in October she moved into her château de Prégny, where she gave dinners and receptions. People flocked to them from Geneva and found the ex-empress a delightful hostess. Etiquette was banished; life, on the surface, was cheerful and light-hearted. But the news from the battlefronts was alarming. Napoleon was retreating from Moscow. Napoleon retreating? It seemed impossible. For twenty years he had always *won* battles. He returned to Paris on 18 December 1812 and left again in April 1813 to repair the disaster of Moscow. 'No one knows his character as thoroughly as I do,' Josephine assured her ladies. 'He fancies himself a predestined being and will bear the frowns of fortune with as much composure as he has exhibited temerity in braving the dangers of the battlefield.'

On other days, however, she felt less convinced. She no longer trusted her cards and summoned the well-known fortune-teller Mademoiselle Adèle Lenormand to Malmaison. Later she went to consult her in Paris. 'Have you noticed that the year begins on a Friday and that it is 1813?' she observed to her entourage as her forebodings increased. People were talking about a Bourbon restoration; her own ladies, particularly

Madame de Rémusat, were said to be plotting with the royalists. 'Had the senators done their duty,' Josephine remarked one day, 'Napoleon would have been less ambitious of that glory for which his thirst is insatiable. His attention would have been more directed to his people, by whom he would have been as beloved as he is by his soldiers.' But even his soldiers were beginning to weary.

Josephine shuttled between Malmaison and Navarre, occupying herself with her flowers and her animals. She had engaged an Italian, Ruccesi, the inventor of *biscuits à la glace* (layer cake with ice cream); her porter's wife was an Englishwoman who made Cheshire cheese – and muffins. She began to put on weight. For the first time in her life she was persuaded to have whalebones inserted in her corsets. 'It took her some time to get used to them,' Mademoiselle Avrillon reported. Napoleon, who heard everything, wrote to her jocularly: 'I hear that you are becoming as fat as a Normandy farmer's wife.'

After spending some time at Saint-Leu with Hortense, Josephine took the children back with her to Malmaison, where they stayed from May until August. The last born, little 'Oui Oui', as he was nicknamed, the future Napoleon III, remembered that his grandmother often took him and his brother to the hothouses and allowed them to suck sugar-canes. She loaded them with gifts, including two little golden hens that laid silver eggs by means of a hidden spring. 'The children enliven everything,' she wrote to her daughter. She played with them and was loving, but was careful not to give the children sweets or interfere with their lessons, as she assured Hortense, who had firm ideas about how children should be brought up, a trait that she appears to have inherited from her father, Alexandre de Beauharnais. Josephine was always careful to conform to the wishes of her loved ones. She was a born peacemaker and restorer of harmony. This role obliged her to tell 'white lies' occasionally. Hortense was difficult and had to be handled carefully. Eugène was different. One could always be frank with him.

At the beginning of 1814 he had a misunderstanding with his stepfather, who was now fighting with his back to the wall. Eugène had appeared to be undecided in his command of Italian troops and was wrongly suspected of coming to terms with the allies. Instead of writing to him directly Napoleon addressed his complaints to Josephine, who begged her son:

Do not lose an instant, dear Eugène. Whatever the obstacles, re-double your efforts to fulfil the orders given to you by the Emperor, who has just written to me on the subject. His wish is that you should march towards the Alps, leaving in Mantua and the Italian fortresses only the troops belonging to the kingdom of Italy. His letter finishes with these words: 'France before all. France has need of all her sons.' Come then, my dear son, hasten. Your zeal will never be of more use to the Emperor. I can assure you that every moment is precious.

The end was very near. Every day brought new defections in Napoleon's entourage. Bernadotte passed over to the enemy. The King of Bavaria sent an envoy to Eugène to offer him the crown of Italy if he would change sides but Eugène loyally declined ; his devoted wife applauded his decision. On 1 April 1814 Hortense sent a courier to Malmaison to inform Josephine that Paris had capitulated and to advise her to go to Navarre, but the ex-empress had already arrived there on 30 March. Napoleon was at Fontainebleau. Hortense refused to join the Empress Marie Louise at Blois and she went to Navarre with her two sons.

In the terrible week from Saturday 2 April to Saturday 9 April, Josephine and Hortense heard that the allies had refused to deal with Napoleon, that a temporary government had been set up, that the island of Elba had been offered to the former master of France, that he had abdicated, and that the Comte d'Artois was daily expected in Paris.

'We are broken-hearted at what has happened,' Josephine wrote on 8 April to Talleyrand, who as usual was very securely on the winning side. 'I wait for the Senate's decision and place my interests and those of my children in your hands. Counsel me in these circumstances and I shall confidently follow your advice.' Josephine had always believed that Talleyrand would outwit everybody, including her husband, and that he had friends in every court and chancellery. As in the post-revolutionary days, she appealed to those in power who, she hoped were still her friends.

Eugène was still in Italy. Josephine wrote to him on 9 April:

What a week I have spent, dear Eugène! How I have suffered at the way in which they have treated the Emperor! What attacks in the newspapers, what ingratitude on the part of those upon whom he showered his favours! But there is nothing more to hope for. All is finished; he is abdicating.

As for you, you are free, and absolved from any oath of fidelity; anything more you could do for his cause would be useless. Act for your family. . . .

In those last words Josephine summarized the driving motive of her entire life. 'Act for your family.' That is what she had always done: before the Revolution, when she had scurried across the beach at Fort-Royal under fire to reach the ship that was to take her and Hortense back to France and Eugène; during the Revolution, when she had placed her children in Aunt Fanny's care; after the Revolution, when she had provided for them by becoming Barras's mistress and finally assured their future by marrying General Bonaparte.

Her only weakness had been to marry Hortense to Louis, but if she had known how great the sacrifice was to be, it is doubtful whether she would have consented to it. It was she who had urged a separation when there was no more hope of their reconciliation and Hortense's attachment to her mother never diminished, though it was not in her nature to be as tender and warm-hearted as Eugène.

'You can stay in France,' Hortense suggested to Josephine, 'since the divorce has set you free, but I bear a name that is anathema now that the Bourbons are coming back. My diamonds are my only fortune. I shall sell them and go and live in Martinique on the plantation that still belongs to you. I recall it with pleasure; it is a lovely place. It will be a great sacrifice for me to leave you, France, my brother and my friends, but I shall be at peace. I shall bring up my children and they will be my consolation.' Josephine was more of a realist than her daughter but, tactful as ever, she advised her to wait and see what the allies would decide. Hortense stiffened. She was not prepared to compromise ; she lacked her mother's sure instinct for survival in the best possible conditions.

Her reader, Mademoiselle Cochelet, who had connections with Count Nesselrode, Tsar Alexander's envoy, went to Paris to try to find out what was happening. She wrote to Hortense from Paris:

Go to Malmaison with the Empress Josephine. The Tsar Alexander will pay you a visit there ; he is most anxious to make your acquaintance and you already owe him a debt of gratitude since he is devoting himself to your interests as if they were his own. The Duke of Vicenza [the title given to Caulaincourt, Napoleon's aide-de-camp] who is behaving so well over the Emperor Napoleon's affairs, also wishes you to go to Malmaison. The future of your children depends upon it. Napoleon has signed a treaty [the Treaty of Paris, signed on 11 April] that assures the position of all the members of his family. They are to remain in France and keep their titles. You have been granted a pension of 400,000 francs. It is said that the Faubourg Saint-Germain is furious to hear that the imperial family has been so well treated. That is the way they show their gratitude after all the good done to them by the Emperor and Empress. You wish, I know, to reside in Switzerland. Monsieur de Nesselrode thinks that you should not give up your residence in France. It is said that Napoleon exclaimed when he left Fontainebleau 'Josephine was right – my parting from her brought me bad luck.'

Josephine had now received Napoleon's last letter to her, dated 16 April 1814:

They have betrayed me ; yes, all of them except our dear Eugène so worthy of you and me. May he be happy under a king who can appreciate the feelings of nature and of honour. Adieu, my dear Josephine. Resign yourself as I am doing and never lose the memory of one who has never forgotten you and never will forget you.

PS I expect to hear from you when I reach the island of Elba. I am far from being in good health.

Josephine returned to Malmaison with Hortense and selected an attractive gown in which to receive the Tsar Alexander. It was like the old post-Revolution days when she had had to begin a fresh chapter of her life and fight for her future and her children with the only arms she possessed: her charm and seductive power. But she was older now, and very weary. The forebodings of disaster that had pursued her all her life were soon to be justified.

Alexander was intensely curious to meet Josephine. He had heard so much about her ; he also retained a great admiration for Napoleon.

There was no hope of making peace with him [he told Mademoiselle Cochelet, who continued to act as an intermediary]. But by placing him in a position in which he could do no more harm we do not forget that he is a great man, whom I loved as a friend and who hurt me deeply by breaking our treaties ; nevertheless I want to know that he is happy, as well as his family. I was in favour of a regency and especially for the country to be consulted, but they rushed to call back the Bourbons without any guarantee or authority. So much the worse for the French if they find it has been a bad bargain for them.

The tall romantic young Tsar went to Malmaison and immediately fell under Josephine's spell. Her languid grace and mysterious smile appealed to his sentimental and mystical nature. Josephine found him gallant and full of thoughtful little attentions that could not fail to please her as a woman, especially as her two husbands had been so sparing of them. 'If Russia suited you,' Alexander told her, 'I should be happy to offer you a palace there, but the climate is too rigorous. You are so loved in France, why don't you stay here? I hear your praises sung on every side. . . .' Hortense began by treating the tsar coldly ; when her mother rebuked her she replied: 'I am not prepared to bow to the enemy of France.' Little by little, however, she became convinced that the tsar was sincerely well disposed towards her and her mother. As he began to spend more time at Malmaison than in Paris, the ladies of the Faubourg-Saint-Germain took umbrage. He told his entourage: 'I find every noble quality in the Empress Josephine, Queen Hortense and Prince Eugène. I find more pleasure in their company than with the ladies of the Faubourg-Saint-Germain.'

Eugène had been well received by Louis XVIII as the son of the Vicomte de Beauharnais, but he had few illusions. 'Everybody is fighting for a share of the cake,' he wrote to his wife, 'and I doubt whether we shall be well treated.' Josephine, too, was beginning to have doubts. Alexander was not the only man to decide their fate; it was in the hands of the Bourbons and their allies. She spoke to Mademoiselle Cochelet about her misgivings, though she attempted to conceal them from her children: 'Sometimes I feel so downcast that I could die of despair. I cannot reconcile myself to Napoleon's fate and to that which threatens my children. They are without support, without money and without any hope of protection except from the Emperor of Russia. Can we rely upon him? He promises much but does nothing.'

The tsar had repeatedly expressed the wish to see Saint-Leu and on 15 May he was invited to dine at the château with Josephine, Hortense and Eugène. The Duke of Vicenza, the Maréchale Ney and Alexander's aide, Count Tchernicheff, were the only guests. They visited the forest of Montmorency, in which Hortense had had roads made leading to a hunting-lodge. On their return Josephine felt tired and went to lie down in a bedroom, followed by Mademoiselle Cochelet, who found her in a state of deep depression.

Again Josephine voiced her fears:

Mademoiselle Cochelet, I cannot repress the sadness that overwhelms me. I am making every effort to conceal it from my children, but I am suffering all the more. I am beginning to lose heart. The Emperor of Russia is full of affection and kind attentions for us but they are only words. What has he decided for my son, for my daughter and her children? What will happen when he leaves Paris? Nothing he has promised will be fulfilled. My children will be unhappy; I cannot bear the thought. I am already suffering enough because of the fate of the Emperor Napoleon, who has been deprived of his greatness and relegated to an island far from France, who has abandoned him. Am I in addition to see my children wandering over the face of the earth without financial means? The prospect is killing me.

Madame [soothed Mademoiselle Cochelet], have confidence in the friendship of the tsar. He reveres you, he is full of attentions for you. He is doing his best to assure your children's future in spite of them ; you know how many difficulties the Queen [Hortense] has put in the way so as not to have to be indebted to him.

Yes, I know, all that is true and the Tsar is behaving to us in a way that we would never have thought possible, but despite all these demonstrations I see nothing positive. You are in contact with Monsieur de Nesselrode. Try and find out from him whether we have grounds for hope. Are the Austrians opposed to my son? I do not think they are. Are the Bourbons against him? They are under too many obligations to me to behave badly towards my children. Have I not been kind to the many unfortunate members of their party? I did not believe for one moment that they would ever return to France, but I was pleased to help their friends ; they were French people who had suffered, many of them were old friends or acquaintances of mine, and the position of princes whom I had known when they were young moved me. Did I not plead with Napoleon over and over again for the return of the Duchesse d'Orléans? It is because of my supplications that he allowed them a pension that was paid to them abroad. I am surprised that they have not come to see me ; only Monsieur de Grammont has come. Monsieur de Polignac, who owes his life to me, has not come near Malmaison.

Josephine was stretched on a chaise longue and looked weak. Hortense came in to find out why she had left the company, so she made an effort and returned to the drawing-room. Hortense was worried. She had noticed how depressed her mother was and she said to Mademoiselle Cochelet: 'She puts on a brave face and is pleasant with everybody she receives, but I have observed that as soon as she is alone she gives way to a sadness that alarms me. I am afraid she is taking present events too much to heart and that her health will suffer.'

Josephine had caught a cold that afternoon but she made light of it. That night she and Hortense went back to Malmaison and Alexander returned to Paris.

On 21 May Alexander wanted to visit Marly, near Malmaison. Josephine was feeling unwell but she was her usual agreeable self and presented the tsar with a cameo that had been given to her by Pope Pius VII. She did not go to Marly but presided over dinner when they came back.

On 23 May she received the King of Prussia and his family, and on the twenty-fourth, Prince of Mecklemburg and the Grand-Dukes Nicholas and Michael of Russia came to pay their respects. Josephine rested on a sofa while Hortense performed the duties of hostess and drove them round the surrounding countryside with Eugène. Josephine was feverish and still suffering from her cold, which she could not shake off, but she insisted on appearing at dinner, attired in one of her flimsy muslin dresses, saying that she never attached importance to such a trifle as a cold. It was unwise but she could not help herself. She had to look her best. 'You should not go down to dinner,' Dr Horeau had told her sternly. He said afterwards that she had looked at him fixedly and said: 'Don't you understand, Monsieur Horeau? I *must*. I cannot do otherwise.' She had, he said, looked almost fierce.

She had read with anguish in a newspaper that the municipal authorities of Paris had decided to remove the remains of little Napoleon-Charles from Notre Dame and put them in a common grave. 'It's like the times of the Revolution – they even dare to violate tombs!' she cried. Hortense took the news more calmly. 'So much the better. I shall place my son's body in the church of Saint-Leu. There he will be near me.'

On 28 May Alexander returned to dine at Malmaison. Eugène was confined to his room with a fever and Josephine was in bed, her cold having worsened. Hortense was hostess at dinner. Mademoiselle Cochelet was seated next to a mysterious English visitor – an enigmatic man whose name has not been recorded but who had known Josephine as a girl in Martinique before her marriage.

It is thirty-nine years since I saw her [he confided to Mademoiselle Cochelet]. It would be cruel, after having wished to see her again for such a long time, to lose her for ever without having seen her.... I knew her in Martinique when, as a lad of fourteen, I used to frequent her mother's house. She treated me very kindly. I always had the presentiment that her eldest daughter would have a great future. She was very elegant even then, and her charming face revealed the loveliness of her heart and mind. I often told myself later that if I had met her afterwards I should certainly have loved her passionately and that that attachment would have decided my fate. I can assure you that it has influenced it, because, recalling the ideal of my youth, no woman has ever seemed to me worthy enough to sacrifice my freedom for her. I have acquired a considerable fortune, I have become a general, and I have remained a bachelor. I saw Josephine leave the island with regret. I continued to visit her excellent mother, where the Empress's letters, portrait and memory were the subject of our daily conversations. From a distance I have followed with lively interest her life, her greatness and then her misfortunes. As soon as I learnt that it was possible to come to France I wrote to ask her permission to present my respects. She replied kindly that she remembered me from the last days she spent in Martinique as a girl and that she would have great pleasure in seeing me if I wished to come and dine with her. She had fixed today, which I was looking forward to impatiently, but my destiny has been such that – I do not know why – but I am alarmed to hear of her illness and to think that death may come between us. . . .

Josephine was indeed beginning to sink. The tsar sent his doctor from Paris. She did not wish Corvisart to be called, for fear of offending her own doctor, Horeau, who applied blisters. But it was obvious that the end was approaching. There was nothing anybody could do.

Hortense tiptoed in to see her mother several times during the night of 28 May. Josephine hardly recognized her. She rallied a little the next day, when the last sacraments were administered by the Abbé Bertrand while her children heard mass in the chapel below. After mass they went upstairs. Josephine stretched out her arms to them and made as if she wanted to speak, but the words never came, and she sank back on her pillow. All was over.

Hortense fell in a dead faint and had to be carried out of the room. Eugène knelt by his mother's bedside and then, rising in a flood of tears, he reeled and fell unconscious. It was not etiquette for them to attend their mother's funeral so they left for Saint-Leu that afternoon. Madame Campan came over from Saint-Germain to console Hortense. She nearly had to have the door forced open before she was admitted to the presence of her prostrate ex-pupil.

Dr Béclard, of the Paris Faculty of Medicine, performed the autopsy and pronounced that Josephine's death had been caused by pneumonia and gangrenous angina.

She would have been fifty-one in June – a short life, and, on the whole, not a very happy one.

When her death was reported in Paris a working man ran up to the Austrian emperor, shouting: 'Have you heard the news? The good Empress Josephine is dead!' To the people of Paris and France she would always remain *la bonne Joséphine*.

Napoleon read of her death in a newspaper. 'Poor Josephine!' he exclaimed. In his memoirs he wrote: 'Her death, the news of which took me by surprise at Elba, was one of the most acute griefs of that fatal year of 1814. She had her failings, of course, but she at any rate would never have abandoned me.' One recalls Josephine's opinion of General Bonaparte shortly after her marriage: 'I am very fond of him, despite his little faults.'

In the course of their life together they had betrayed, hurt and humiliated one another, yet a deep, intangible bond united them even after their divorce, by which time Josephine had given her heart to Napoleon – or perhaps it would be more accurate to say a third part of her heart ; the other two parts belonged to Eugène and Hortense.

When she heard that Josephine was dead, a lady belonging to the Faubourg-Saint-Germain's aristocratic set drawled : 'What an interesting woman she was – what tact, what a good heart she had, what a sense of proportion and taste in all she did.

She even had the good taste to die at the right moment. . . .'

Was there not a grain of truth behind the flippancy of that remark? What more could Josephine have expected from life had she lived? Her son Eugène, who was given the title of Duke of Leuchtenberg (a Bavarian enclave near Munich, in his father-in-law's territory) died ten years later ; Hortense, who had been given the title of Duchess of Saint-Leu, died in 1837, after spending the rest of her life in exile in Switzerland. It would have broken Josephine's heart. No, that is not true ; her heart was already broken when she died.

EPILOGUE

When Napoleon returned from Elba in March 1815 he told Hortense that he wished to go to Malmaison. She asked to be allowed to spend the night before he arrived for lunch at the château, which she had not revisited since her mother's death. She was afraid her emotions might overwhelm her.

At Malmaison Napoleon summoned Dr Horeau, whose conversation with the emperor was later recorded by Mademoiselle Cochelet.

'So . . . you let my poor Josephine die!' Napoleon exclaimed. 'You were with her during illness, weren't you?'

'Yes, Sire.'

'What was the cause of her illness?'

'Anxiety, grief. . . .'

'Do you really believe that?'

'I do, Sire.'

'Was she ill for long? Did she suffer?'

'The illness lasted a week, Sire. Her Majesty did not suffer very much. She knew that she was dying. A sign she made when she could no longer talk left me without a shadow of doubt that she felt her end was near. She contemplated it without weakness.'

'You say she was sad. What was the cause of it?'

'Events, Sire. Your Majesty's position. . . .'

'Ah, so she spoke of me?'

'Often, very often.'

Napoleon passed a hand across his eyes and tears rolled down his cheeks.

'Good woman, good Josephine. She really loved me, that one . . . she was French. . . .'

'Oh yes, Sire, and if the fear of displeasing you had not restrained her, she would have proved it to you.'

'How?'

'She once said that if she had still been Empress of France she would have crossed Paris in a carriage drawn by eight horses with her entire household in full livery to join you at Fontainebleau and thereafter never leave your side. She would have done it too, Sire ; she was quite capable of it.'

Napoleon walked away, visibly moved.

After lunch he told Hortense that he wished to see Josephine's room. As she rose, trembling, he put out his hand and bade her be seated. 'No, Hortense, stay there, my dear daughter. I shall go alone, it would upset you too much.' When he came back, his eyes were swimming with tears ; he took her hand and they walked silently through the gardens. Napoleon stopped before a rose-bush. 'I cannot get used to the idea of being here without her,' he murmured. 'I seem to see her coming along the path, picking one of the flowers she loved so much. Truly, she was the most graceful woman I have ever seen.'

Almost simultaneously they turned to look at the swans gliding on the lake – the bird that Josephine had so aptly adopted as her emblem and with which she had such an affinity : languid, sinuous in its movements, radiant in its snowy plumage, quick to defend its young, subject to violent outbursts of temper. . . .

Napoleon paid a last visit to Malmaison on 29 June 1815, after Waterloo, before his final exile to St Helena. He spoke briefly with Frère, Josephine's first valet :

'Malmaison is so beautiful,' he said, looking round him sadly. 'Josephine spent a lot of money on it. I used to shout at her a lot, didn't I ?'

'Yes, Sire – and if only they had completed what she had begun before she died !'

'What was that ?'

'The alley you must have noticed near your little garden, to join Boispréau.'

'What's Boispréau ?'

'The park that belonged to Mademoiselle Julien.'

'Ah yes, yes. That must be completed.'

'The Empress liked the idea, and it employed poor peasants.'

Napoleon then asked about Josephine's tomb. 'She lies in the church of Rueil, doesn't she?'

'Yes, Sire.'

'Has a monument been erected?'

'Not yet, Sire. A plan and an estimate have been drawn up for a fine mausoleum but circumstances have prevented its execution. We have been waiting for the Prince. The Empress lies in a chapel hung with black draperies, where masses are said.'

The monument was completed in 1825 after many difficulties. The epitaph, moving in its simplicity, consists of only five words:

À JOSÉPHINE

EUGÈNE ET HORTENSE

In spite of her spendthrift ways, Josephine left money: over 8 million francs after deduction of her debts, shared equally between Eugène and Hortense. Malmaison was left to Eugène. Two years after his death in 1824 his widow, Princess Augusta, sold it to the Swedish banker Hagermann. The furniture, library and paintings were dispersed. Tsar Alexander had already bought many of the pictures.

One day in the month of August 1831 Hortense paid a visit to Rueil with her twenty-three-year-old son, the future Napoleon III. They both knelt reverently before Josephine's tomb and were touched to see that it was covered with fresh flowers. 'What a drear feeling came over me,' she wrote in her memoirs, 'when I knelt before that cherished image and sadly thought that of all whom she had loved I alone remained with my son, isolated and compelled to flee the spot where she reposed. The great number of flowers covering the monument, which my brother and I had such difficulty in getting permission to build, proved to me that at any rate she was lying among friends who held her memory dear. . . .' Later they walked up to the gate of Malmaison:

I stopped at the gate and insisted upon entering. It is from there that the Emperor started on his way to exile to leave France for ever. . . . It was impossible to secure any remission of the orders of the new proprietor, who had forbidden entrance to the château without a card. My sister-in-law had sold Malmaison to a banker, who kept a part of the gardens and château and had sold the rest. It was difficult to recognize the place and I could not believe I was at the same spot that I had left so beautiful, where I had always been so gladly received, when admission to it was so cruelly denied me.

In 1842 the morganatic husband of Marie-Christine de Bourbon, widow of Ferdinand VII of Spain, bought the château and the grounds, by then reduced to 106 acres. Then in the spring of 1861 Napoleon III bought back the château he remembered so vividly from his childhood days, and a museum was opened in 1867. With his own hands he hung the pictures on the walls where he remembered having seen them as a child. His wife, the Spanish Empress Eugénie, tried to restore the interior to some of its former splendour.

During the 1870 war many battles took place in the surrounding area and the château was badly damaged. In 1877 a speculator bought Malmaison and the grounds were sold in lots. The château passed from one owner to another until the financier Daniel Osiris bought it in 1896, restored it at great cost and gave it to the nation in 1904, on the condition that it should house a Napoleonic museum. This was inaugurated in 1906 and has gradually been added to until the present day.

BIBLIOGRAPHY AND ACKNOWLEDGMENTS

Most of my material has been taken from eyewitness accounts of the events described and from the various editions of letters from Napoleon to Josephine. Memorialists, nearly all of whom are referred to in the text, include Mademoiselle d'Avrillon, the Duchesse d'Abrantès, Mademoiselle Cochelet, Madame de Rémusat, Madame Campan, Mademoiselle Ducrest, Hortense, Queen of Holland, and Prince Eugène de Beauharnais. Memoirs written by members of Napoleon's entourage include those of Bausset, Bourrienne, Constant, Fouché, Méneval and Louis Bonaparte.

I have also consulted the classic biographies of Frédéric Masson, *Josephine de Beauharnais* (Paris 1898), *Josephine imperatrice et reine* (Paris, 1899), *Josephine repudiée* (Paris, 1900), and *Madame Bonaparte* (Paris, 1920) ; and of Arthur L. Imbert de Saint-Armand, *La Cour de l'imperatrice Josephine* (Paris, n.d.). Other useful works were :

André Castelot, *Josephine* (Paris, 1964)

Jean Hanoteau, *Le Ménage Beauharnais* (Paris, 1935)

Louis Hastier, *Le Grand Amour de Josephine* (Paris, 1936)

E. J. Knapton, *The Empress Josephine* (Cambridge, Massachusetts, 1963; London, 1964 ; Harmondsworth, 1969)

G. Manguin, *L'Impératrice Joséphine* (Paris, 1924)

Carola Oman, *Napoleon's Viceroy* (London, 1966)

In addition I am grateful for the material kindly provided by Miss G. M. Grainger, Assistant Librarian, Royal Botanic Gardens, Kew ; Monsieur Gérard Hubert, Chief Curator, Musée National de Malmaison, Rueil ; Monsieur J. Pons, Conservateur de la Bibliothèque Municipale de Brest.

INDEX

INDEX